PELICAN BOOKS

THE FAMILY LIFE OF OLD PEOPLE

After leaving Cambridge Peter Townsend undertook research into social policy for Political and Economic Planning, helped to produce reports on poverty, the cost of social services, pensions, primary and secondary schools, and investigated the problem of unemployment in Lancashire. In 1954 he was appointed research officer of the newly founded Institute of Community Studies in Bethnal Green, and wrote this book as a result. In 1957 he joined the London School of Economics and embarked on a national study of old people's homes, published in 1962 as *The Last Refuge: A Survey of Residential Institutions and Homes for the Aged in England and Wales*. He undertook a national survey of old people in Britain which was part of a cross-national survey carried out also in the United States and Denmark. One book on the British findings (with Dorothy Wedderburn) was published under the title *The Aged in the Welfare State*. The next, giving the cross-national findings (with Ethel Shanas, Dorothy Wedderburn and others), *Old People in Three Industrial Societies*, was published in 1968. In 1965 he published a study of poverty, *The Poor and the Poorest* (with Brian Abel-Smith). Since 1963 Peter Townsend has been Professor of Sociology at the University of Essex. He is married and has four children.

PETER TOWNSEND

THE FAMILY LIFE OF
OLD PEOPLE

*

AN INQUIRY IN EAST LONDON

PENGUIN BOOKS

Penguin Books Ltd, Harmondsworth, Middlesex, England
Penguin Books Australia Ltd, Ringwood, Victoria, Australia

—

First published by Routledge & Kegan Paul 1957
Abridged edition, with a new postscript, published in Pelican Books 1963
Reprinted 1968, 1970

—

Copyright © Peter Townsend, 1957, 1963

Made and printed in Great Britain
by Cox & Wyman Ltd,
London, Reading and Fakenham
Set in Monotype Times

For my grandmother and mother

Contents

Contents

APPENDIXES

List of Tables and Diagrams

TABLES

DIAGRAMS

Introductory

CHAPTER 1

The Study in Outline

THIS book is in two parts. The first describes the family life of people of pensionable age in a working-class borough of East London; the second discusses the chief social problems of old age against the background of family organization and relationships.

Concern about the growing number of old people springs partly from an assumption that many of them are isolated from their families and from the community. It is widely believed that the ties of kinship are much less enduring than they once were and that as a consequence the immediate family of parents and unmarried children, of which the individual is a member for only part of his lifetime, has replaced the larger family of three or four generations, of which the individual is a member for the whole of his life, as the fundamental unit of society. Such an assumption is of very great importance and demands careful examination.

The first trial interview I had when I started this study was with an old man whose situation suggested the assumption might be right. He was an old widower of seventy-six years of age who lived alone in two rooms on the third floor of a block of tenement flats. His wife had died two years previously and he had no children. He was a very thin, large-boned man with a high-domed forehead and a permanent stoop. His frayed waistcoat and trousers hung in folds. At the time of calling, 5.30 p.m., he was having his first meal of the day, a hot-pot of mashed peas and ham washed down with a pint of tea from a large mug. The living-room was dilapidated, with old black-out curtains covering the windows, crockery placed on newspapers, and piles of old magazines tucked under the chairs. In one corner of the room by an open fireplace (a 'kitchener') stood a small table covered with worn lino cloth and in another corner stood a broken meat-safe with scraps of food inside. There was a photo of his wife in her twenties on the mantelpiece together with one of a barmaid and a pin-up from a Sunday paper. His wife's coat still hung on a hook on the door and her slippers were tidily placed in the hearth.

For most of his life he had worked as a commercial artist. 'I did a bit of tickling' – delicate lettering and design for advertising blocks. In his late sixties he experienced long spells of illness. When he was able to work he went as bottlewasher to a dairy. He was obliged to give up work finally because of ill-health and growing infirmity at the age of seventy-two. Since the death of his wife his social activities had contracted. He did not get up for long and rarely went out, except at week-ends for his pension and his shopping. Even his visits to an infirm brother living some miles away had fallen off. 'I used to go over and see him every Tuesday night last year – up to that fog we had in November. Then I just lay on my bed coughing and coughing. Coughing all day and night, thinking my time had come. But it wasn't to be.'

He regretted not having children, especially a daughter, who 'might have stood by me when I got old', and he had no nephews or nieces living in London. The neighbours saw little of him. Next door was 'Mrs Lipstick and Powder, that's what I calls her, always going out.' On the other side was 'Mrs Fly-by-night. She rushes past me on the stairs now, like some of the others, without asking how I am. Not that I mind. But they used to do it and since I came out of hospital and go around just like a decrepit old man – decrepit, yes – I suppose they don't like to ask how I am in case they feel they should do something. But there – life's like that, isn't it?'

He had lost touch with all his friends and did not approve of old people's clubs. 'They're all clicks of decrepit old people.' His opinion of national assistance officials, doctors, almoners, and nurses was favourable, except that sometimes they 'kept you in the dark' or 'treated you like a little child'. He had refused offers of a home help, mainly, it appeared, from a sense of privacy, shame of his home, misunderstanding about payment, and suspicion of the sort of woman who would come. His memories of contacts with doctors and hospitals were extremely vivid and he recalled at length some of his experiences. He talked about an almoner who was 'a lovely looking party', about his new dentures, 'I don't wear the top, it's more comfortable', and with pride about his one perfect faculty, his eyesight. On occasions when he could scarcely walk it never occurred to him to ask his doctor to visit him; he preferred to make painful journeys to the surgery.

*

I have chosen to begin this book with a description of the life of this one individual because he typifies what so many observers regard as the social 'problem' of old age. In his case we would find it impossible to ignore the crucial facts of bereavement, absence of children and other relatives, infirmity, and virtual social ostracism. If we mean anything by isolation from society he must be the sort of person we keep in mind. But is he exception or rule? Are there many others like him in our society? Many sociologists and administrators believe there are. One administrator expressed it in these terms:

> Provision for old age has emerged as a 'problem' largely because of the loosening of family ties and insistence on individual rights and privileges to the exclusion of obligations and duties which has developed so markedly in recent years. Whereas families used to accept responsibility for their old people they now expect the State to look after them. . . . The care and attention which the family used to provide for them must be provided in some other way.[1]

The separation from kin is supposed to be one of the features which serves to differentiate the industrial from the so-called primitive societies.

But do old people in Britain lose touch with their married children and lead an isolated life? Are the bonds of kinship of little or no consequence, especially in urban areas? We have only to pose these questions to realize the need for more facts. What few there are do not confirm many current suppositions. Sheldon, in a pioneering study, drew attention to the important part played by relatives of old people in Wolverhampton and said that too little was known about their role.

> There are therefore 192 subjects (forty per cent of the sample) whose happiness and domestic efficiency are to a greater or lesser extent dependent on the ready accessibility of their children or other relatives. . . . No solution of the problems of old age will be acceptable

1. King, Sir Geoffrey, formerly Permanent Secretary, Ministry of Pensions and National Insurance, 'Policy and Practice', *Old Age in the Modern World*, 1955, p. 45.

to the people themselves or to their children which does not take the family factor into account.[1]

Studies in other places such as Hammersmith, Acton, and Northern Ireland have also produced some evidence of close ties between old people and their relatives and of a willingness to bear the burden of nursing care. But the evidence gained in these inquiries was incidental to their main purposes. There has been no specialized study of the place of the old person in the family. Yet such detailed knowledge may be fundamental to any understanding of old age or of its problems. That is the starting point of this study. How often do old people see their children and their brothers and sisters, and do they live near or far? What services do relatives perform for each other every day and at times of crisis? What is the difference in family role of an old man and an old woman? Can a more precise meaning be given to loneliness and social isolation and what does it mean to be widowed, single, or childless? Is the status of old people undergoing change? Which old people make the greatest demand on the social services and why, and how far can and should the State aid or replace the efforts of the family? These are some of the questions which will be discussed in this report.

Plan and Method

They are not easy questions to answer. One area was sought in which a detailed study could be made. The metropolitan borough of Bethnal Green was chosen, partly because a companion inquiry into family life had already started there, undertaken by my colleagues, Michael Young and Peter Willmott.[2] In many respects the two studies are complementary. One considers family life through the eyes of middle-aged couples with children and the other largely through the eyes of the elderly. Both lay great emphasis on intensive interviews with random samples of the population. The two studies were planned together but the subsequent work was carried out, and the reports written up, independently. My colleagues and I have, quite deliberately, made no attempt to reconcile the findings in the two books. Since our chief informants belonged to different age-groups, the impres-

1. Sheldon, J. H., *The Social Medicine of Old Age*, 1948, p. 156.
2. Young, M., and Willmott, P., *Family and Kinship in East London*, 1957 (Penguin Books, 1962).

sions we gained were also bound to be different. Any reader (if there be any with the stamina) who studies both books side by side will therefore notice the disagreement on certain subjects as well as the great measure of agreement on most of the important features of the local kinship system.

The borough where the studies were carried out is relatively small, is near central London, and has a predominantly working-class population. In 1951 fourteen per cent of the people were of pensionable age – the same proportion as for the County of London and England and Wales. The borough had lost population to new housing estates on the outskirts of London, and a small minority of people were Jewish.[1] With these two reservations there was no reason to suppose that family life would be very different from that in other long-settled working-class urban areas.

After trial interviews had been carried out in Westminster and Hampstead the names of individuals of pensionable age in Bethnal Green were obtained at random from the records of general practitioners. Seven of the general practices in the borough were themselves selected at random for this purpose. The procedure was to work through the medical cards for all patients on a doctor's list, picking out every tenth card and, where the card referred to a man aged sixty-five or over, a woman aged sixty or over, or a person whose age was not specified, to note down the name and address. After eliminating those who were subsequently found to be below pensionable age (or to have died before the sample was drawn) 261 names remained. The result of visits paid to all the addresses was as follows:

Died before interview	9
Moved out of the borough	24
Untraced	5
Hospital or residential home	8
Ill	2
Refused an interview	10
Interviewed	203
	261

1. Five per cent of the old people interviewed in 1954–5 and eight per cent of a random sample of the whole population interviewed in 1955 (for the purposes of the companion study) were Jewish. Young, M. and Willmott, P., op. cit., p. xvii.

Of the 203 people interviewed two-thirds were women, half of them widowed. Just under a fifth had no surviving children. Table 1 outlines the numbers of different marital status, distinguishing those without children.

TABLE 1

MARITAL STATUS AND CHILDLESSNESS

	Without surviving children			With surviving children		Total
	Unmarried	Married	Widowed	Married	Widowed*	
Men	6	3	3	38	14	64
Women	12	5	7	52	63	139
Total no.	18		18	167		203

* Including a few who were divorced or separated.

The main interview lasted for an average of about two hours. After an explanation of the reasons for the call, the interview itself was not so much a search for short answers to formal questions as a guided conversation. An interview schedule was taken out and extensive notes taken. A kinship diagram was drawn for each informant, the Christian names, ages, occupations, and districts of residence of husband or wife, children, grand-children, brothers and sisters, and so on being noted down, together with an estimate of the frequency of contact with each of them.

Information about the family often proved difficult to obtain – sometimes because the number of relatives was very large, some-times because people were infirm, deaf, forgetful, or unwilling. Too much should not be made of such difficulties. Most people were remarkably generous and indulgent and went to great lengths to find an answer to questions – searching out birth certificates, funeral cards, family photos, insurance agreements, and supple-mentary assistance books. The kinship diagram usually gave information about more than fifty relatives, including all those in frequent touch with the old person. Facts about income, health, household management, retirement, neighbours, and friends were also sought. After the interview a report of from two to four thousand words was written. A further note on method, together with examples of interview-reports, will be found at the end of this book. In the illustrations from interviews throughout the text fictitious names have been used and details have been altered to prevent identification. In the quotations no attempt has been made to convey dialect.

Apart from a few early interviews all the people were seen between October 1954 and November 1955. I interviewed 160 myself and the remainder were interviewed by my colleague, Peter Marris. Nearly all were visited a second time, some three, four, or more times, partly to round off interviews that were incomplete and partly to secure additional information. Separate interviews were also obtained with some relatives of the chief informants.

Later in this book I will describe information gained from other sources. Twelve old people in the sample were kind enough to keep a diary of their activities for a week in the spring of 1955. Four of these diaries are reproduced in an appendix. Special surveys were made of the social and family background of old people seeking help from the social services: a sample group of some 200 people originating in East London who spent the last period of their lives in L.C.C. homes; a group of 300 people in the care of a local geriatric hospital; and finally, 400 people being visited by home helps in Bethnal Green. The object of these surveys was, first, to explore the respective functions of relatives and of the social services in helping to meet the needs of old people, and second, to pinpoint those groups who make the heaviest demands on statutory and voluntary provision.

In presenting the results I have tried throughout to keep individual people in the forefront. The research worker is so anxious to establish patterns, uniformities, and systems of social action that he is tempted to plan questionnaires that can be filled in simply and to confine his report largely to classificatory lists and tables of statistics. The uniqueness of each individual and each family is probably the fundamental difficulty about this. However those to be studied are selected, whether on grounds of likeness in age, situation, occupation, or class, once one meets them and begins to talk to them one becomes aware of the diversities of behaviour, relationships, attitude and interpretation. Standard questions, prepared beforehand, mean different things to different people; they are sometimes appropriate, sometimes inappropriate; by themselves they do not provide an adequate means of thoroughly investigating subjects as complex as this. Before one can apply or interpret the reliability of answers to set questions, one needs a fair idea of the most important relationships, activities, and characteristics of each person approached, important, that is, as they are judged by him. Too many of the principal features of social life might otherwise be missed or misrepresented.

Although I believe with conviction that the methods of interviewing should be flexible and that reports on social research should convey the quality and diversity of individual and social behaviour, I am not suggesting that the search for patterns of behaviour, through statistical analysis and correlation, is not important. I am submitting only that once a social inquiry moves beyond simple description and measurement, for instance, of facts of a basically demographic kind, the build-up of statistics and indices of behaviour becomes a subtle and complicated process that can only proceed in the context of a wide knowledge of the societies concerned. And such knowledge cannot be gained unless there is direct and continuous acquaintance with the people who are being studied.

*

I owe much to the elderly people of Bethnal Green who were generous of their time and patience, and also to colleagues at the Institute of Community Studies during the period of this study (1954–7) – Michael Young, Peter Willmott, Philip Barbour, Daphne Chandler, Polly Kasserer, and, particularly for helping so much with the interviewing and the planning of the report, Peter Marris. Among many others to whom I am indebted are Richard Titmuss, Brian Abel-Smith, J. H. Sheldon, F. le Gros Clark, Geoffrey Smith, and C. S. Walton.

CHAPTER 2

Place and People

THE Metropolitan Borough of Bethnal Green is a flat, roughly rectangular area lying in the heart of East London, less than a mile from the City and only a mile or two north of the Thames. It is one of the smallest boroughs in London, being less than two miles wide by three-quarters of a mile deep. Adjoining it to west north, east, and south are the boroughs of Shoreditch, Hackney, Poplar, and Stepney.

The housing does not give the impression of being monotonous, nor is it, broadly speaking, squalid and dilapidated, nor unrelieved by spacious parks and squares. There are patches devastated in the war and still neglected. There are pockets of semi-derelict and congested dwellings, particularly in the western part of the borough, bordering the railway and lying to the north of Roman Road. And there are the empty shells of houses awaiting demolition. But visitors expecting confirmation of what they have been told about London slums are usually surprised by the width of some of the streets of terraced cottages, by their neatness and dignity and by the number of small back-yards and gardens. These rows of two-storey cottages, mostly dating from the early part or middle of the nineteenth century, are broken up by intervening blocks of tenement flats, built towards the end of the century by private trusts and companies and later by the L.C.C., huge, forbidding buildings set in narrow paved yards, rather like outcrops of granite overlooking unpretentious escarpments. Since the war this landscape has been made even more varied by large-scale building of new council flats of varying design and colour.

The variety of housing is one expression of change. The continuity and rapidity of physical and industrial change within the borough has been one of the most important facts in the lives of its people, and particularly its old people. Two hundred years ago Bethnal Green was described as a parish with 'the face of a country, affording everything to render it pleasant, fields, pastorage, grounds for cattle, and formerly woods and marches'. In 1800 over half the parish was still farmland. Yet by the 1870s its overcrowded slums were attracting public attention and censure. In 1901 there were nearly 130,000 people in the borough, about half of whom were over-crowded and just under half in poverty. By 1931 the population had declined to 108,000 and in 1943, after bombing and evacuation, there were only 40,000 people in the borough. After the war the population increased to over 60,000 but fell to 54,000 in 1955. The movement has not only been outward, to new housing estates on the fringes of London, but also from district to district within the borough. In recent times whole groups of streets have been demolished and replaced by many new flats. The population as a whole, therefore, has been much less stable for several decades than in many other places.

To a casual eye the customs of life of the population are not so varied as the housing. Attachment to flowers and pets is almost universal. The back-yards or back-gardens of many old houses are filled with masses of flowers and sometimes with hen-runs, rabbit-hutches, and aviaries. One old man who was interviewed grew prize dahlias and others had sheds in which they repaired shoes or furniture. The balconies of many of the modern flats are also ablaze with colour in the summer. And in the windows of both flats and houses hang cages of budgerigars. Well over half the old people interviewed had a pet, most of these a cage-bird. One man kept an aviary on the balcony of the tenement block in which he lived.

It is as difficult to look from the street into the homes of those living in modern flats with spacious windows as of those living in old houses. Lace curtains or ornaments intervene, and doors are not usually left open except when children are playing round the doorstep or when an old man is sitting on a chair watching the passers-by. Sometimes a wooden gate is fitted into the doorway to prevent a young child from venturing into the street. The privacy of the hearth seems to be sacred to all but a very few families with children – these few usually living in dilapidated property.

Old and modern flats as well as old terraced houses have the whitened or painted doorsteps covered with strips of lino; the bells beyond the reach of any child; the sparkling windows cleaned weekly or fortnightly; and the pot alsatian dogs, vases of artificial flowers, and gaudily dyed curtains.

Neighbours often imitate each other. In one street is a row of six houses with an aspidistra in each front window, rarely found elsewhere; in another a line of four alsatian dogs and, in a third, a succession of curtains of a particular hue, dark blue, rose pink, yellow ochre. For young children the modern flat with its doorkey dangling on a piece of string from the letter-box seems to be just such a home as the old house with its grimy piece of cord tied to the latch and protruding through a makeshift hole in the door.

One difference between old and new in Bethnal Green is the separation of home and workplace. New housing does not provide workrooms, although elsewhere, scattered among the back-streets, are hundreds of small workshops, mostly converted from houses and some retaining one floor as living quarters. Some of the oldest houses have very wide windows on the first floor. These were the homes and workshops of the Huguenot silk weavers and their descendants. Most people still live close to their work.

The back-street workshops make furniture and woodwork of all kinds, shoes, and clothing. For old people tied to their windows there is a great deal to watch. One of the commonest noises in the streets is the wood-turner's lathe or the sewing-machine. In summer there are glimpses of men or girls at work in tiny workshops and of furniture frames, boxes, and rags piled high on the pavement. At night, in some streets, sombre lines of vans or huge transport lorries are drawn up, bumper to bumper.

If one major feature of the borough is its small industry, another is its commerce. In the back-streets are the characteristic cornershops, easily accessible to all but the most infirm people. On the main thoroughfares are few of the familiar chain-stores found elsewhere in London, but many small shops and market stalls. Three general markets open every day, with three hundred stalls lining Bethnal Green Road, Brick Lane, and Roman Road. Special markets open on Sunday mornings – flowers and plants in Columbia Road, pets of all kinds and especially budgerigars in Club Row, wireless and electrical equipment in Cygnet Street, and second-hand clothes in Cheshire Street. The intimacy of contact between seller and buyer among the market stalls extends also to many of the shops. A number of grocers and ironmongers, for example, display their wares on the pavement. The individuality of shops and stalls is striking: 'Sam's fish: quality and civility'; 'Gent's hairdresser: please note our only address'; 'The Little Wonder' and 'Kelly for Jelly'.

The outward character of Bethnal Green lies in its back-street workshops, its colourful markets, and its rows of terraced cottages interspersed by grim sentinels of Victorian solidity – those gloomy blocks of flats built up to and around the turn of the century. The place comes alive with its people, short, jocund, and familiar; plump women on the move with their shopping bags, old women showing off their daughters' prams, men loading a lorry with furniture frames or leaning against it with their feet idly crossed, bantering with the passers-by. Children and teenagers seem to be arrogant, confident, and sparkling. Girls are not afraid to wear extravagant plumage, hobble skirts, purple coats with princess collars, and imitation gold ear-rings, and some even wear make-up to do their shopping (though they seem to keep their nylons for the evenings). Boys combine suits of Edwardian cut with American swagger and there is nothing subtle or discreet in their advances to the girls. Young children are remarkably self-possessed, if shrill, and quick to take advantage of their opportunities, whether they prove to be a pile of wood-chippings left unattended, a lorry edging too slowly down a street, or a sudden issue of sunlight at a moment when they have some broken bits of mirror.

The Old People

All this provided the setting within which old people in Bethnal Green led their lives. What, to a visitor, did they and their homes look like? Looks often belied age. Most people visited were short in stature and some were lined and bent and rooted like withered trees, but others were swift and spruce and sly as the experienced fox. Some were exhausted by life but others seemed barely to have started it. A woman in her early sixties had resigned herself to her room, her stick, her black cat and her fire. Yet a man in his late eighties still talked alertly and moved swiftly about the house and neighbourhood. He had not seen his doctor more than three times in ten years. And a woman in her mid sixties said she liked evenings out. 'I like dancing. There, you wouldn't believe that, would you?' She did a little jig in the room. 'I bet I'm the wildest one you've met.'

The women ranged in age from sixty to ninety and in physique from the grotesquely fat to the painfully thin. They curled their hair or swept it back from the face and ears, only two or three wore make-up of any kind and few wore other than woollen or lisle stockings. Many of them were in bedroom slippers and some in curlers. Usually they wore flowered cotton dresses or woollen skirts and cardigans and often a colourful apron or overall. The men varied in age from sixty-five to eighty-seven but few were either fat or thin. They usually had their hair cropped short and a number had walrus moustaches but none had beards. The arms of some of them were tattooed. In the home many wore a waistcoat over collarless shirts and unlaced boots and some a silk scarf. The clothes of many people, particularly those over seventy, were well-worn and old.

The homes revealed a great deal about the occupants. Photos of relatives, distributed over tables and sideboards and walls, were one of the best indications of the size of an old person's family as well as one of the most natural cues for talking about it. A clock which was an hour slow or two hours fast proved, in practice, to be one of the most impressive expressions of isolation, loneliness, or weary resignation. Unusual items of furniture were often found to be the gift of children or an inheritance from dead relatives. It was impossible to ignore a huge chromium-plated fender (made by a son) or a copy of Holman Hunt's picture 'The Light of the World' (passed on from the old person's parents). In many simply-designed modern flats the old-style possessions seemed to be out of place but they recalled the history and expressed the unity of the family.

In one widow's small kitchen was a television set with two Toby jugs below it and a budgerigar in a cage standing on top. There were photos of two sons on the walls, one in police uniform. At least eight photos of other children and grandchildren were on a small sideboard. The back window overlooked a tiny yard, where, she said, 'the flowers look a picture in the summer'. There was a framed piece of embroidery made by a granddaughter on the wall. The inscription read 'I have got a sweetheart – I would have no other. She's more than all the world to me – Because her name is "Mother".' The ironing board was up and she was about to do her daughter-in-law's and her own ironing.

A widower cooked and ate in a small room at the back of the house. At the time of call he was just beginning his breakfast. This was a pint mug of tea and one piece of toast with margarine. The room was untidy and the wallpaper peeling. There were two wooden chairs, a kitchen table with newspapers on top and a zinc bath hung on the back of the door. The china on the dresser obviously had not been dusted since his wife's death three months before. The floor was scattered with bits of rubbish and in a corner was a pile of jute or hemp material intended to stuff furniture. On the mantelpiece was an accumulation of various boxes of pills, bottles of medicine, bits and pieces of cotton reels, and a few old-fashioned china vases. Under the table were two large enamel bowls full to the brim with slops. There were no photos. He had no children. There was no radio.

The homes contained abundant evidence not only of the presence or absence of family relationships but also of the customs and standards of daily life. In a number of homes doormats were laid in parallel in the hall-way, which was often curtained off from the kitchen. Lino, or 'oilcloth' as it was usually called, was the common form of floor-covering, upon which were laid coconut mats, and less often, woollen rugs or carpets. In better-off homes suites of imitation leather furniture, sideboards, and upright pianos replaced the Windsor or cane chairs and the folding tables of the poorer homes. In the older houses the polished iron fireplace or kitchener with a white hearth was common. The ownership of a radio was usual but not universal (eighty-five per cent of the old people had a radio, a substantial minority of these, about one in five, having only relay sets). One in five owned, or had access to, a television set in the home.[1]

The old people were visited without previous warning at all times of the day and year. One woman of seventy was found kneeling on the pavement chatting to two of her neighbours, all three scrubbing their front doorsteps. A man had just had a bath and two or three were slipping their braces over their shoulders, having just got up from a nap. One woman was doing her washing with a neighbour in the washroom shared by the occupants of five flats. Another was

1. In 1955 a third of all households in Bethnal Green had television sets. See Young, M., and Willmott, P., op. cit., p. 117.

soothing a tearful grandchild on her lap. A man wept copiously as he explained that his wife could not be seen because she had just died. Another widower lifted a finger three or four times during an interview when he heard a door slam. 'That's my Rosie. That's my daughter now,' but there was no sound of steps ascending the stairs. Rarely did a man ever open the front door to me if there was a woman or girl in the home. Three people were ill in bed and invited me to sit at their bedside. Others were very deaf. Sometimes, after knocking, I heard the tapping of a stick for two or three minutes before the door opened, and another few minutes elapsed while I followed an aged man or woman labouring upstairs to a room on the first floor.

The relationship between several husbands and wives was such that the interview was constantly in danger of getting out of hand. One man and his wife disagreed violently, the man repeatedly telling his wife to shut up. 'Leave the gentleman to me, I'm telling him all the answers. He doesn't want you interrupting.' A severe-looking woman attempted to squash her husband, a small, tooth-less man in baggy trousers. He said, 'All right, if I'm not wanted I'll go into the kitchen', but he returned after a while. Some women, particularly those in their early sixties, made it plain they would prefer me to call when their husbands were at home.

One wife went into her kitchen to make a cup of tea. When she returned she said, 'What's he been doing, telling you the tale of the old iron and the pot?' A man explained what clothing he washed on a Monday, 'one dickey dirt, one 'oller, boys, 'oller, and one pair of almond rocks' (shirt, collar, and socks). A widow said her husband had 'done a guy'. Some people were anxious to pass on the lessons they had learned from life. One woman put an arm affectionately round my shoulders and said, 'My son, cut your grass and you'll never want. . . . Chance your arm. . . . persevere and you'll get your reward.'

The home was often warm and convivial. One married woman was visited by her daughter and granddaughter. The daughter immediately began washing up in a bowl and from her came a crackling stream of back-chat, cheery, ironical, and humorous. Her mother seemed to be uncertain whether I should be treated courteously and seriously but her daughter's remarks, like fire-crackers, overlaid any embarrassment she had. 'Come on, she fancies herself really, we'll give you something to put in your book. . . . Help her with the shopping?' she asked with mock amusement. 'Don't put those ideas into her head. I want her to keep on getting *mine*.' Later, hunks of bread pudding were taken out of a pan in the oven and were handed round with a cup of tea.

Again and again people drew attention to their unimpaired faculties, to their individuality, and to the compensations they recognized for things they had lost. One man in his late seventies said, 'When people come here they think they are going to meet a tottering old man. But by the time I've finished with them they've said very little, and I've said a lot.' This, alas, was only too true. The first interview lasted three-and-a-half hours. It was impossible to keep him to the point. A question whether he liked reading would lead on to historical studies, Queen Elizabeth the First, whether she was a virgin and whether red-haired women were often virgins. In the course of the interview he touched on how much money Tottenham Hotspur had in the bank, whether Gordon Richards was a real jockey, the iniquities of American tariffs, whether Ernest Bevin deserved the credit he got for his work for the dock labourers, how his father used to buy Russian ponies, and why Keir Hardie died of a broken heart.

In any group of people selected at random from the population a few are so out of place, in most respects, as to be virtually unclassifiable. One was the retired prostitute who 'hit the road' in the summer and secluded herself in one room for the winter. Another the man who had served prison sentences for the greater part of his life and who now depended on his former accomplices. Another the Russian émigré who spoke scarcely a word of English and had practically no contacts in the locality.

Altogether there was great diversity – of people warm-hearted or reserved; illiterate or well-read; enthusiastic, garrulous, witty, or disconsolate; sociable or isolated from nearly all human contact. Some things people had in common. They were, for instance, rarely self-pitying. They bore pain with surprisingly little fuss. They were anxious to appear honest and fair-dealing, liked a joke, were easily pleased, disliked formality or affectation, and were rarely content unless they were of use to others and had company. This was written into their manner, their conversation, and their homes. They thought of themselves, first as members of families and workgroups, as grandmothers, aunts, or housewives, as grandfathers, uncles, and cabinet-makers, and only second as individuals old in years.

This brief description of the place in which the old people lived and of their appearance and home environment is the background to the following report.

PART ONE

The Family Life of Old People

CHAPTER 3

Home and Family

THIS book started by asking how far in fact old people were isolated from family life. The first step in attempting to give an answer is to consider the home and its membership. To what extent and why do old people live with their relatives? And what do they think of living with married children? These are the main questions discussed in this chapter.

Of the 203 people in Bethnal Green twenty-five per cent lived alone in the household, twenty-nine per cent in married pairs, thirty-eight per cent with unmarried or married children, and eight per cent with others, mostly relatives. Rather more women than men lived entirely alone, largely because more of them were widowed, but about the same proportion of both men and women lived with relatives. Altogether, forty-five per cent shared a household with relatives other than a husband or wife.

This proportion does not appear to be exceptional. Indeed, fewer in Bethnal Green seemed to live with relatives than in other parts of the country, but detailed comparison is obscured by the different classifications and definitions of the living unit that have been used. Census data refer to all people over sixty and not those just of pensionable age. In Great Britain as a whole, twelve and a half per cent aged sixty and over were living alone in 1951, and only a further twenty-eight to twenty-nine per cent in married pairs. Roughly four and a half million people of sixty and over, or about fifty-eight per cent, were living with people other than a husband or wife, nearly all of them with relatives. At that time, so far as the Census material can be interpreted, at least forty per cent of people of that age were living with children unmarried, married, or both unmarried and married.[1] If the single or childless are excluded, perhaps as many as sixty per cent of those with surviving children were living with at least one of them.

1. Calculated from Part II of the *Census of 1951: One Per Cent Sample Tables* V.1, VI (1–8). Only vague estimates can be made from the Census data of the number of old people in different types of household in 1951.

Conditions vary from one locality to another. According to the report on a field survey carried out just after the war for the Nuffield Foundation, forty-six per cent of people of pensionable age in the London boroughs of Wandsworth and St Pancras, fifty-three per cent in Oldham, sixty-two per cent in York, and seventy-five per cent in mid-Rhondda, were living as householders with their children or lodgers, or living as guests of their children. In 1947 almost fifty per cent of old people in Wolverhampton were living with their children and a further ten per cent with other relatives.

Clearly, in spite of the inexactness of available information about the households of old people, many live with relatives, particularly their children. This appears to be true even of the oldest people. A special analysis of the 1951 Census showed that in Bethnal Green forty-five per cent of women over eighty, compared with forty-three per cent in their sixties, lived with relatives other than a husband.[1] Much the same was true of both men and women interviewed in the sample inquiry, although, because of the small numbers in the advanced age groups, the information is less reliable.

This is not to say there is no change with increasing age. The special analysis also showed that the proportion of women living entirely alone in the household was twenty-six per cent of those under seventy and forty-eight per cent of those aged eighty and over. This is largely accounted for by the rise in the number of widows, balancing the fall in the number of married women. Four in five of women over eighty were widows, compared with two in five of those in their sixties. An increase with age in the proportion living alone is also found in other parts of the country, though it does not affect such a large part of the elderly population.[2]

1. The author is indebted to the Registrar-General for his assistance in providing the results of a special twenty per cent sample analysis of the Bethnal Green household schedules.

2. For Great Britain the Census reports do not distinguish the proportions of different age groups over the age of sixty living alone. The previously mentioned survey carried out for the Nuffield Foundation just after the war shows that old people interviewed in York, Wolverhampton, Oldham, mid-Rhondda, Wandsworth, and St Pancras eleven per cent of the women aged sixty to sixty-nine, twenty-two per cent aged seventy to seventy-nine, and twenty-two per cent aged eighty and over were living alone. For men

Household and Dwelling

This description of old people in terms of households cannot, however, be accepted unreservedly as an adequate account of living arrangements. Relatives sometimes live in the same dwelling even when not in the same household. Information in reports on the Census and in most social surveys is about the household, meaning by that a number of people sleeping under the same roof and eating together at the same table. There may be two or more households in a structurally separate dwelling which, according to the Census definition, 'generally comprises any room or suite of rooms intended or used for habitation, having separate access to the street or to a common landing or staircase to which the public has access'. The definition is extraordinarily difficult to apply in practice. In Bethnal Green there was a single man living in the same flat as his widowed mother but eating all his meals out and spending most week-ends away from home. There was a married woman living in the same house as two married daughters, each with their husbands and unmarried children, where most of the domestic arrangements, including midday meal for all the women and children, were communal but the three wives separated for evening tea when the husbands returned. Who is in the same household, and who is not? For relatives in a single dwelling, the difference between those sharing most meals and those eating separately was often extremely slight. They did not divide naturally into two. Even those old people who ate all meals by themselves sometimes had relatives 'on call' in the dwelling who helped them in all kinds of ways. These facts deserve more scrutiny than they have had. While necessary for much social analysis, a working definition of 'household' that is applied too rigidly may cause part of the truth about people's home relationships to be missed or misrepresented. In this book more account will be taken of dwelling than of household.

Table 2 compares two definitions of the living unit, so far as they could be applied to the Bethnal Green sample. When reference was made to dwelling as well as to household, the proportion of old

---

aged sixty-five to sixty-nine, seventy to seventy-nine, and eighty or over the percentages were four, eight, and ten respectively. Those living in lodgings were not included. (*Old People*, Nuffield Foundation, 1947, pp. 140–1.)

TABLE 2

OLD PEOPLE SHARING HOUSEHOLD OR DWELLING WITH
RELATIVES

Number of generations	Relations present	Household %	Dwelling %
One	No other relative	26† ⎫	23† ⎫
	Spouse only	29 ⎬ 59	23 ⎬ 53
	Other relatives	4 ⎭	7 ⎭
Two*	Unmarried child(ren) only	24 ⎫	22 ⎫
	Married or widowed child(ren) (and others)	4 ⎬ 31	7 ⎬ 33
	Other relatives	3 ⎭	4 ⎭
Three*	Unmarried child(ren) and grandchild(ren)	2 ⎫	2 ⎫
	Married or widowed child(ren) and grand-child(ren)	8 ⎬ 10	12 ⎬ 14
	Other relatives	0 ⎭	0 ⎭
	Total	100	100
	Number	203	203

* With or without husband or wife.
† A few people shared the household with non-relatives. The proportion living entirely alone was twenty-five per cent, in terms of households, and twenty-one per cent in terms of dwellings. The latter were alone in that no one else lived in the household and no relative lived in other households in the same dwelling.

people found to be living with relatives increased from forty-five to fifty-four per cent. Nearly a half lived in dwellings containing two or three generations of relatives. Of the 203 eighty-seven lived with at least one child and another twenty-four with various relatives, a number of them with brothers or sisters and nephews or nieces, a few with a cousin, a grandchild only, or a sister-in-law. Forty-three people, or twenty-one per cent, lived alone, in the sense that there was no other relative or non-relative in the household and no relative in the dwelling. Most of these were widowed.

The Wish to be Independent

When old people lose their husbands or wives it seems many of them go on living alone. What causes them to do this? Do children neglect them or do they choose to live alone? The short answer is that, on the basis of the interviews carried out, most of them choose to. They wish to be independent and they are attached to their own homes.

The great majority of old people in Bethnal Green believed that to live together was to invite that open conflict with the child's spouse they preferred to avoid, to interfere with the marital obligations of man and wife, and to lose their own privacy. They thought they best served their own interests, and those of their children, by living near them rather than with them. Both parents and children were then able to preserve deeply-rooted kinship ties without prejudicing the new ones formed by a child's marriage.

A widow living alone said, 'This is my idea. A mother's a mother no matter how old she is. She's got something she doesn't want the children to know, and they've got something they don't want her to know. There's that little something about your life you want to keep on your own. When I feel I'm in the way I just go.'

A sixty-three-year-old woman said of her unmarried children, 'I'd rather they got a place on their own. They get into married life. If you live with your parents you're upstairs to mother. One [the child] would be downstairs and leave the other one [the spouse] upstairs moping. You're more your own master when you're independent. But it's nice to be near.'

A married woman was visited by her daughter and grandchild every afternoon for four or five hours. She did not think it right to live with married children. 'I don't, as much as I love my girl. You should live on your own. There comes upsets between you. They [husband and wife] have a cross word and you get to thinking about it and perhaps you can't keep quiet. It's nice when you come and see one another fresh. There's more privacy, definitely there's more privacy.'

A widow of eighty-three who lived alone said, 'I can go to bed when I like and come back when I like. There's no one to say "where've you been?"' She slapped the table with laughter at the thought of this reversal of role of mother and child.

Much of the same kind of thing was said by many of the people actually living with married children. A majority of those with married children at home were against living with them (fifty-one per cent) or were uncertain about the arrangement (fifteen per cent). One married man, sharing his flat with his married daughter and son-in-law, was asked whether he thought it a good thing to live with married children. He said:

> 'No. They like to be on their own. They like to do their own cooking, and my youngest daughter can't get a place. She's been on the [housing] list four years but she hasn't got a family [children] yet.' Later his wife added, 'No, although we get on marvellous, they want a place on their own.'

Sometimes it was difficult to get a clear indication of the old person's attitude. Children were present at a number of interviews and disarming remarks, such as, 'It's all right if you can agree all right' or 'We've had our little ups and downs naturally', made it hard to ascertain true feelings. Another complication was that some old people did not regard themselves as 'living with' children although they shared their dwelling, and much of their lives, with a married child. One woman spent much of the day with a married daughter and grandchildren living in another part of the same house, sharing meals and housework. But evening tea was taken separately with their respective husbands. The old woman agreed with the general preference. 'She doesn't live in with me. You don't want to be together in the same flat. It wouldn't be fair.'

Others expressed themselves in the same way: 'It's right to be independent'; 'You need a private place'; 'It's nice to be near but not too near'; 'Familiarity breeds contempt' – these were the kind of phrases used. They held to an ideal of non-interference in the marriage of their children. They recognized it imposed obligations not only on a man and wife but on themselves.

Old people's wish to live independently was reinforced by a deep attachment to their homes. It was rare for widows or widowers in the district to join a married son or daughter. Only three, all widows, had done this, and even these three had been reluctant. Others said they were invited but had refused to go. Home was the old armchair by the hearth, the creaky bedstead, the polished lino with its faded pattern, the sideboard with its picture gallery, and the lavatory with its broken latch reached through the rain. It embodied a thousand memories and held promise of a thousand contentments. It was an extension of personality. To the married children it was also the reminder of their history and achievements – this the chair scorched by a sparkler on Guy Fawkes night, this the wallpaper where you looked for animal shapes, that the doormat which had to be lifted at the corner if the door was to be shut. 'We always go over *home* to see Mum on Sundays,' said a married daughter. Part of what the children felt for their parents was what they felt for the parental home. It was not only the place where associations with the past and long usage provided comfort and security in old age. It was a symbol of family unity and tradition.

Although wartime bombing and recent demolition had forced many people to move out of the borough, the old people interviewed had lived in the same home, on average, for twenty-four years. Twenty-seven per cent had remained for over forty years, as compared with only fifteen per cent for less than five. The home had sometimes been in the family for more than three or four generations. One person in six had inherited their tenancy from parents. Several women said their mother's parents had lived in the house before their own parents. One sixty-year-old woman, after explaining she had lived in the one house all her life, added, 'My mother died in this room, my father died in this room, and so did my grandmother'. Both men and women frequently said that a younger brother or sister was living in the parents' old house. One married woman said she visited an unmarried brother and sister nearby. 'Yes, we still say we're going "over home" when we go there, even though Mum's been dead ten years.'

The home stood partly for relatives known to have lived there and many people reported parents, aunts and uncles, brothers and sisters who had lived in it after their marriage. Throughout life, as changes took place in the family, changes had taken place in the membership of the home. Such changes continued to take place in old age. Over a third of the sample had experienced a change in the previous three years. For one reason or another at least one relative had left or joined the home. This applied almost as much to people in their seventies and eighties as those in their sixties.

Reasons for Living with Relatives

The desire to be independent of a child's marriage; the attachment to the home and its traditions: each of these helps to explain why many people preferred to go on living alone after the death of their husbands or wives. Why, then, in spite of this preference, did a substantial minority share their homes with married children? People do, of course, choose to share their homes or are obliged to do so because of housing shortages, but an independent answer is that certain kinds of family structure favour relatives living together. Variation in the size of the family and in the sex, age, and marital status of its members produce special household and personal relationships for young people as well as old.

Throughout this book attention will be called to structural variations among families as providing one of the chief means of insight into family life. The variation is certainly great. The Bethnal Green sample ranged from an unmarried woman who was the only child of an only child to a woman who had had seventeen children, nearly as many as her mother's eighteen and her husband's mother's twenty-two. Many people were widowed, single or childless, and the age difference between old people and their children varied between seventeen and fifty years. Such variations are, naturally enough, reflected in variations in household membership.

In Bethnal Green, only children were more often found living with their elderly parents than other children, not so much because they delayed marriage as because they continued to live with their parents afterwards. Of those with two or more children, twenty-two per cent lived with at least one married child, compared with thirty-six per cent of those with one child. Of twenty-six people with only one surviving child ten were living with them, and another nine lived within a mile. Only one of these was unmarried.

Old people more often lived with married daughters than sons. Of the 203, eight per cent lived in the same dwelling with married or widowed sons but eleven per cent with married or widowed daughters. The numbers living with daughters rather than sons would have been greater but for the fact that a third of the old people had children of one sex only, and these tended to live more often with their married children.

Relatively more widowed people than married lived with married children. Besides having no spouse, a number were infirm or had only one surviving child. This helped to make a joint household more practicable.

Mrs Bates was almost stone deaf. She went to live with her daughter, an only child, on the death of her husband. Her daughter said, 'Naturally, she came to us. I used to be there with her all day. We were always together. So naturally she came to us. . . . We get on well together. To tell the truth I find it a help. I wouldn't like anything to happen to her.'

A much higher proportion of old people lived with unmarried than with married children. Many of these had had children late in life. The average age at birth of the last child was thirty-five for women and thirty-nine for men. This was not the chief factor, however. Only one in six of the unmarried children had not reached the average marrying ages and over half were older than thirty-five. And of those who still had at least one unmarried child at home many, particularly widows, were of advanced age.

Of the sixty-seven widows in the sample only twenty had lost their husbands in the previous ten years, and thirty-three more than twenty years ago. Although both widows and their children were older on average than married women and their children, a slightly higher proportion of widows were living with unmarried children. The special Census investigation referred to earlier showed that in 1951 twenty-seven per cent of widows over sixty were living with unmarried children, compared with twenty-five per cent of married women of that age. In the present small sample there were eleven widows in their seventies and eighties living with unmarried children, nearly all of whom were themselves over forty years old. While difficult to confirm it seemed that if the children were in their teens or early twenties when their father died one or more of them put off marriage altogether to act as a kind of substitute for the lost father,[1] or postponed marriage till late and stayed on thereafter in the same house with their widowed mothers. The special responsibility for a widowed mother was frequently acknowledged. 'She stayed with Mum when Dad died.' 'We didn't want to leave Mum.' 'He said he didn't want to get married. He'd rather stay with me.'

A widow of eighty whose husband died young and who had just lost her sixty-year-old son said he had never married because 'he always thought too much of his mother. He was always so proud of his

1. This is discussed in Chapter 7.

mother. When he was at the hospital, they said he never talked about anyone else. They said they'd never heard a son talking about his mother like that. He never got worried about women. I miss him, oh, how I miss him. We used to keep the home going. We were never apart. We always used to sit together in the afternoon in the two armchairs. We were always going out together.'

The facts cited in this chapter show how wrong it would be to assume that the household passes through three simple stages over the life cycle, from a first stage where there are only young parents and young children to a second stage of middle-aged parents and adolescent earners, and thence to a third stage where the old parents are on their own. It does not pursue a simple cycle of development but adjusts to the needs and facts of family relationships. As a result married relatives often live together, and unmarried ones join forces or remain with parents. We have seen that over half the old people lived in the same dwelling with relatives other than a spouse. At the highest ages more lived alone, but the proportion living with children remained about the same. Old people were not against living alone. In fact most preferred it to living with married children, because they could maintain their own independence and avoid imposing on the privacy of the children's marriage. They made one big qualification. They did not mind living separately from their children, so long as they could live *near* them. Most parents mentioned this spontaneously. They spoke as if the proximity of relatives meant they were not really living alone.

CHAPTER 4

Living near Relatives

THE handicap of living alone loses its force when relatives live nearby. This is often overlooked in discussions of the circumstances and problems of old people. We have seen that many old people live with relatives. We shall now see that relatives often live nearby.

Between them the 203 people interviewed had approximately 2,700 relatives living within a mile. As it was not possible to obtain full genealogies, these were mostly near-relatives, meaning relatives by blood or through marriage no more distant than first cousins or nephews and nieces and their children. Each person had an average of thirteen living within a mile, but the range was great, one person having as many as ninety and a few none at all. Only twenty-one per cent of the old people had fewer than four within a mile but, at the other extreme, twenty-four per cent had more than twenty. Only a fifth of those living alone had no relative within a mile; some had more than twenty.

The Nearness of Children

To what extent were children living near? This is clearly a vital question. Although many of the people in the sample married in the ten or twenty years before the 1914 war, fewer than a third had large families. Death had claimed a high proportion of children. Information was supplied altogether about 818 (discounting still-births), of whom nearly a quarter had died. Ten per cent of those who were married, widowed, or separated had no surviving children, thirty-five per cent had one or two, and thirty-one per cent had five or more.

A strikingly large proportion – eighty-five per cent of those with children – had a child living with them or within a mile. Over half of those not living with a child had one in the same street or block of flats, or just round the corner. The figures remained impressive, even when unmarried children were excluded. Although only a quarter lived with a married child a further half had one within a mile. Very few people had become so separated from their children that none were living in or around London. These facts are shown in Table 3.

TABLE 3

PROXIMITY OF NEAREST CHILD

Proximity	Unmarried or married child	Married child only
	%	%
Same dwelling	52	24
Within 5 minutes' walk*	25	38
More than 5 minutes' walk but less than a mile	8	12
East London region†	8	16
Elsewhere in London	3	6
Elsewhere in Great Britain or abroad	4	5
Total	100	100
Number	167	164

* Same or next street or block.
† The eastern boroughs of the Administrative County of London plus the eastern districts of Outer London, north of the Thames, served by London Transport.

For most people what was true of one child was true of others. As shown by Table 4, fifty per cent of *all* children lived within a mile. A high proportion was living in other parts of East and Outer London. Most had migrated to L.C.C. housing estates before and after the war and most were within an hour's journey by bus or underground railway. Only eleven per cent of the 626 children did not live in or around London.

Rather more married daughters than married sons lived within a mile, forty-seven per cent compared with forty-two per cent. How so many married children came to be living near, and why there were slightly more daughters, deserves some comment. The couple usually began their marriage in a home near the wife's parents. Often this happened to be near the husband's parents too, but whenever a choice presented itself the wife's parents were generally favoured. Just as the bride's mother was expected to play a greater role than the bridegroom's mother in the preparations for the marriage so she was expected to play a greater role thereafter. She had first claim on the married couple at Christmas and other festivals and later she had first claim on the visits of the grand-children. The ascendancy of the wife's parents, and particularly her mother, was generally acknowledged by men and women alike. 'He had to go near his wife's people. It's only natural.' 'At Christ-mas I go to my daughter's and my son goes to his wife's mother. She's got the right to do that, hasn't she? You couldn't expect him not to, could you?' 'We don't see much of Lucy [her son's wife]. The last time she came up and brought Carol [her son's child] she screamed at me, and tried to hide behind her mother! She is such a quiet girl. She is shy. I suppose she sees more of her other grannie.'

TABLE 4

PROXIMITY OF ALL CHILDREN

Proximity	Sons	Daughters	Sons and daughters
	%	%	%
Same dwelling	15	23	19
Within a mile	31	31	31
East London region	30	28	29
Elsewhere in London	12	8	10
Elsewhere in Great Britain or abroad	12	11	11
Total	100	100	100
Number	314	312	626

By general acknowledgement of this principle many questions of choice involving a wife's and a husband's parents were settled. It was one rule by which two families could adjust to a marriage. Many daughters found a home near their mothers. If living in ter-raced cottages or blocks of flats owned by private trusts, such as the Guinness or Peabody Trusts and the Industrial or East End Dwellings Companies, it was the mother who approached the land-lord or superintendent on behalf of her daughter. Preference for vacant accommodation was usually given to the married children of tenants. Even when living in council-owned property the mother and her daughter often went to extraordinary lengths so that they might live near one another, repeatedly visiting the local housing offices and arranging complicated 'exchanges' with third parties.[1] 'My girl was on the housing list for eight years and in the end she got a place in Bethnal Green.' 'My girls wouldn't go out of Bethnal Green. After the war a couple of them got into those Nissen huts – they kept them like dolls' houses and then when the time came they were able to get places in these new blocks.'

But not all the daughters were successful. One widow said, 'A daughter used to be able to get a house in the next turning. I remember when I had the key of one house for weeks and nobody wanted it. But now they can't do that and they have to go out miles and miles.' One man said his youngest daughter had tried hard to find a place in Bethnal Green after the war but in the end had gone out to Letchworth, some miles from London, even though her husband had a long journey to his work in the London docks. A woman explained that her only daughter lived in South London. 'She would have loved to be in Bethnal Green. She would live next door if she could. She put her name down for ten years. But in the end she went to live with her mother-in-law because her mother-in-law had a big place. She comes up to see us every week, sometimes twice a week. And we go there on a Saturday evening and come back Sundays.' There were many instances of this kind. Housing was short and local authorities, unlike many private landlords, did not give preference to the children of existing tenants for houses or flats falling vacant. Moreover, the parents of children moving to a new estate were not allowed a claim on any housing falling vacant in that estate. Although families worked to preserve their cohesion there is no question that, so far as the Bethnal Green sample was concerned, more married daughters would have lived near their parents if the choice had fallen to them and their families.

The usual practice of establishing a home near the wife's parents therefore ran into difficulties. The practice was also modified by family structure and circumstances. The wives of some sons had lost their mothers and this explained why they were living near their mothers-in-law. Many sons had married local girls and were near their own as well as their wives' parents. And finally, there

1. See Interview Report 3 in Appendix 2.

was some recognition of the needs of the mother, particularly the widow, who had sons but not daughters. At least one of her sons usually remained at home or nearby. Several references were made to such a circumstance. 'My son comes with his wife at Christmas. He's all I've got. Her mother had seven [children] so she lets her come.'

Migration was influenced by family structure. If there were brothers and sisters at home or in the district a married child seemed more likely to move to a housing estate outside London. Youngest and only children (whether sons or daughters) tended to stay in Bethnal Green, and other children, particularly the eldest, to move out. Elder children did not have to worry about leaving their parents on their own, and anyway now depended less on their parents, and particularly on their mothers, than previously in their lives. As the eldest children's children grew up the grandmother turned her attentions more to the younger sons and daughters and their initiation to marriage and childbirth. The tie with the eldest became weaker. Moreover, with two, three or more children of their own they were allotted more 'points' by the housing authorities and so qualified sooner for a house on an outside housing estate. There were fewer pressures on them to remain in the borough.

Seeing Children

Despite the inevitable demands placed upon young people by changing family structure and despite all the practical difficulties of getting a house or flat locally, one or more of the old person's children usually lived with them or near them, as we have seen. Indeed, altogether, nearly half the married daughters, and over two-fifths of married sons, lived within a mile. This was a noteworthy fact in a borough which had lost more than half its population in the previous twenty or thirty years.

With so many living near it was no surprise to find that old people saw a great deal of their children. How often they saw them and what went on when they met is plainly a central part of this inquiry. A preliminary sketch of the data is given here. The general question of contacts between relatives, if it was to be an exact means of social discovery, had to be approached carefully. 'Contact' was understood as a meeting with another person, usually pre-arranged or customary at home or outside, which involved more than a casual

48

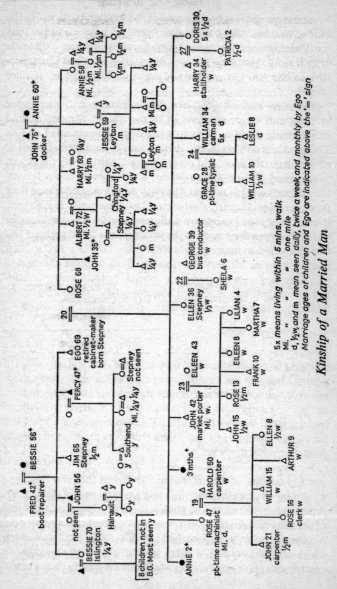

Kinship of a Married Man

5x means living within 5 mins. walk
Mi. " " one mile
d, ½w, and m mean seen daily, twice a week, and monthly by Ego
Marriage ages of children and Ego are indicated above the = sign

exchange of greetings as between two neighbours in the street. People were asked *how often* they saw each of their relatives. Wherever possible they were also asked, as a check, when they *last* saw them. The diagram on p. 48 shows how this information was recorded. On the whole the answers were straightforward. They were often consistent with answers to other questions on such things as care during illness, looking after grandchildren, and holidays, with the occasional testimony of the relatives themselves and with the interviewer's direct observation. For example, one widow, who said her youngest daughter often spent a good part of the day with her, was seen on six subsequent occasions: on four of these her daughter was in the house.

Most people kept in frequent touch with their children. Table 5 shows that two-thirds saw at least one of their daughters daily and nearly half saw one of their sons. Although fifteen per cent had no child within a mile, only four per cent did not see at least one of their children once a week.

TABLE 5

THE GREATEST FREQUENCY WITH WHICH OLD PEOPLE SAW
AT LEAST ONE OF THEIR CHILDREN

Frequency	Old people seeing a		
	Son	Daughter	Son or daughter
	%	%	%
Daily	48	67	78
Not daily but at least once a week*	37	25	19
Less than once a week	15	8	4
Total	100	100	100
Number	137	144	167

* Most in this category were seen at least twice a week.

So far the information does not cover all their children. How many of *all* the children were seen every day or every week? When looked at in this way it turns out that, of the total of 626, a third were seen every day, nearly three-quarters once a week or more and only one in ten less than about once a month. The difference between sons and daughters was marked. As Table 6 shows, forty-five

per cent of daughters were seen daily, compared with twenty-six
per cent of sons. Nearness obviously affected visiting. If the children lived in the same district the old person often spent one or two
days of each week, particularly Sundays, with them, quite apart
from any visits the children made on other days. If the children
lived several miles away in London suburbs or housing estates he or
she often spent a weekend with them. And if they lived far outside
London he or she often spent a week or more with them once or
twice a year. Thus a widow with a daughter living a mile away said,
'My grandson comes over to fetch me on Sundays and I stay the
day with my daughter.' Another widow with a son living twelve
miles away said, 'Often I go over on a Friday and stay until Monday morning. At Whitsun I stayed four or five days.' And a third
widow who had a son and daughter living near her said she had
just spent a month with a son living in North Wales. 'I scraped and
scraped for months before July. It's a big fare but they wanted me
to go.' Even those living abroad were sometimes seen. One woman
had two daughters in Canada. 'They've each been over to see me
for a holiday two or three times (staying a fortnight on each occasion) and two years ago they clubbed together for my fare and I
went to live with the youngest one for seven months.'

TABLE 6

FREQUENCY WITH WHICH ALL CHILDREN WERE SEEN

Frequency	Sons	Daughters	Sons and daughters
	%	%	%
Daily	26	45	36
Not daily but at least once a week*	42	33	38
Not weekly but at least once a month	19	15	17
Not monthly but at least once a year	9	5	7
Not seen	4	2	3
	—	—	—
Total	100	100	100
Number	314	312	626

* Most in this category were seen at least twice a week.

Distance divided the children into intimates, week-enders, and holiday companions. Children and old people meeting every day or nearly every day exchanged all kinds of services and helped one another in the daily problems of life. Children seeing their parents from once a month to once a week exchanged news, brought gifts, contributed sums of money, gave help in emergencies, and generally reinforced their ties with parents and brothers and sisters through regular visiting. And those seeing least of their parents and living farthest away provided free holidays and maintained family unity by attending weddings, funerals, and golden weddings.

One common feature of the contact with children was its regularity.[1] Again and again, when asked how often he or she saw a particular child, an old person said, 'Ivy calls every Tuesday and Friday', 'Bill comes on Saturday', 'Sundays I have lunch at my daughter's and spend the day with her', 'My daughter comes every day on her way to work'. The individual members of the family relied on routine.

Mrs Mayhew was a widow of seventy living alone. That morning her daughter-in-law had visited her. This happened six days of the week. Just before I left her daughter arrived (a regular call after she finished a part-time job). Mrs Mayhew saw these two every day, and her son, who had a market stall, nearly every day. In addition to these visits there were the following rituals: Monday afternoon, old people's club; Tuesday afternoon, tea with her son, his wife and children; Wednesday, visit to cinema with sister; Friday, old people's club; Saturday, tea with daughter; Sunday, day with daughter.

Two Groups of Kin

Such routine in day-by-day activities involved other members of the family too. When account was taken of various relatives and not just children an impressive picture emerged of contacts with kin. The average old person saw three of his relatives once a day and another seven once a week. A further nineteen were seen during the year. This is shown in Table 7. The total number of relatives claimed to be seen in the course of the year and about whom information was obtained was nearly 6,000.

1. This was shown very clearly by the diaries kept by some people. See Appendix 3.

TABLE 7

NUMBER OF RELATIVES SEEN BY AVERAGE OLD PERSON

Frequency	*Number of relatives seen*
Daily*	3
Not daily but at least once a week	7
Not weekly but at least once a month	8
Not monthly but at least once a year	11
Total seen by the average person	29
Total number for sample of 203	5,898

* Relatives living in the same dwelling are included, and counted as seen every day.

Usually there were two sets of kin – the distinction between them being fundamental. First were those relatives in the same dwelling or nearby who were seen regularly and frequently. This was the group of intimate kin, who did each other's shopping and household tasks and cared for each other in illness. They included the daughters who came to wash and polish the floors; the sons who came to a midday meal from work, brought gifts, and repaired broken chairs and hinges on doors; the grandchildren who came while their parents were at work, and the sisters who dropped in for an afternoon chat. Of all ages, from a few days to ninety years of age, they depended on each other for their everyday needs.

Second were those relatives who were seen less frequently and usually on ritual or holiday occasions. This was the group of recognized kin with whom there was some association in the course of a year. These were often brothers and sisters, nephews and nieces, cousins, and so on living some distance away who were seen at funerals, weddings, birthdays, and christenings and over the Christmas, Easter, Whitsun, or summer holidays. A rough idea of the size of these two groups is gained by comparing the number of relatives seen at least once a week with those seen less frequently in the year. Table 7 shows that these numbers were, on average, ten and nineteen respectively. There were, of course, other recognized kin not seen during the year.

In subsequent chapters we shall consider what these statistics mean in terms of relationships and services. This chapter has examined the extent to which relatives, particularly children, lived near old people and the *frequency* of contact (as distinct from the function or intensity of contact) between the two. The analysis must not be interpreted baldly as stating that every old person in Bethnal Green was at the centre of a cluster of relatives. In the nature of things, if there are no children or grandchildren to replace relatives of the same or of ascending generations, then some families must dwindle. Of those interviewed eighteen per cent were single or childless and seventeen per cent had no surviving brothers or sisters. A few had no near relatives at all. We shall discuss such isolated people later. Yet for the most part the evidence does not support the general assumption noted in Chapter 1. These people were not separated from their relatives. Over a half lived with them. Nearly all of them, including four-fifths of those living alone, had relatives nearby. The great majority saw a number of relatives, particularly their children, with impressive regularity and frequency. Three quarters even of those living by themselves saw at least one relative every day or nearly every day; some of the others had no relatives.

CHAPTER 5

The Family System of Care

THE proximity of relatives greatly affects the way the domestic affairs of old people are managed and how they are looked after in illness and infirmity. As old people may be members of a home containing three generations of relatives, two, or one, the first step in describing the pattern of care is to see whether we can distinguish between these three types of home in their functioning.

Of the 203, twenty-nine, or fourteen per cent, lived in homes containing relatives of three generations. With one exception – a bachelor living with his sister's daughter and her children – they all lived under the same roof with their children and grandchildren.

To say they were living together does not necessarily mean that they formed part of the same household for all purposes. Married couples in their sixties usually ate separately from their children and grandchildren and pursued some evening interests independently. Almost invariably they had separate kitchens. But the wives often joined forces in the day when the men were absent from the home. The latter were sometimes unaware of the extent of this.

> Mrs Belliers said she did most of her own shopping, cooking, cleaning, and washing, although her married daughter living in the house 'mucks in with lots of things, especially the washing'. The two couples ate meals separately, 'unless we're invited upstairs' [usually meaning week-ends]. But there was much coming and going. While I was there the son-in-law came in and immediately had his habitual evening cup of tea with his parents-in-law. She said, 'My grandson is more down here than upstairs. We don't know whether he's their son or ours.' Later her husband expressed surprise when she said she often had her midday meal upstairs with her daughter and grandson and sat with them afterwards.

The pattern was not the same for widows. They shared much more with their children. Fewer of them maintained separate kitchens and more sat down to eat all meals with their children. The difference in home arrangements once a person was widowed rather than married was shown most clearly in one home, where the grandfather had died only a year previously. The married daughter, who shared the cooking and housework with her mother, 'never interfered with Mum while Dad was alive. We each had our own kitchen and got on with ourselves.'

> Mrs Lyons, a widow of sixty-eight, lived with her married daughter, son-in-law, and four grandchildren. She did the cooking, bathed the baby and the next youngest child, and looked after the baby when her daughter went to collect two other children from school. Her daughter said, 'It helps me really, having her. She keeps an eye on the children for me.' And she added, as if her mother had a proper and rightful share in the children's world, 'My husband likes messing about in the garden. . . . I don't like leaving her on her own.' The daughter did all the shopping, managed the household and, in partnership with her mother, attended to the children, besides working four hours a day as a machinist.

Married sons and their wives, when living in the home, maintained more of a separate establishment than married daughters. One widow, for example, usually took her meals separately from her son, daughter-in-law, and grandchildren. 'We don't make a habit of it.' And the widow had less to do with the twin grandchildren. 'I don't look after them. "You've done enough," my son said. She takes the babies round to her sister.' But she did not lose sight of them altogether. 'Sometimes she brings the twins in here to give them their supper. That's when it's a bit cold to take them upstairs.'

The Two-Generation Home

There were sixty-eight people, or over a third of the sample, living in two-generation homes. Fifteen lived with married or widowed children, forty-four with unmarried children and nine with other relatives, including nephews, nieces, and grandchildren. Illustrations will be taken from the first two of these three groups.

When married children were at home but not grandchildren, the two generations were on the whole less dependent on each other and their relationships were more strained, particularly when the married child was a son. It seemed less easy for old people to reciprocate a service such as shopping or cleaning performed by their children when there were no small grandchildren to be watched, dressed, and fed. They had fewer natural interests to share, and so spent more time on their own.

> Mrs King was a widow of seventy-five living with a recently married son in a small council flat. Her daughter-in-law paid the rent and most bills. 'I turned everything over to her when she moved in. It's only right. The wife has to do it.' The daughter-in-law did the shopping and the cooking at week-ends. Mrs King did the washing and pre-pared tea during the week for the young couple when they returned from work. 'They have theirs in their own room and I have mine in my room.' At one point, in answer to a question as to her evening activities, she said, 'I don't enjoy myself. I keep to my room and listen to the wireless.' She was anxious not to disturb the first few months of marital bliss and so prejudice her own delicate position in the house-hold.

Such examples of widows sharing a home with married sons, although comparatively rare, suggested that the mother's authority was delegated to the younger woman and her role sometimes be-came that of a subordinate housekeeper. She tended to be divested of domestic power and her responsibilities were much more con-sciously (and narrowly) defined. Only in this way was harmony pre-served and the rights and responsibilities of a wife honoured. This shows some of the difficulties to be contemplated by some old people not able to live alone.

We can see that married children living in both two- and three-generation homes had varying degrees of independence in their home activities. They were more independent if both mother and father were present in the home and not only a mother. They were more independent if the parents were active rather than infirm and if no grandchildren were in the home. And they were more indepen-dent if the parents in the home were parents of the husband and not the wife.

When unmarried children lived with old people the situation was much simpler. The right of the old mother to have a controlling say in the home was never in doubt. Even so, the distribution of res-ponsibilities varied according to state of health, whether the hus-band was alive, and whether the children were sons or daughters. An active woman in her sixties, for example, often did most of the housework.

Mrs Tout, an active woman of sixty-five, allowed her husband and son to do little in the home. She prepared the meals, cleaned the flat, did the shopping and washing and many of the odd jobs. Talking of her husband she said, 'He's tired when he gets back and he makes a fuss if I ask him to. He's never been used to it. If I'm not well, of course, they do it. That's the top and bottom of it.'

When the old people were infirm or ill the unmarried children took a greater responsibility.

Mr Anchor suffered from chronic bronchitis and became breathless at the slightest exertion. His wife was infirm and had not left the house for some months. Mrs Anchor did most of the cooking, but her single daughter at home did it at week-ends. This daughter also did most of the cleaning. 'Last night she scrubbed all the place through, and tonight when she comes home she'll say that perhaps she wants to do the other room.' Mrs Anchor and her daughter did most of the washing between them, but 'the heavy is sent out'. As for shopping, a married daughter living about ten minutes' walk away did that every day.

Some widows living with unmarried children treated them as they had treated their husbands. The unmarried son, or indeed, daughter, having taken the place of the husband as wage-earner, was not expected to do much in the home.

Mrs Wiles cooked during the week but 'my girl does the cooking on Sunday. She says, "I'll make it, Mum." We work together.' She admitted her daughter did some cleaning and washing, but she tried to do most of it. 'I do the dirty. Her hands have to be kept for dressmaking. They have to be just so. So I always do the dirty.' She was very aware that her daughter was the breadwinner. 'You've got to put yourself out for the one who gets the wages. They've got a right to a bit of peace and quiet in the evening. It's a hard job and the girl gets tired.'

The One-Generation Home

Just over half the old people lived in homes containing no relatives of any other generation: forty-three were alone, forty-six in married pairs, fourteen with other relatives, mostly brothers or sisters, and the remaining three boarded with non-relatives. For the great majority of these people the management of their domestic affairs could not be understood solely by reference to their own capacities and their activities at home. Few of them were obliged to be self-sufficient. In the previous chapter we found that most people living alone in fact saw relatives frequently. Now we find that most received much help from them, not only in times of illness, but every day.

> Mrs Tilbury, sixty-nine, lived in a small cottage with her husband. She managed most of her own household affairs but not all. 'My daughter does some. She's a bit rough and ready like me. She wanted to stop off work. She said she wanted to turn her job up so that she could look after me. But I didn't want to stand in her light.' The daughter worked as a waitress in the City from 10 till 3.30 p.m. and lived nearby. 'She comes over here before she goes and cooks me a bit of dinner. My two granddaughters come from school and have it with me.' Mrs Tilbury fetched the younger granddaughter from school. Indeed on one call she came in with the younger granddaughter and the elder one followed later. Once a week when her daughter went out with her son-in-law to the cinema she had the two granddaughters to stay with her. She said, 'I like to make things for my grandchildren. Everything they've got on is what I made.' If she were ill, her daughter would look after her. 'When she comes in here she says, "I'm going to scrub up", and nothing you can do will stop her.'

> Mrs Rilk, an infirm widow in her early sixties, lived alone. A married daughter living nearby regularly did her cleaning and gave her meals on Sundays. Her shopping was done by a thirteen-year-old grandson. 'He comes every morning before school.' As for washing, another grandson 'calls in when he's on his milk round on Sunday and collects it. My daughter gets it done on a Monday and Charlie [the grandson] brings it back.' Her grandchildren chopped firewood for her, exercised her dog and took her to the cinema or to the bus-stop. Her daughter collected the pension. But Mrs Rilk prepared a meal for her daughter and grandchildren six days of the week, often entertained her relatives in the evenings, and once or twice a week she took a meal to an old lady in the same block of flats.

Most people living alone considered themselves part of a family circle spread over neighbouring streets in Bethnal Green, or sometimes over greater distances.

Some of the people living alone or only in married pairs did not have children, but where they had sisters or nieces living near they produced similar evidence of domestic cooperation between related households. Childless people were not necessarily handicapped.

Mr and Mrs Marshall had no children and they lived alone. The last time Mrs Marshall was ill in bed one of her married nieces nearby looked after her, and she said she could depend in future on any one of at least four nieces in Bethnal Green. A large number of relatives lived nearby and they were seen throughout the week and at week-ends. The previous Saturday they had had eleven to tea. Mr Marshall said proudly of his wife, 'She's always helping one or another of them out. She's always going to one or another when they're ill. There's her brother who was living round the corner and is now in hospital, she always used to do his washing and give him meals every day before he went in hospital. Now she goes round and cleans out his place. We've always helped one another in the family. That's how it should be.'

Those with no available relatives were in the worst position. They were acutely conscious of what they considered to be a misfortune. In describing their own feelings they gave perhaps the strongest, if most indirect, testimony to the dependence of old people on available relatives of other generations.

Miss Kabel, aged seventy-seven and very infirm, lived with a single brother aged eighty and a single sister aged seventy-one. Their parents died when they were in their teens and they had no relatives in England. The brother had looked after his two sisters and he and one of the sisters used to go to work while the other sister looked after the home. The pattern of their lives had not altered until Miss Kabel and her brother retired. Her younger sister managed the household and they paid a cleaner 4s. for a weekly visit. They looked after each other in illness and had no help from friends or neighbours. 'Single folks, they don't bother with you. They'll ask how you're getting on. One even visited me in hospital. . . . But that's all.' They talked at great length of their lack of relatives and many remarks were of the kind, 'How can you feel happy with no family behind you?'

Mrs Frazier, an infirm widow of seventy-five, lived alone in one room. Her husband died three years previously. They had no children and none of their brothers or sisters were alive. Her parents had died when she was a child and she had no knowledge of any aunts or uncles or cousins. 'I can't help myself.' She envied other women who had surviving children. 'If I'd had a couple of daughters they'd have been a help to me. If you've got children at the back of you you're all right.'

Evidence of the way people's lives were bound up with those of close relatives was so often forthcoming in the interviews that one is forced to reconsider what is meant by old people 'living alone'. The concept had little value in Bethnal Green when applied only to the dwelling. It was wrong to consider the domestic affairs of the elderly in terms of the bricks and mortar of a structurally separate home as much for those living alone as for those living with relatives of two or three generations. This became clearer upon detailed analysis of the help received and given by people in their own homes, regularly and in emergencies.

Regular Help in the Home

Old women surrendered their household duties unwillingly. Determination and vitality often overcame serious physical handicap: of 139 women in the sample, only five had virtually given up playing any part in the management of the home, two of these being bedfast and the others infirm. Many women continued to perform household tasks which put a great strain on them, occasionally because they felt they had no available source of help but usually because they felt that only in this way could they preserve their self-respect and demonstrate that their lives still had a purpose. Children who would quite readily have assumed responsibility for all these tasks recognized that housework gave the mother something to live for and which she would be unhappy without. One woman said, 'A woman's principal part is her kitchen'. The kitchen was the place where she worked, where she reared her children and entertained her close relatives and friends. It was, to a large extent, the symbol of her life. One very infirm married woman could do no housework but her daughter respected her need to appear useful in the household. 'We [a son and herself] give our wages to Mum and she gives it to me for the shopping and suchlike.' One old widow of eighty-three lived in the same house as a married son and married daughter. Her daughter-in-law said, 'She's well taken care of. I only wish when I get old I get looked after like she does. She has all of us. Loneliness is the worst thing. She's never lonely. Yet she likes her independence. She likes to do her own cooking. There wouldn't be anything left if she didn't have that. She used to have us up in the night when she was taken bad. Her daughter sleeps with her door open so she can hear if Mum wants anything. Mum has a little hammer so she can bang on the wall without getting up.' Another widow, aged eighty-four, depended on a widowed daughter at home. She was able to undertake only a few odd jobs, such as peeling the potatoes. 'I don't like the word old. I don't like to be old. I like to be doing. I took after my mother. I can't do anything, I'm sorry to say.'

Over two-thirds of the women interviewed had main charge of household affairs and half the remainder did something like half the work in the home. It is difficult to be more precise than this because domestic work consisted of a variety of tasks which, to a lesser or greater extent, were shared out among several people at home or nearby, depending on availability and infirmity. When these tasks were examined one by one, relatives were found to be doing most of the shopping, cleaning or washing for between a quarter and a third of the old people, and they were assisting a further proportion. But three in four of the old people or their wives or husbands did all their own cooking.

As women got older and more infirm their relatives took over first the shopping, then the heavy cleaning and washing, and only in the last resort the cooking and the payment of rent and other regular outgoings. One service for infirm people was the collection of the pension from the Post Office. In the sample 163 people had a pension or other State benefit and twenty-six of them, or sixteen per cent, had this collected by relatives. More than half those helping with home tasks were daughters, and most of the remainder were daughters-in-law, sisters, and nieces. A number of neighbours, friends, or employees of the home help service gave substantial help.

Some people had help only with their shopping and others only with their cleaning. Altogether, sixty-eight per cent regularly had help in the management of their homes from relatives living with them or elsewhere; twenty-one per cent had occasional and eleven per cent no help.

Regular Help for Others

Why were there so many? The essential answer is that they were members of a tightly-knit family group and as such they received help because they also gave it, or had given it in the comparatively recent past.

In previous surveys the fact that old people perform services for others has had less attention than the fact that others perform services for them. What seems to be an essential principle of the daily renewal of an intimate bond between adult relatives is the reciprocation of services between them. Children, for example, shop for their old parents; the latter give them meals or look after the grandchildren. It was suggested earlier that relations in three-generation homes were easier than in two. Old people with no grandchildren may find it difficult to justify themselves to a married child at home. In the same way people seeing a lot of grandchildren in the locality may, on that account, attract more help from their children.

What services do old people in fact perform for others? There are those for other people at home. Excepting individuals living entirely alone, ninety-one per cent of the women, and sixty per cent of the men, performed at least one service every day or every week for others. Most women did a great deal; a few, who were very infirm, could do no more than share in the preparation of meals.

Then there are services for people living outside the home, ranging from daily shopping and preparation of meals to such things as fetching a pension once a week for a blind sister. Altogether forty per cent of the women in the sample, and fourteen per cent of the men, performed at least one regular service for relatives not living with them. Regular services for neighbours or friends were undertaken by eight per cent of women and two per cent of men. Besides those performed regularly there were many occasional tasks, such as shopping for a sick neighbour, looking after a relative's child for a time after the death of one of the parents, or taking a relative to hospital.

The care of grandchildren was one of the most important tasks of all. As many as 105 women and fifty men had grandchildren. Of the women, sixty-six, or sixty-three per cent, performed some or many regular services for at least one of their grandchildren, such as fetching them from school, giving them meals, looking after them while their parents were at work, or sitting in during the evenings. This is perhaps one of the most significant findings of the whole inquiry. Of the old men, twenty per cent shared in the care of grandchildren, baby-sitting, fetching them from school, or accompanying them on regular expeditions to the park. They usually did much less than grandmothers.

Few old people took no part in helping others, only one in eight of the women and two in five of the men undertaking no regular domestic or personal services. Some of these in fact made an indirect contribution to the welfare of others through their work, as Table 8 shows.

TABLE 8

OLD PEOPLE PERFORMING SERVICES FOR OTHERS

	Men %	Women %
Performing regular domestic or personal services* for others (including those also at work)	59	87
Not performing regular domestic or personal services		
(i) At work	17	1
(ii) Not at work	23	12
Total	100	100
Number	64	139

* Such as shopping, cleaning, and preparing meals; washing the windows, chopping firewood; minding a grandchild, or fetching him from school; collecting a pension. Some men performed only one small service. By 'regular' is understood at least once a week.

While it is hard to find a criterion which allows exact comparison it is clear that in general there were almost as many old people helping others as were themselves being helped during the weekly round. This evidence compels us to look more critically into the assumed 'burden' of old age. We may be attaching too little weight to the contribution to society made by the aged and too much to their claims on it.

Health of Old People and Help in Illness

When relatives of the three generations lived in close proximity a balanced system of family care thus tended to evolve. It was put to one of its greatest tests when the old people were infirm or bedfast. A precise definition of infirmity is impossible but this investigation took account of the following: severe limitation of movement, difficulty with stairs and in kneeling, trouble with feet, and tendency to giddiness and to falling. According to these criteria forty-two of the old women in the sample, or thirty per cent, were infirm or bedfast and fourteen of the men, or twenty-two per cent. Of the married people seven wives who were infirm, and thirteen who were not, had infirm husbands. For married men the numbers were five and ten respectively. For the whole sample thirty-nine per cent of the old people were infirm or living with a husband or wife who was infirm. Naturally enough, this high incidence of physical incapacity among the aged creates many problems and imposes strict limits on the ability to maintain social activities.

Altogether eight per cent of the sample were confined to their homes; a further forty-two per cent were limited in their outside movements. A third had marked difficulty with stairs; nearly a quarter experienced pain in the feet; just over a quarter had experienced a fall within the previous few months; and a fifth, although they had not had a fall recently, complained of occasional periodic giddiness.

There was a higher incidence of each kind of disability among women than among men – a finding which accords with previous research. Relatively fewer men were house-bound, fewer had difficulty with stairs and pain in the feet, and many fewer had experienced a recent fall. The group of women included a substantial proportion in the age-range sixty to sixty-four and also included more at the advanced ages, because of women's greater expectation of life, but there was still a broad difference between the sexes when like age-groups were compared.

This difference between men and women seemed to apply to a number of specific ailments. Just under ten per cent of women complained of severe or marked deafness, compared with six per cent of men. Women complained more often of arthritis and various rheumatic complaints, men more often of bronchitis. Although the information is not supported by any medical observation, it accords with Sheldon's important finding that whereas old men are mostly in either very poor or very good physical health a much higher proportion of the women are poor in health but have a more tenacious hold on life.[1]

This could be seen in the rate of medical consultations. As Table 9 indicates, the variation among men was slightly greater (although,

1. Sheldon, J. H., op. cit., p. 13.

TABLE 9

FREQUENCY WITH WHICH OLD PEOPLE SAW THEIR DOCTORS

Doctor consulted the following no. of times in year	Men %	Women %
0–3	61	57
4–10	14	27
over 10	25	16
Total	100	100
Number	64	139

on this small sample, the difference was not statistically significant). On the whole the men had a better capacity for physical movement, yet slightly more of them saw doctors frequently and more had experienced a recent spell in hospital. The average old man had seen his doctor seven and a half times in the year, the old woman just over five times. Forty-three per cent of the men, compared with thirty per cent of the women, had had a spell as a hospital in-patient within the previous five years. These are high proportions and merit further investigation. Yet a fifth of the men and nearly two-fifths of the women had never (excluding confinements) spent a day in hospital.

With increasing age both sexes saw more of doctors, as would be expected. Men in their sixties saw their doctors about seven times in the year, women about four. In their eighties they saw the doctor fifteen and ten times respectively. The incidence of physical inca-pacity also increased with age. For example, about a quarter of the people in their sixties, compared with nearly two-thirds of people in their eighties, had difficulty with stairs. It was noticeable, how-ever, that the group of men in their late seventies and eighties con-tained relatively more vigorous but also relatively more incapaci-tated people than the similar group of women.

All this evidence shows the heavy incidence of incapacity and ill-health among the sample. This fact underlies much of this report and partly explains why family life was so important. People were limited to the immediate environment of their homes and, in one way or another, they required some support. Half the women and half the men had been confined to bed because of an illness in the previous two years. They relied greatly on their relatives for help at

such times, providing meals and drinks, making the bed and assisting with personal toilet. Daughters were the chief source of help for
fifty-eight per cent of women, other relatives (mainly sisters,
daughters-in-law and nieces) for twenty-six per cent, husbands for
ten per cent and neighbours or friends for the remainder; three per
cent had no help. For men, wives usually were the main, and daughters the second, source of help. It is worth noting, however, that over
a third of both men and women had no reserves of help. These were
chiefly single and childless people and those, with children, who
had sons but not daughters.

Statements from all the people in the sample about sources of
help in *future* illness broadly corresponded with these figures.
Reliance on daughters was very marked. Of the 144 people in the
sample who had at least one surviving daughter 128, or eighty-nine
per cent, named a daughter as a primary or secondary source of
help in future illness. (Some of these old persons had no daughter
living in London.)

> A widow living alone said her youngest married daughter was her
> main standby. 'When I'm ill I stay here till one of them comes. I don't
> see Bob more than once or twice in a month but if I'm not well he
> always comes.' When she was ill last year for eleven weeks her
> daughter called every morning and evening. 'The children were pop-
> ping in all the time to see if everything was all right. My family does
> what they can.'

The Old Woman's Place

The pattern of care was greatly influenced by the structure and
nearness of the family. If daughters were available, particularly the
youngest, they were the ones to help. If they were not, then the duty
passed to daughters-in-law, sisters, and nieces. If a close female
relative was not available or was herself infirm (or if there was a rift
with the only available relative, such as a daughter-in-law) then
the duty tended to fall on a husband, if he was still active.

While some men performed valuable domestic and personal services for their families, this was usually when female relatives were
not available. Men, young as well as old, rarely occupied a vital role
in family care. The system was chiefly organized around female
relatives. At its focal point stood the old woman. As we have seen,
she usually retained important functions as housewife, mother, and

grandmother. In her social and occupational life she had experienced much less change than had the man. These differences between man and woman corresponded with the sharp differences in health and physical capacities already described. The man experienced more violent and unsettling changes. These were largely connected with his retirement from work, which we will discuss later.

By contrast the woman was eased more gradually into an awareness of her age. Final retirement from *her* job in life rarely occurred. When it did, it was usually after the relinquishment of one small job after another, by easy stages, over many years, until she was bedfast. Usually she ran her own home, although with increasing assistance from her daughters and other relatives. Of the forty-two infirm women in the sample, most received help with household tasks from relatives, but nearly two-thirds of them retained complete control of the cooking and nearly half of them of the washing. Two-thirds performed some services for others. It is hardly possible to over-emphasize the way in which old women, even when infirm, continued to occupy an important place in the family.

Mrs Plum, a widow in her mid sixties, was almost stone deaf. She complained of headaches, severe arthritis in her legs, and incontinence, and one of her feet had to be bound with bandages each day. A married daughter living with her said, 'She's not been out for more than a month. She's frightened of going out on her own. And she doesn't like it because if people speak to her she doesn't understand what they say. She gets embarrassed about it. She went out last Easter Sunday and that's when her leg first gave way. She was up all night with the pain. I had to get a taxi Monday morning and take her round to the hospital [for treatment].' Yet the widow did nearly all the cooking for the household, a lot of the washing, and she often looked after her three grandchildren. One was a baby. When the widow and daughter were asked who bathed the baby the widow indicated herself and rocked with laughter. Her daughter said, 'She baths the baby, nine times out of ten. The other night I took the child up to sleep and she wouldn't go to sleep. I had to bring her downstairs and *she* took her up. I suppose she's used to her putting her to bed.'

Mrs Blenkinsop was in her early sixties. She said she contracted pneumonia one winter a few years previously and the doctor was dumbfounded when she did not die. A year later she was found to have TB. 'They took half one lung away and then they had to take the rest. I came out of the hospital and then I had a relapse and vomited blood and had to go back.' She was very thin, suffered from arthritis and giddiness, and could not sleep. She also said her husband was 'not fit to go to work. He has to be up at 5.30 and has to use that pump for his asthma and take tablets, to get himself right for the day.' Her married daughters came in to help with the shopping and cleaning and her grandchildren ran errands. But she looked after her husband during a recent illness and she provided a midday meal for two of her children and usually two or three of the grandchildren. On two later calls I found five and possibly seven grandchildren in her home. They were so much on the move it was not easy to make a count.

Some older and more infirm women had not been able to withstand such a pace. To them their children were a comfort. A woman who was crippled and had not left her house for ten years delighted in the daily visits of her son and daughter-in-law living locally. A widow in her eighties had had a long spell of illness. One of her daughters said that six or seven of the children then called every day. Between them they got her shopping and gave her meals. 'Mary stopped there and nursed her. And Annie and Rose were always over there helping. She had a bottle of brandy every three days. We all clubbed together to get it. She still likes a nip, and says that's what pulled her through. I have to go there, because I can't rest.' Another woman in her eighties was housebound and had just spent months in hospital. She was glad to be out. 'The nurses have not got the feeling of your own.' Her daughter looked after her. 'She used to lift me so that I could go to bed but that got too much for her and [pointing at an armchair] I sleep here.'

Among the oldest infirm people those without children were worst off, particularly if they were confined to the home.

A married man explained that his wife, in her mid seventies, depended on an elderly niece for help and company while he went to work. 'I don't know what I'd do without her. I could not go to work if she wasn't here. The old girl has a lot to bear and I don't know what she thinks stuck up here every day. [They lived on the fourth floor of a tenement block and his wife had rarely left the flat in the previous four years.] Sometimes I come home and there she is sitting in the corner of the room and she doesn't say a word. She just looks at me. She goes on looking at me as I go about getting the tea and I say, "What's the matter? Are you thinking how it was years ago?" And then sometimes she will burst into tears. I don't know how she stands it. It fair breaks your heart to see her hobbling about. Mind you, if I didn't have her here I'd pack up and go. There'd be nothing left for me, would there?'

Such people were in a small minority. For the majority of women increasing age was a gradual unwinding of the springs of life. They gave up part-time occupations, visits to the cinema, shopping, cleaning, and washing, services for neighbours and associations with them, friendships outside the family, holidays and week-ends with relatives, the care of grandchildren, the provision of meals for children, and finally their own cooking and budgeting, one by one as their faculties grew dim and age took its toll. Their last refuge was their family. They did not want to escape from their homes, to a cottage in the country any more than to an institution. They wanted to spend their last months in their homes and among their families, where possessions and faces were familiar and where an unsteady foot was most secure.

Their activities became adjusted to a limited routine. They went out little and slept longer. They bemoaned their frailty but even when wholly incapacitated they kept, because they were women and not men it was said, 'a closer touch on things'. They knew what was happening to their relatives, had a finger on the details of family history, and were respected and admired for their canniness and insight into what went on. 'She's a marvel, really,' said more than one daughter, 'she's got such spirit and she can still have a laugh.'

The Limits of Care in Illness

The shortcomings of this system of care must not be overlooked. Much depends on whether or not there is a family and, if there is, whether help is readily available. Nearly a fifth of the old people in Bethnal Green were, after all, single or childless and several of the others had relatives unable to help. If there were only one or two female relatives living at home or nearby, and if they themselves had young children or were at work, the care of the old could not always be properly undertaken or could be undertaken only at the cost of severe strain. 'I wouldn't expect her to. She's had TB.' 'My daughter's got her own worries. She's got three kiddies and her husband's been off work for three weeks.' 'It's such a long way for her and she can't afford the fares.' 'My daughter's husband has got artificial legs. She's got enough to do looking after him.' 'He's got his job and he couldn't give that up. They've got to study the work.' These remarks each referred to an only child.

Two other limits to the care available to the aged are less obvious and arise more from the nature of family relationships than from family size, structure, and circumstances. As we have seen, part of the strength of family relationships comes from individuals receiving *and* returning services. Some old people can no longer reciprocate the services performed for them and this seems to make them less willing to accept help and their relatives sometimes less willing to give it. Among infirm people in the sample it was noticeable that a few getting least help were not in a position to give anything in exchange. For example, a man and wife in their late seventies who were both infirm had little help from a married son and daughter-in-law living in the same house. The wife had a wheel-chair and the younger couple rarely volunteered to take her out. Son and daughter-in-law were at work in the day and their only child, a son, was on National Service. The old couple's other married children and grandchildren no longer lived in the borough although some were seen fairly often. The old woman said she was happiest when she had her grandchildren around her but 'that isn't so often now'. The cause of the separation between the generations was, it seemed, not so much the infirmity of the old couple as the absence of common interests and responsibilities.

The second limit concerned the union between man and wife. A number of people who were ill or infirm were in need of bodily care, such as dressing a wound, providing and emptying bed-pans, and washing soiled linen. Some old people refused to allow anyone except a spouse to do such things. This was particularly true of men. The care of a man's body was felt to be the prerogative of his wife and it was thought to be a break with propriety, if not vaguely incestuous, for a female relative, even a daughter, to undertake such an intimate task. She could do the shopping and fetch prescriptions; rarely, if ever, was she allowed to wash his body or make his bed. Some married women also preferred an infirm husband, rather than a daughter, to look after their personal toilet. Old widows were less reserved, perforce, and were often grateful for the personal services of a devoted daughter. The inhibitions of men, who were more reluctant than women to accept care from daughters, may be one explanation why more old widowers and bachelors enter hospital in England and Wales than widows and spinsters, though fewer married old men than women. In sickness married men are mostly looked after by wives and when they do not have them it may be hard to find a substitute among female relatives.

Except for the widowed, what the children could do often stopped short of bodily care. This was why old people often experienced enormous strain in caring for a spouse in a final illness.

A widower in his mid seventies explained that before his wife died two years previously she had been bedfast. Although his children came every day and helped with all the household chores he had attended to most of her personal needs. 'I had to sit with her for months. The last two or three months, her motion was coming away from her all the time and it was terrible, I can tell you. She wouldn't go away to hospital although the doctor tried to get her to.'

I visited one man three times during his final illness. His single daughter living at home and his married children who visited him frequently took over nearly all the shopping and cleaning from his infirm wife. But his wife washed him and did all the 'messy' jobs. He bled continuously from the chest. He said, 'Mum changes the dressing at least twice a day and we wouldn't want our daughter to do it. You couldn't expect it.' And his wife added, 'It even turns my stomach sometimes seeing poor Dad's chest. It's like a bit of raw meat.' She washed bloodstained sheets every day, lifted him on to bedpans, washed him and dressed his wounds, despite her own frailty.

An infirm widow gave a long account of her husband's death, in which she said, 'It happened all of a sudden. Jack had been strong and healthy all his life and he suddenly went to nothing. For over three months I never had any rest.' She sat with him, washed him, and gave him his meals, though her daughter prepared them. 'He kept talking about the pain in his chest in the night. One day he came in here and lay down on the bed with his coat on. He said, "I'm done, Nan." I said, "Come on, Jack, don't get depressed." But we were crying our eyes out before the ambulance came. He wouldn't get into the chair for them to take him to the ambulance. He said, "I can walk." I was as ill as I could be but I told him, "Don't walk, Jack," and of course I was breaking my heart, but he said while he had legs he was going to use them. He was in hospital three weeks. Bad as I was I tried to get along to see him. . . .'

When the husband or wife was dead one relative rather than

several tended to assume responsibility for the survivor. Often this seemed to be understandable because no other suitable relative was available. The old person had one child only or one daughter only; other members of the family did not live nearby or were themselves sick or disabled; and other members of the family had young children of their own or husbands with disabilities. In particular it seemed wholly natural for the remaining unmarried child at home to take on the care of a parent. When all this is said, it still seems to be true that one person in the family was singled out to carry more than a fair share of the burden of care simply because the old person found a need to replace a spouse with someone in almost the same intimate standing. A particular child sometimes undertook tasks of a personal character which no other child was expected to undertake and which were previously borne by the husband or wife. All these reasons perhaps explain why the care of the old seems too often to be unequally distributed among their children.

The Strain of Illness

Severe difficulties and strain often resulted. One measure of this was whether relatives had been obliged to give up paid employment. In the interviews there were many instances of relatives giving up work to care for one another during illness, for both long and short spells, but most instances mentioned by old people related to the past. At the time of first interview fourteen people, or seven per cent of the sample, were causing relatives to lose time from work (only three of them from full-time work). This figure would have been higher but for the fact that five people postponed first interview because they were ill and two people refused an interview altogether (or rather, relatives refused for them) because they were ill. The families of most people organized help in ways that allowed the breadwinners to go to work. The wage of a single child living at home was often vital to the standard of life of a retired person's household and the wage of a married child to that of the child's household. In talking about help from children in illness a qualification repeated most often by old people was, 'They've got to study their work.'

Other strains were imposed on relatives not only by the incapacity of the old, but also by their own disability or ill-health and by conflict between, for example, their responsibilities to their children and those to their parents. Such difficulties were not always admitted and were difficult to define precisely. If by strain is meant to overtax mentally or physically or make excessive demands on a person's resources because of efforts involved in having to work, look after a home, nurse someone or care for several people at once, or any combination of these, without sufficient help, then thirteen per cent of the old people were imposing strain on their relatives at the time of the interview. These cases could be classed as severe in three and a half per cent and moderate or slight in nine and a half per cent. In addition fourteen per cent of the husbands or wives of the married people interviewed were experiencing strain at the time, classed as severe in two per cent and moderate or slight in the remainder. How severe the strain could be is shown by the following example.

A widow lived with her only daughter and grandchildren. She became increasingly infirm over the previous year and was no longer able to do anything in the home. Her daughter managed the home with the assistance of the youngest granddaughter, who was at work. She also had the care of a sick husband (who later had a leg amputated). The only grandson was in the Army and the eldest granddaughter, who was married and lived nearby, was expecting a child. The daughter was now in her mid fifties and she said to me when we were alone, 'Sometimes I think this is getting too much for me. With the old man at home and my mother, it's as much as I can do to keep the place going. I'm getting that I can't get up and down stairs and run about like I used to. Sometimes I think to myself that I'd like a break, to get away from the place for a while. But we've always been home-loving people and you don't like leaving anyone who's always looked after you.'

When there were several children the main burden of care often fell on the daughter who lived nearest, but she usually had some support from her brothers and sisters. The following is fairly typical of what happened in large families.

Mrs Bliss was first interviewed a year before her final illness, and visited briefly many times. In her late seventies, she had five surviving sons and four daughters, all married. All except the youngest daughter and youngest son were living outside the borough. These two were both in the same block of flats, but she and her husband lived alone. When first interviewed she was still fairly well. Her youngest daughter did much of her cleaning and washing, and during a previous illness lasting ten weeks had left work to look after her. Her youngest son did various odd jobs for her. Her remaining children, whom she saw once a week or once a fortnight, did no regular jobs for her, but brought gifts and most gave her 2s. 6d. or 5s. when they came. When Mrs Bliss had a succession of strokes her doctor tried to persuade her to go to hospital. She was very weak indeed. She and her family pleaded against this and her children organized a night service for several weeks. On several occasions I saw a makeshift bed her son had put in her room. Her youngest son and daughter took it in turns to sit up with her for about two nights in three, but the other children gave them a break the remaining nights of the week. All the children visited her much more frequently and news was passed on daily from one telephone box to another. The youngest daughter left her work and the youngest son for a time too. Between them they did all the shopping and cleaning. The son lifted his mother when necessary and the daughter prepared meals and washed her. The husband, now very infirm, attended to some personal needs. On every visit I saw evidence – food, vases of flowers, sheets and blankets – of the devotion of her family.

Old people themselves were sometimes under considerable strain in caring for their husbands or wives or other relatives. In the care of their spouse twenty-two per cent of the married people were experiencing strain at the time of the interview (six per cent severe and the rest moderate or slight). In the care of relatives other than a spouse, usually children or grandchildren, a few of whom were crippled or mentally defective, twelve per cent experienced strain, none of it severe, however.[1]

We started this chapter by examining the three types of family home, three, two, and one generation, as a first step in finding how domestic affairs and illness were managed in old age. We found that one person in one dwelling was rarely living alone in any real sense. The domestic unit was generally spread over two or more households in proximity. We found old people getting a great deal of help, regularly and in emergencies, from their female relatives, particularly their daughters, living nearby. The remarkable thing was how often this help was reciprocated – through the provision of meals, the care of grandchildren, and in other ways. The traffic

1. A fuller discussion of the strains imposed on relatives and old people in the management of illness will be found in Sheldon, op. cit., pp. 164–85.

was not all one-way. This exchange of services seemed to be an essential feature of the relationship between the generations; this is one of the main conclusions of the book. The family system of care was mainly organized around female relatives, with an old grandmother at its centre. To find that there were limits to what it could do for old people, that it sometimes produced strain and that a minority of people fell outside its scope, simply because they had few or no surviving relatives, modifies, but does not alter, this conclusion.

CHAPTER 6

Man and Wife and the Home Economy

THE financial relationship between man and wife and parent and child at home was crucial. Even so, there were important exchanges of money and gifts between people in one home and those in another. Many old people had financial help from children living elsewhere and the day-to-day provision of meals and care of grandchildren led to many exchanges of money and goods in kind. These various financial arrangements, symbolizing, as they do, other relationships within the family, are the subject of this chapter. The standard of living of old people, and pensions, national assistance, and the last wage before retirement will be discussed later.

Altogether, sixty-one per cent of the people in the sample lived in households where the economy depended on, or was assisted by, regular contributions from relatives living at home or elsewhere. The figure becomes seventy-five per cent if regular help in kind is included as well as monetary contributions. These contributions were of three general sorts. First were the payments of board money by single or married children and other relatives living in the same household towards its upkeep. Second were the sums or gifts given to old people by relatives, usually married children, living elsewhere. Third were the payments, in money or in kind, for services performed by old people, such as meals for married children and the care of grandchildren.

Board Money

The most important was board money. Altogether forty-five per cent of the old people received board money from relatives and others. Payments by unmarried children living at home varied from £1 5s. to £4; £2 or £2 10s. were the figures most frequently mentioned and the average was just under £2. Some children had meals out and contributed little. Others paid for shopping and all kinds of incidentals as well as making a weekly contribution. Sons tended to pay more than daughters, the reasons for this being threefold. Daughters often gave domestic help and so contributed more in kind; daughters were felt to need a larger sum for clothes or 'bottom-drawer' savings for marriage; and daughters earned less on average than sons.

Mrs Clay, whose husband had retired, had £1 10s. each from her two unmarried daughters. They sometimes gave her more and frequently brought home cakes or fruit and other things they paid for themselves. At Christmas they had ordered a television set for the home and were paying the weekly instalments for it.

Mrs Flamm, whose husband was still at work, received £1 10s. from an unmarried daughter, £2 from her son, and £1 5s. from her youngest daughter, 'I don't take much from the youngest. She's got her clothes to buy. I give her 2s. back each day [towards fares].' And her eldest daughter was getting 'married this year so she's got to save up for that. The wedding will cost a lot. There's fifty on her side of the family, not counting her husband's.'

Grown-up grandchildren, single brothers and sisters, and nieces who sometimes lived in the home paid roughly the same as unmarried children. A single sister and a niece living with a widow, for example, added £2 each to her pension of £2. Married children, however, often kept their finances independent of their parents. Of the thirty-nine people living with married or widowed children twenty-two shared housekeeping money in part or in full. A young married couple usually gave about £4–£5 to the mother, but the amount was not always fixed.

Mrs Dyke had about £4 from her married daughter at home, but she found it difficult to give an exact sum. 'When me and my daughter go up the road [to the market] she always gets the shopping when I haven't any money. She buys anything I want. It's like that, isn't it?' she asked of her daughter, who was present. The latter nodded and said, 'Oh yes, we always mix in'.

The sums given for board money often appeared to be small. An unmarried child was normally expected to contribute no more than a bare minimum to the mother, so that he or she had enough money left for teenage pursuits, courting, and preparations for marriage. But when the parents retired the contribution was increased or supplemented by gifts. While it was hard to determine how far old people benefited personally from the board money paid to them by their children, it seemed that retired people, unlike those who were still at work, often benefited considerably, particularly if they were widowed and living with married children.

Contributions from those Living outside the Home

Money or gifts given by married relatives living elsewhere, usually children, made up a second kind of help regularly received by old people. Such contributions varied greatly in size and nature. Few people still at work received money from their children living elsewhere, though the mother often received presents from her sons. And those with children at home did not usually have money from other children too: they could maintain a reasonable standard of living without help. But retired people, particularly when living alone, usually accepted help from their children as a matter of course.

Mr and Mrs Angel lived on their own near four of their six married children. Although not yet retired Mr Angel had been off work for seven months because of illness. His firm continued to pay him a small allowance in addition to £2 12s. sickness benefit. Income from their children varied from 10s. to £1 10s. a week and Mrs Angel emphasized this would increase if her husband's firm stopped its allowance. Of the children she said, 'They're very good. One will come in and give me 2s. 6d. or 5s. Another puts 2s. in the gas and they bring round a box of chocolates. They'd all help me out if I was in trouble. It would be their duty, just like we did for our parents.'

Occasionally a fairly large sum was given by children not living at home. One widow said she had £1 a week from each of three children. But usually the amounts were small, and not always regular: 2s. 6d., 5s., or 10s. a week from two or three married children were the amounts most often specified. Widows often made remarks such as, 'He's a good boy, he is. He gives me 5s. every week.' 'My daughter gives me 10s. She told me once, "That's what I go to work for, Mum."' Children living some distance away and seen every month or so occasionally gave £1 or £2. A married man said of his son living in Surrey, 'When we go on holiday he always sends us a fiver'. A widower said he had no regular income from his children but could count on them for support from time to time. One would give him £1, and if he dropped a hint he needed a pair of boots, all of them would have a whip round. 'They club together whenever I need anything.' There were instances of old people being subsidized members of family loan clubs. One widow said her son paid 4s. a week for her eight shares. There were also instances of money given by more distant relatives. A widow without children said a nephew and niece living nearby dropped a couple of shillings into her hand once or twice a month. In addition to money, there were gifts in kind, ranging from fish brought regularly by sons working in the fish market, and vegetables by sons working as market porters, to the remains of a family joint.

It was not possible to exhaust information about the various kinds of help received and sometimes old people preferred to generalize, 'My children are good to me,' rather than make specific statements. The main question was to establish whether they received money or gifts *regularly* from relatives, particularly when living alone. Table 10 shows how many of those living alone received such help. The money value of services performed by relatives, such as shopping, window cleaning, and washing, is ignored. Two points should be borne in mind in interpreting the table: a few people may not have disclosed monetary help, and, of the sums stated, many were not large, as the above examples testify. Nearly half the old people living alone, who did not depend on a working wage, received regular sums of money from relatives,

TABLE 10

OLD PEOPLE LIVING ALONE AND RECEIVING REGULAR SUMS OF MONEY OR HELP IN KIND FROM RELATIVES

Nature of regular help from relatives	Old people living alone	Non-earning old people living alone
Money (and help in kind)	17 (40%)	16 (47%)
No money but help in kind	12 (28%)	10 (29%)
None	14 (33%)	8 (24%)
Total	43 (100%)	34 (100%)

mostly children, and nearly a third more received regular help in kind. Less than a quarter had no regular help, and a number of these people were childless and had no relatives living near.

There were few open complaints from the retired people who did not receive any money from children. References were made to sons and daughters who could not afford to give them money because they had young children or were ill or unemployed. Although an old person sometimes seemed to be protecting a child from outside criticism it was apparent that a good deal of information about family life had to be obtained before one could be sure that a child was indifferent to the financial needs of his parents.

A widow at first said she had no help from her children. 'I'd sooner go without than ask. They shouldn't need to be asked, should they?' A son lived outside London and a daughter in the next street. It turned out she had just spent a month at her son's home, at his expense, and apart from staying with him from time to time in the year he had helped her buy clothing and linen recently. It also turned out her daughter's husband had artificial legs and lived for frequent spells on sickness benefit. Later, when asked, 'Do you get as much help as you think you should?' the widow replied, 'I don't see how they can help me. They can't give anything. They haven't got anything.'

A married woman had two married sons. 'When the married ones have got children they've not got the means to help you. They decorate the place out or do my repairs. But my son in Dolcis Street, he's got three young children and when he gets home from work he goes out giving out library books. He does that three nights a week. So you can see if he does that [to get extra money] he hasn't got anything left over to give his parents.'

In talking of children's contributions some people drew attention to the 'freedom' of married sons. They remarked that sons were more likely than daughters to give money. One woman said a married son gave her 4s. every week and another son 2s. 6d. Her married daughter used to give her 3s. 6d. but no longer does so. 'It's difficult for the daughters, as it's their husband's money. The sons still give me money because they're more free.' Many wives and husbands were not aware of exchanges of money and gifts between married child and parent. When they were, they sometimes objected. A married woman said her two married sons sometimes put £1 in her hand, but 'their wives don't like that'.

Payments for Family Services

Many old people received payments, in money or kind, for the services they performed, such as preparing meals or minding grandchildren. Rarely did it appear that any profit was gained. A widow received £1 a week from her daughter for giving a grandchild his midday meal and tea five days of the week. Another received about 2s. a day from each of two relatives for their dinners. A single woman visited an infirm married sister several evenings of the week and at week-ends to help her with the housework and cooking; in return she had most of her meals there. These were characteristic examples.

As a result transfers of income within the families of old people were sometimes extremely complex. Such transfers could not be subjected to minute scrutiny but data suggested that principles by which household budgets of elderly people are normally collected and evaluated may require re-examination. For example, a widow lived in one house with her two married daughters, and had a house-keeping allowance from the youngest of them, while the eldest contributed to the rent. The youngest daughter's allowance was roughly £4 for herself, husband, and child, and in addition she paid her mother between 10s. and £1 for looking after the child. Sometimes the widow had a meal with her eldest daughter. A nephew was given a bed in the house four nights of the week and the nephew's mother paid 10s. in addition to the sum he paid for meals. Two married sons living nearby gave the widow a few shillings each week and she had meals in their homes at week-ends. She quoted instances of one or the other of her family paying for an oil stove, a dress, and club subscriptions.

Finances of Man and Wife

Close relatives, therefore, often played an important role in the financial affairs of old people. But the pattern of financial behaviour in the family depended most on the economic relationship between man and wife. This is a difficult and tangled subject but one which is important to an understanding of family life.

In the entire sample forty-five people, or twenty-three per cent, were husbands still working or women whose husbands were still doing so. They largely depended on a working wage. The average man earned £6 16s.[1] This average was rather low, partly because

1. The information was usually supplied only when the men could be interviewed alone. A few of them, even after several visits, could not be seen alone or would not give the information. In such cases (ten out of the forty-five) an approximate figure was gained by reference to the earnings of men in similar jobs in the district.

the information was faulty, overtime earnings and bonuses being rarely included. In any event, one would expect the average to be lower than for other men because some men had in later life taken jobs, such as lavatory attendants, at a low wage of about £4 a week. Only a few men earned £10 or more. The housewife was given an average of £4 8s., so that about two-thirds of the man's wage went to his wife as housekeeping money.

Married people revealed the true state of their financial affairs, if at all, only when they could be questioned separately. Few wives knew what their husbands earned; many did not think they had a right to know. Of the forty-five wives seven said they knew how much the husband earned, twenty-seven said they did not. For the remaining eleven it was not possible to ascertain the facts, usually because the wife was not alone for any part of the interview or interviews.

> Mrs Tubbly was asked her husband's wage now he had taken a less well-paid job, but she answered with a laugh, 'I've never known his money. He's a very quiet man. I couldn't tell you that. He gives me £5 for the housekeeping.'

> Mr Perrier said, 'I don't think a wife ought to know her husband's earnings. If she's got a good living wage for the house she's got nothing to grumble about.'

> Mr Snape told me his earnings and savings when his wife was not in the room and he was most anxious that this information should be treated as private. Two or three times he repeated, 'This is between you and me.'

The wife regularly received a round sum as housekeeping money, £4, £4 10s., and £5 being the sums most frequently stated. To this she added any earnings or pension of her own, or board money from her children. She regarded the housekeeping allowance as *her* money. Her claim on this sum was thought of in distinctly personal terms. There were many references to 'his money', 'her money' and 'what a wife does with her money is her affair'. A widow said in answer to a question about her husband's insurance, 'Well, my husband was a man and I was a woman. I never knew what he earned or whether he was insured [by his parents].'

This division of the wage into two parts and the personal, rather than joint, claim over each part allowed man and wife to spend their money separately, with relatively little consultation about day-to-day expenditure. The wife paid the rent, insurances, and fuel bills and bought all the food and household sundries for the home. She also set aside regular amounts for clothing, loan, and Christmas clubs. Husbands for their part often did not know how housekeeping money was spent. This was evident from the number of married men interviewed who had to turn to their wives for information about rent, insurances, and sums spent on coal. One wife, for example, said, 'If you asked him how much he was insured for he wouldn't be able to tell you'.

Wives had little scope for manoeuvre in their budgeting. Their expenditure was mostly determined in advance. After paying fixed amounts for rent, insurances, fuel, and clubs nearly all the remainder of the housekeeping money had to be reserved for food and household goods. A good housewife was economical and careful and, as she often had to make do with a small sum, she knew the value of weekly repayments for all those items, such as clothing and bed-linen, which she could never buy with one week's money.

Mrs Kreddick was visited every week by a clothing tallyman. 'I've dealt with him for thirty-eight years and his father and grandfather before him. I've always got my boots and shoes through him and now I get things for the grandchildren. I'm getting some blankets for my granddaughter when she gets married. It all comes out of the house-keeping – two or three shillings a week.'

Careless or bad budgeting was sometimes referred to in the same breath as the wife's ignorance of the husband's wage. One remark was made spontaneously by a number of wives, particularly when husbands were present. 'I've never got into debt' or 'I've never owed a penny.' They regarded this as the test of their efficiency in the role of housekeeper, which justified their husband's confidence in them.

Mrs Blake, justifying husbands who concealed their wage from their wives, said, 'Some men are greedy towards a woman, and some are jealous. A woman should know near enough, but some women get themselves into debt.'

There is in this example a hint of competition between man and wife for the available wage. Some people certainly looked at it in these terms. A married daughter said of husbands in general, 'They

give you all you can get. You've got to put up with it.' Some remarked that quarrels and fights between man and wife, 'bundles'
as they were called, were more frequent a generation or two ago
when housekeeping money was relatively smaller and less regular,
but that arguments still arose.

The wife's ignorance of the husband's wage was often equalled
by his ignorance of what her children gave her. When one man was
asked how much his two daughters paid on board money he said,
'They give it to Mum. I don't even know how much they give her.'
Women spoke of financial arrangements between themselves and
their children as though the husband was not a party to them at all.
A few couples who were interviewed together were very evasive
about their respective incomes. (An example is provided by Interview Report in Appendix 2.)

The husband's share of the wage was more than pocket money.
He spent it on fares to work, midday meals (though the money for
this was sometimes returned to him by his wife), trade union subscriptions, haircuts, his own clothes, tobacco, drink, and betting,
and usually he provided the cash for family entertainments, holidays, and some household goods, such as a carpet, a new strip of
lino, linen or a radio or television set.

> Mr Agnew bought his own clothes and lunches and paid his fares.
> When he and his wife went out together he paid for everything. His
> wife laughed when I asked whether she ever contributed on such
> occasions. 'Oh, no. When we go out he treats me. That's what we
> have him for.'

To some extent the husband was looked on as the family banker.
A few wives mentioned that if they ran short of money in the middle
of the week they could ask their husbands for extra. 'He'll leave a
few shillings on the mantelpiece.' 'Even with £5 or £6 a week a wife
is sometimes singing "Do not forget me" on a Tuesday.' One wife
showed me the new lino and curtains in her flat. 'I don't know
where Dad found the money, but he found it.' Some men undoubtedly saved 'for a rainy day'.

When the husband retired his wife was no longer mainly dependent on him for her housekeeping money. Hers became the presid-
ing financial influence in the household. His share of the total
income was cut to a few shillings. Generally he kept, or his wife re-

turned to him, from 2s. 6d. to 5s. of his pension. This was enough
only for a haircut and a few cigarettes or a little tobacco, and perhaps one week-end drink in the pub. Only when he had another
source of income, such as a pension from his former employment,
was his income anything like maintained.

> Mrs Spanner said, in an aside when her husband had left the room,
> 'All the money goes on the table. He has £2, I have £1 5s. He gives me
> £1 17s. 6d. and I let him have 2s. 6d. Well, I've got to do that. He has
> to have a bit of tobacco, doesn't he?'

> Mr Ketch had a non-contributory old age pension of £1 6s. and a
> pension of £2 a week from his former employers, a local hospital. He
> gave his wife £2 10s. of his total income of £3 6s.

Of great interest was the personal interpretation of the retired
person's claim on a pension. When couples were asked the exact
amount of their retirement pensions they never stated the total
amount, but first the man's and then the wife's pension. 'I get £2.
My wife has £1 5s.' This was her money, that was his. This was
underlined in a few revealing cases where the couple were dependent, not on a retirement pension, but on sickness benefit. The wife
thought it was her husband's money. When one woman was asked
whether she or her husband collected the sickness benefit from the
post office she said, 'My husband, of course, that's his money.'
Unlike the pension, for which separate pension books are issued
for man and wife, the sickness benefit for a man and his dependants
is issued on production of a single cash voucher.

The personal interpretation of the claim on the pension was evident from what married people said about collecting it each week.
Of sixty-six married people interviewed where both man and wife
received a pension twenty-seven, or over forty per cent, said the
pension was collected by each partner of the marriage independently, or by both together. Considering that in most of the
remaining cases either the man or his wife or both were infirm and
were unable to walk easily to the post office, this proportion was
very high. One man said, 'We go to the Post Office together and
I give in the books. Then I stand back and let her take the money.
I see that I get the books back. There's the cashier in the family,'
he added, nodding towards his wife.

Segregation in Role

After retirement, as well as before, an attempt was made to divide personal income into the part that belonged to the husband and the part that belonged to the wife. The outlay of housekeeping money was still the wife's responsibility. To a large extent the traditions of working life were preserved. A tradition of segregation between man and wife in their financial roles had been built up and was not easy to lose. The division of income, and a relative unawareness of the other's income and expenditure was closely related to, and partly explained by, their roles in home and family.

The working husband often had, as breadwinner and as nominal head of the household, considerable authority. He was consulted over any official form-filling, and many crucial decisions affecting home or family, such as a housing application, a visit to hospital, or the date and period of a holiday, had, in the final analysis, to be either taken by him or, at least, taken with his consent. This must not be forgotten. But he had little to do with domestic affairs before retirement, and not much more afterwards. 'I'm finished when I come home from work.' 'He just sits down and reads the papers. He puts his feet up on the sofa. I don't ask him to do anything.' 'My husband doesn't do a hand's turn. He doesn't even clean the windows. He only did that in the first year of our marriage.' Such remarks were common. In some homes, indeed, the wives implied their their husbands had the privileges of a hotel guest.

When interviewed alone some housewives may have exaggerated how little their husbands helped them but if the subject arose when both man and wife were present the picture that emerged was only slightly less sharp. One woman said, 'Well, you see, there's no need for him to do anything because by the time he gets home there's nothing left for him to do.' Another faced her husband squarely, 'I've never had no help yet but I expect I'll have to have some later on.' A third, like so many people in Bethnal Green, thought that the young generation of husbands gave more help to their wives than the old. Giving her husband side-glances she said, 'I know that they do, these young fellows, according to my own.'

Of course it would be wrong to give the impression that the older man was completely idle in the home, for sometimes he did minor household tasks, like lighting the fire or making a cup of tea and he often grew flowers or did repairs in the backyard or garden. Sometimes he did much more, such as shopping or cleaning windows, but this was usually when the wife was infirm and no close relatives were available. This qualification is important, for it appeared to hold in retirement as well as before. There seemed to be little change in the proportion of men helping in the home after retirement from work.

TABLE 11

HUSBANDS HELPING IN THE HOME WHEN DAUGHTERS WERE
AVAILABLE

Help in the home*	Daughters at home or within 5 minutes' walk	
	At least one	None
All husbands		
Husband helping	15	31
Husband not helping	34	18
Total number	49	49
Husbands at work		
Husband helping	4	15
Husband not helping	16	10
Total number	20	25

* 'Help in the home' is defined as the acknowledged performance, daily or at least once a week, of at least one domestic task, such as shopping, washing up, cleaning windows, making the fire. Hobbies, gardening and occasional repair jobs, such as mending a door-hinge or an electric fuse, are excluded. Some men counted as 'helping' had only one small job.

When female relatives lived at home or nearby, the husband, whether retired or not, had a limited domestic role. Sometimes no domestic job was acknowledged to be his. But when female relatives were not available he tended to give more help. Table 11 gives a crude measure of this. It refers to married men and the husbands of married women in the sample, and distinguishes the men still at work. It shows that when daughters lived at home or nearby significantly fewer men helped their wives in the home.

This fact has wide implications. It suggests that a division of labour between man and wife was not simply a matter of personal adjustment. The particular form of their relationship was greatly influenced by the proximity of female relatives, especially married daughters. Because she shared so much of daily life with children and grandchildren the grandmother did fewer things jointly with her husband. In the first place she shared the domestic round with them in the daytime when her husband was at work. Second, even in the evenings the couple spent little time on their own, because relatives either lived with them or paid them visits. Third, man and wife often went their own separate ways in their leisure time. Men spoke of going to pubs, sports grounds, and clubs with brothers or workmates; women of going on holiday, to the pictures, and to clubs with daughters or sisters. 'We don't go out much at all together. He likes a drink but it doesn't appeal to me, and then he's got his work.' Visits were made singly to some married relatives, particularly brothers or sisters. Even when retired a husband or wife often, though not always, continued to have separate interests and activities. Segregation of the sexes was particularly noticeable in old people's clubs or on outings organized by pubs and clubs. The following example illustrates several of these points.

Mr Cowell retired three years previously. As he had worked beyond the pensionable age he received a pension of £1 17s. 6d. (This was when he was first interviewed in 1954.) 'Thirty-seven and sixpence. It's a lousy sum to give her.' His wife returned him a few shillings. She did most of the shopping, cleaning, and washing, with the assistance of a single daughter. 'I don't do much in the house. If I do a job it's never done satisfactory and they do it again. The daughter is even more precise than her mother,' he said, as if that were scarcely possible. His wife worked part-time and was an active member of two clubs. She saw much more of their relatives. He played little part in her activities. They went separately to the pictures and she met a sister every afternoon, leaving her husband to sit by himself or go for a walk. She also visited and stayed frequently at week-ends with their married child, a daughter living some miles away. He rarely accompanied her.

When husband and wife shared as little of life as this, friction was likely to arise between them. A number of women admitted greater loyalty to their married children than to their husbands. One said, 'Some wives put their husbands first, but I, now, I've always been the other way. I'm all for the children, and I leave my husband to himself.' Others made it clear they did not want the man's retirement to interrupt their daily routine. One woman's daughter said, '*She* wouldn't want him to [retire]. She couldn't stand him here all day. She wants him out of the way.' A number of other wives were scornful or critical of their husbands and sided with their children in arguments. Occasionally, a husband was ridiculed by his wife and her children even when he was present. In contrast, only one wife was ridiculed by her husband and no example was encountered of children criticizing the mother publicly.

Asked whether man and wife seemed to get closer together as they got older Mrs Wenton said, 'No. Me and my hubby don't get on well. If he's sitting at the table, and I ask him to pour me out a cup of tea he says he won't, and that irritates me. He's never been a man for helping in the house. And now that I can't do things he creates because I can't. He goes on at me.' She spoke fondly of her daily relationship with her two married daughters and their children and said she spent most of her evenings with them, her husband going off to meet friends.

Mr Blazes showed me with pride a framed certificate acknowledging his service for the borough council. While he was showing me this his wife and son nudged each other behind his back and winked at one another. The wife went purple with suppressed laughter. 'He used to have it hanging over his bed.'

The husband did not have a full awareness of the extent and depth of his wife's associations with married children, grand-children, and other relatives. And she did not fully compre-hend his need to maintain his standing among workmates and friends and visit the remaining members of his family of origin. Possibly each may not have understood the other's responsibilities and activities outside the marriage and each may have recognized the need not to draw too much attention to them.

Retirement produced frustrations in men, because they could not fill in their time and because they felt they were useless, and it also produced frustrations in women, because they had been used to a larger income and to a daily routine without interference from the husband. Friction could not always be dispelled by a new formulation of the division of occupations. A wife said of her retired husband, 'It's different with him at home. Because he's at home he wonders what you're doing. Before that he wasn't here and you could get on with things. Now he's asking you what you're doing this for and what you're doing that for.'

Excluding minor frictions, six of the married women whose husbands had retired, or one in five, revealed marked hostility in their marital relationships.

> Mrs Bassy was in her late sixties. Her husband had been a cabinet-maker and he retired two years previously after a spell in hospital. She said he hadn't been the same since. 'We don't sleep together, we don't. He has his room and I have mine. He hasn't spoken to me for more than a fortnight. He's often like that and all over nothing. Even when he *is* on speaking terms he's no company. He sits reading his papers and goes out at night with his pals. It's no life at all. There's nothing for me to stop here, with a fidgety man about the place like that. He can't let nothing be.' When I had called for the interview the husband had opened the door, knocked on the door of a front room occupied by his wife and had then retreated, without a word, into the depths of the house. Mrs Bassy did all her own housework. 'I gets the meals ready and nowadays I puts his in his room and I eats mine in here.'

Some of the difficulties between man and wife in old age were due, possibly, to unsatisfactory sexual relationships, particularly if one but not both were infirm. The impression was gained that some women had rarely experienced sexual satisfaction and found it difficult to give a husband 'his rights' when they became infirm. There is little doubt that sexual intercourse is maintained into old age but is less frequent and may be discontinued altogether in infirmity. One man in his seventies with a wife who was too infirm to leave the home said, 'Well, the woman don't want too much of it. Any decent woman at all, well, my wife she never says anything to me because she knows that I never touch her, not for three or four months at a time, then when I do she don't say nothing because she knows I've been waiting all that time. See what I mean? Some people say they go with their wives just as though they were youngsters, once a week, but I don't get that in my head. I don't believe them. You know what I mean, I don't feel like it.'

Quite apart from the special circumstances of infirmity and retirement, this discussion brings out the way the existence of a localized group of three or four generations of relatives seems to involve a conception of marriage different from that of a married couple living in isolation from relatives. A balance has to be struck by an individual between his responsibilities as a marriage-partner and as a member of an extended family. The maintenance of separate loyalties outside the marriage is a possible source of continuous friction between man and wife. Such friction is reduced or avoided by respect for the need of a couple to live in their own household, by a fairly strict division of labour and of income, and by segregation in associations with relatives and others. In this way the marriage adjusts to the needs of extended family relationships and so helps to preserve them.

It is important not to dismiss such evidence of separation between man and wife in their financial, domestic, and family roles simply as evidence of working-class male or female 'authoritarianism' which stands in poor contrast to so-called middle-class 'partnership'. Customs symbolize and express social relations and segregation in role can solve problems as well as create them. Perhaps the marriage necessarily adjusts in this way to its complex social environment.

In this general context it may become easier to understand the financial relationship between man and wife. In this chapter we have considered (i) the division of income, (ii) the personal responsibility for each share of income, and the uncertainty or ignorance of the other's exact income and spending habits, (iii) the regularity of housekeeping outlay from week to week, (iv) the underlying competition between man and wife when the wage is small, (v) the alignment of wives and their married and unmarried children over financial and domestic affairs and the exchange of money between them, and (vi) the division of labour and segregation in spare-time pursuits which may have contributed to unawareness of the marriage partner's financial needs and responsibilities. The evidence may justify the conclusion that the husband tends not to reveal his wage to his wife when each have strong loyalties outside the marriage, she to relatives living nearby who are seen frequently and he to relatives on his side or to workmates and friends. When the wage is small this may be a particularly effective way of avoiding or reducing conflict. A wider conclusion is that segregation of roles between husband and wife depends on the degree to which they are members of a three-generation extended family in the locality.

CHAPTER 7

Sons and Daughters

IN previous chapters we have been concerned with the extended family largely as a domestic and economic organization. Before we can sum up its characteristic features we also need to examine more closely some of the principal relationships between its individual members. The strength and the character of these relationships help to explain the strength of the family.

We shall first consider the tie between old people and their children. Over four in five of all the old people interviewed had at least one child. A man had married, on average, at twenty-five and a half, his first child was born when he was twenty-eight and his last child when he was thirty-nine. He was about sixty-two before his last child reached the average marrying age. A woman had married, on average, at twenty-three, her first child was born when she was twenty-six and her last child when she was thirty-five. She was fifty-nine before the last child reached the average marrying age. Now these averages, crude though they are, indicate one crucial fact about the adult life of these people. For about thirty-four years of their lives both man and woman had had at least one unmarried child at home. Both were not far short of pensionable age before the last child would normally expect to marry. This suggests a major reason for the maintenance of strong ties between child and parent in Bethnal Green: the prolongation into late middle-age of parental care of children, and the consequent shortness or non-existence of the interval between the period when the youngest child depends on his parents and the period when, because of increasing infirmity, they are likely to depend on him.

Averages conceal the diversities of family structure. One in five of the people with children had six or more and nearly one in five one only. One in three of them had children of one sex only. Some married at seventeen and had their children young and others did not marry and have children until their late thirties or forties. A number of children had not yet married, although many of them were in their thirties, forties, or fifties. Account has to be taken of such variations in understanding the relationship between child and parent when the parent is old.

Unmarried Children

The relationship between old people and unmarried children is of special interest in two respects. First, the strength and kind of the bond between parent and child prior to the child's marriage provides a means of understanding the extent to which the bond may be maintained after marriage. Second, some children defer marriage or do not get married at all. Of the 626 children reported by the people in the sample eighty-three, or thirteen per cent, were unmarried. Only one in six of these was under twenty-five years of age and less than a half under thirty-five. A fifth were over forty-five.

Despite the large number in their thirties and forties all but seven of these unmarried children, five being sons, lived at home. Of the seven, two were in mental hospitals and the others comprised a social worker, a primary school teacher, a seaman, a mechanic working in his married brother's garage, and a car maintenance engineer in America. The last visited his mother in Bethnal Green every year for a month.

It was therefore rare for a working-class child to leave home before marriage unless he took a non-manual occupation. Until he began courting seriously many of his activities were shared with his family or indirectly determined by his family. Despite an apparent relaxation of parental discipline in the last two generations children, particularly daughters, were expected to be home fairly early and to participate in many family activities and gatherings. They often performed jobs of various kinds in the home and looked after a younger child. In this period some of them also helped to look after ageing grandparents and kept them company, spending a lot of time in their homes and sometimes going on outings or visiting a cinema with them. They usually had holidays with their parents or other members of the family and entertained friends at home. A parent often helped a child to get his first job, either by approaching his own employer or by accompanying the child to make an application for a job. The mother often supervised her children's spending money and their purchases and she had a right to a fixed share of their wages. When courting, boy and girl spent many of their evenings in the girl's home and her mother was prominent in arrangements for the marriage. When living in privately-owned property she usually 'spoke for' her daughter in seeking from her landlord the tenancy of the next flat or house falling vacant. In these various ways the bond between child and parent, especially between child and mother, was maintained through adolescence into early adult life.

The mother often gave the impression she was flattered if her children were reluctant to marry. There were various references, by old people and children alike, to unmarried children or siblings who were 'too comfortable at home' or 'didn't want to leave Mum'. While the mother sometimes acted and talked as if she would have liked one or more of her children to stay on at home for as long as possible before marriage, her husband seemed to be much more anxious for them to marry and leave home. 'Dad says the sooner they marry the better but I don't like to see them rush into it.' The potential challenge to a man's authority that existed when grown-up sons and daughters were present in the home may be one reason for this difference between man and wife. The illness or infirmity of parents made it difficult for some children to contemplate early marriage.

The children's sense of duty and attachment was particularly strong when the father was dead. A high proportion of people of pensionable age are widows. In 1951 in Great Britain the proportion was twenty-eight per cent. In the Bethnal Green sample thirty-three per cent were widows. Just over one in ten had no surviving child. Of the rest nearly a third had at least one unmarried child living at home. The strong bond between a widow and her unmarried children, particularly her sons, was frequently mentioned in the interviews.

Mrs Pinkerton thought it right for one child to stay on with the widowed mother. Her eldest son had married only a year previously, at the age of forty. 'My Teddy stayed long enough with me. One child should cling to a mother. I do miss him.'

Mrs Vixon had no sons and she lived with an unmarried daughter aged thirty-five. 'After all these years I wouldn't like to be parted from my daughter. But if she does get married I wouldn't stand in her light. But I'd hardly like to part from her.'

When they were seen separately children often said much the same. One of two unmarried daughters caring for an infirm mother said they could have married but did not because they were so fond of their mother. A married daughter said of an unmarried brother, 'My mother pampers him. No wonder he's single.'

Similar evidence arose when old people talked of relatives other than children. A woman explained that an unmarried nephew and niece continued to live in the old home. 'They live only for their mother.' Another woman explained that a niece had not married because 'her mother had such bad health. She wouldn't go and leave her mother.' A man said he had an unmarried nephew. 'His mother only died a year ago. They went about together. He was like a husband to her. He told me he didn't want to live.' And an elderly spinster said, 'I miss every hair of my mother's head. We were always together. We were like two sisters.'

Delaying Marriage

The evidence suggested that widows' children often delayed marriage, sometimes indefinitely. This appears to be one of the ways by which a family adjusts to the loss of one of its members and compensates the individual who is most affected. The children, to some extent at least, substituted for their fathers. Occasionally it also seemed they substituted for mothers. One widower said, 'My daughter acts as mother used to do. She looks after me, buys everything and pays everything.' Now it is hard to devise an adequate test of postponement of marriage. The widows in the sample had lost their husbands from a few weeks to forty-five years previously. Sometimes the husband had died leaving them with several young children and sometimes he had died when one child only remained unmarried. Because of such variations it is hard to distinguish a set pattern in their relationships with children. But, as we have seen already, a slightly higher proportion of widows than of married women were living with unmarried children, despite their higher average age. This seems to be part of any attempt to test the validity of statements about postponement of marriage. Another part is to seek a means of establishing whether children who do marry, marry later. It was found that both sons and daughters marrying after losing their fathers married later than average. By itself this is not a conclusive criterion of postponement of marriage, however, but taken with other arguments it is persuasive.

There was a difference in age at marriage between children who lost their fathers when very young and children who lost their fathers in adolescence or young adult life. Thirty-six married children had lost their fathers before they were ten years of age. They married at roughly the same average age as children whose parents were both alive. Fifty-three other married children had lost their fathers between the ages of ten and their middle twenties. Of these, sons married over one year and daughters two years older than children whose parents were both alive. This suggests that the bond between widow and unmarried child may have been particularly close if the father died when the child was in his teens or twenties, rather than if he died when the child was an infant or only a few years old. The adolescent child is much more conscious of what the loss of the father means to him and to the family and of the consequent needs of his mother, especially her financial needs. Compared with a child who grows up without ever knowing or barely knowing what it was to have a father, he may make a more conscious effort to take on the father's role and responsibilities. It is possible also that the loss of his father at such a time may reduce the number of his social activities outside the home and result in a slower approach to maturity. He will thus be less ready, in his middle twenties, for marriage and for setting up a home independently of his mother.

The Predominance of Mum

Many instances of the special feelings of children for their mothers have already been given. Both sons and daughters expressed a greater affection for their mothers than for their fathers. It was chiefly Mum they visited and Mum they supported, materially and emotionally. The men indeed often accepted this. One married man, a pensioner, in talking of his children's visits to the home said, 'They come up every week to see their mother.' Although he was at home at the time of their visits he did not say his children visited both *him* and his wife. Another said, a little wistfully, 'If his mother's little finger ached, he'd be in pain all over his body.'

T – D

A married woman said, 'The mother always comes first in every child's life. It's always the mother. Sons and daughters alike. I suppose they're with them all day.'

Some evidence for this closer attachment to the mother arose when people talked about divorce or separation. The children usually sided with the mother, and even when the separation took place not when the children were young or in their teens but after they were married they appeared to have little or nothing more to do with their fathers. In two cases the father continued to live in the same district as mother and married children. The children never visited them although they lived alone. One father had left home largely because his wife had a child by another man. Yet I was told at the interview, 'The children won't speak to their father if they pass him in the street.'

The crucial position of the mother could be seen in the way her children depended on her in many of the emergencies of life. Several women looked after unmarried daughters and the daughters' illegitimate children. Three women said they had had the main care of a mentally defective grandchild for several years. A number of children returned home after losing a spouse by death or separation. Often they depended on the mother for the care of one or more of their children while they went to work. It was the same in illness. One son, who was in the home at the time of the interview, said, 'When my wife was in hospital with bladder trouble a couple of years ago, me and my nippers made a bed on this floor.' The mother's home was the reception centre for many of the major problems of the family.

On one occasion an old widow produced two burial cards, on which were printed the names and addresses of her brother and sister, both of whom had died within the previous few years. The inscription on the sister's card said:

> Rest on dear mother, thy labours o'er,
> Thy willing hand will toil no more:
> A faithful mother, true and kind,
> No friend on earth like thee we find.

The brother's inscription merely asked the Lord to forgive him for all his sins. There was no reference to his labours, nor to his toiling hand.

Keeping in Touch after Marriage

A daughter expected her mother to accompany her over the threshold of marriage. She did not think of marriage so much in romantic terms of starting a home in a new district where she was to spend nearly all her time, centring all her interests, affections, and activities first on her husband and then on both husband and young children. She remained a member of her family of origin, and inevitably there was friction, latent as well as revealed, between in-laws and between man and wife because of the proximity of their relatives. An extract from an interview will help to convey what sometimes happened.

Mrs Bloom was a widow in her late sixties living alone in a tenement flat. Her married son lived a few minutes' walk away and he had a midday meal with her three days a week. She rarely saw his wife, although his children visited her on Sundays. Her daughter, aged twenty-eight, lived in a nearby flat. 'I spoke for her to the superintendent. Her husband comes from Stepney. She wanted to get married at nineteen but I had a little talk with her. He was five years older than her and he was old enough but I said to her, "I wouldn't stand in your way, Mary, but you mustn't make a mistake. You want to be sure." They were courting three years. She's a good daughter to me. I see her every day. At her wedding his mother wasn't very nice. She was off-hand. When I came in and they introduced me I felt they were all looking at me. It was like coming under a cloud. And they cut the wedding cake, it was a lovely one, like bits of wood, and there were no speeches. My son gave her away. He took the place of her father. I don't think his mother wanted to lose him. He was twenty-seven. She said to him, "Whatever you do I want you to keep your own home." I felt that. I felt that was said in front of me. Well, he wanted her, didn't he? My daughter says they come to see the baby and they always bring her something. He's a very good husband. He helps her in the home and he takes the baby out on Sunday morning. I think he takes her [the baby] round to see his family. When I see my daughter I always come home at five o'clock. Well, he comes home at 5.30 and I say, "Mary, you want the place to yourselves." She'd like more children but I say, "Think what would happen if your partner goes." She'd have to go out to work. It was a hard time for me. I stayed with my mother [she was the youngest of a large family] and I didn't want to get married. I didn't look for it. [Her mother died and she got married late in life.] My daughter was only six when my

husband died. He was at work one Wednesday and in his coffin the
next. She stayed with me after my son got married and when she was
sixteen she said, "Mum, you have a rest, I'll look after you." She
brought money home but I saved it for her in her name and when she
got married I gave it to her. But you don't know what a girl will do
when a fellow gets talking to her.' [She implied her son-in-law would
deprive her daughter of the money.] Throughout the interview her
year-old granddaughter was sitting on her lap and the grandmother
sang to her, 'She wore a little bonnet.'

This example illustrates most of the characteristic features of the
relationship between old people and their married children and
children-in-law: the special tie between mother and daughter; the
way married sons visited their parents unaccompanied by their
wives; the tactful avoidance of children-in-law; the tensions
between in-laws, particularly between husband and mother-in-
law; and the close relationship between maternal grandmother and
grandchild. Marriage was more than the marriage of two persons
free to devote themselves to each other. As one woman put it,
'Before they got married my son said to me, "I'm not marrying
her family, Mum, I'm marrying her." But she creates if he comes
to see me and I think he's found I was right.'

The tensions between in-laws were often mentioned in the interviews. Old people sometimes said sons-in-law were contemptuous
of them, refused to speak to them in the house, or did things
deliberately to upset them. Sometimes they said daughters-in-law
tried to weaken the relationship between them and their sons. In
one extreme family a daughter-in-law forced an old widow to
move out of the home, and so caused a rift between the widow
and her son. Frequently a mother made such a remark as, 'If my
sons make a fuss of me the wives get annoyed. They get a bit
catty.' Old people who liked to think their children had very strong
loyalties to them despite the claims of marriage contrasted
children-in-law unfavourably with children. A widow living with
her married daughter said, 'At first my son-in-law thought he
was going to be the boss but he's found out that I'm the guv'nor.
I've only had one guv'nor in my life [her husband] and I wasn't
going to have another one now.' She continually told how poor a
showing her son-in-law made against her son. 'My son would do
anything if I was queer. But my son-in-law,' she said scornfully,

'he sleeps all the time. He wouldn't do anything unless you asked him to.'

This conflict with in-laws is reduced or avoided in several ways. One is by acknowledging the primacy of the wife's mother's claims. Another is by maintaining reserve in the relationship with sons-in-law and daughters-in-law. Old people recognized that since many of the open clashes between in-laws occurred when they lived in the same home, it was better to maintain an independent home if possible. When this was achieved they saw less of children-in-law than married children although, because of close proximity, they could not avoid seeing them sometimes. Compared with twenty-seven per cent of married children fourteen per cent of children-in-law were seen every day. Repeatedly during the inquiry a person would say, 'I see my daughter every day, but I only see her husband on Sundays.' 'My son calls in on his way home from work. I don't see his wife.' 'My daughter and I feel we belong to one another. I don't interfere with man and wife.' One woman said, 'My daughter-in-law in Stepney says I'm the best mother-in-law you could wish for. I hardly ever see her.' Things were made easier because the wife was able to see her parents while the husband was at work, and he was able to see his parents either in the lunch-hour or on the way home from work or by taking his children to see them on a Sunday morning when his wife was preparing the dinner.

These activities led to a certain alignment of blood relatives against affinal relatives. Loyalties to parents were maintained by individual associations with them and these loyalties were passed on to grandchildren. A widow, for example, criticized her son-in-law in front of her eight-year-old grandson. 'He's a difficult man to live with. I'm saying this in front of you confidential like,' she said, looking at her grandson, 'but your Dad's a very funny man. We don't get on well. He didn't like me being there. I had to be careful not getting in the way. He had his own likes and dislikes and he thought I was interfering. He thought I was having too much to do in the house.'

Old people were not always so reserved in their relationships with children-in-law. Some claimed they were as fond of them as their own children and saw them every day. This was often when, firstly, they had no children of the same sex and, secondly, when the parents of the children-in-law were dead. Table 12 provides some support for the first proposition. Old people saw a significantly higher proportion of children-in-law daily when they possessed no children of like sex. To some extent daughters-in-law substituted for daughters, and sons-in-law for sons.

The second proposition can merely be illustrated, without being supported statistically. One woman said, 'I've always been like a mother to my son-in-law. His mother is dead. He told a friend of mine that he had a mother-in-law in a million because when he's ill I look after him.' Another saw her son-in-law every day. His parents were dead. 'He's an angel from heaven. He'd do anything for me – he's only a little fellow too. I don't know what I'd do without them two.' A third, in her early sixties, had a mother-in-law nearby although her own parents were dead. 'I always like taking his Mum round something. Don't matter what elaborate flowers you buy her if anything happened to her, she couldn't see them. What you take round now, she can taste and she can eat.'

TABLE 12

CHILDREN-IN-LAW SEEN DAILY (AND WEEKLY) BY
OLD PEOPLE

Old people with children	Children-in-law seen		
	daily	weekly*	Total number
	%	%	
Sons-in-law			
those with son	13	52	217
those with no son	35	71	34
Daughters-in-law			
those with daughter	10	45	244
those with no daughter	23	67	40

* Those seen once a week or more, including those seen daily.

Large and Small Families

So despite the claims of marriage many children continued to see a lot of their parents. What difference did it make if they came from a large rather than a small family? We have seen that as high a proportion as thirty-one per cent of married and widowed old people had five or more surviving children. Such large families are becoming rarer and in the future an increasing proportion of old people will have only one or two children. It is of particular interest to consider people of this kind in Bethnal Green; they made up thirty-five per cent of the married and widowed.

Table 13 shows the contacts per week between old people and their children, according to the number alive. Those with one or two children saw a child, on average, significantly more often than those with three or more. These averages naturally conceal variations between and within similarly constituted families and it must be emphasized that four in five of the old people with large families were in daily touch with at least one of their children.

TABLE 13

FREQUENCY OF CONTACT WITH CHILDREN, BY NUMBER OF
SURVIVING CHILDREN

Number of children	Old person's total number of contacts per week with all children	Average contacts per child per week	Total children	Total old people
1	5·2	5·2	26	26
2	8·5	4·2	78	39
3–4	11·7	3·4	158	45
5 and over	19·1	3·1	364	57

An outstanding feature of the whole inquiry is the intensity of relationship within the one- and two-child family. Of the twenty-six people with one child, eighteen saw them every day and another five from once to three or four times a week. Only three saw their children less frequently than once a week, one of these being a step-child. Of the seventy-eight children in two-child families only eleven were seen less frequently than once a week.

This conclusion was more striking when account was taken of how the figures were influenced by the inclusion of unmarried children and by differences in age between old people and their children. All but one of the only children were married. They were older on average than others. Their age at marriage was near the average and all but two of them had been married for ten years or more, a third of them from twenty to thirty-five years. The presumption from the evidence was that people having one or two children, as compared with those having several, partly offset the possible handicap in old age by a more intense relationship with those they had.

Eldest and Youngest Children

Contacts with children also varied according to their birth-order. Youngest sons and daughters lived nearer and were seen more often than eldest children, comparing eldest and youngest only when *both* were married. Fifty-six per cent of youngest sons and forty-five per cent of youngest daughters lived nearer than eldest and twenty-three per cent and twenty-seven per cent respectively lived further away. The others lived at the same distance. More youngest children were seen every day, as shown in Table 14.

TABLE 14

ELDEST AND YOUNGEST MARRIED CHILDREN SEEN DAILY BY OLD PEOPLE*

Married and widowed children	*Eldest*		*Youngest*	
	% seen daily	*Number*	*% seen daily*	*Number*
Sons	9	70	31	70
Daughters	28	71	44	71

* Only cases where there were at least two sons or two daughters and where each was married, widowed, or separated.

Why was there a closer link with the youngest? In the first place an emotional preference was sometimes expressed for a youngest child. An effort was made to find out from old people whether they felt greater affection for one child rather than another. Many took refuge in an ideal which to them was very important. They said they always made it a rule not to pick and choose between one child and another. They often made remarks like, 'I always treat them the same. That's only right. I always have done. It's not fair to make fowl of one and fish of the other.' On closer inquiry a number admitted special feelings for the youngest. 'Well, really, I hoped he wouldn't marry yet. He helps in the home. . . . I'm fond of them all but you do like to do something for the youngest.' These feelings were often voiced by the children themselves. 'She's the baby of the family. She's the favourite.' 'When Mum lost Ben she couldn't get over it. He was her favourite. He was the youngest.' 'It knocked Mum a bit when Rosie [the youngest] got married.'

Sometimes the tie with an eldest child had become weakened in childhood. A few women whose husbands died when they had young children asked relatives to look after their eldest. In old age they gave this as the reason why they saw little of them. One woman, in explaining why she saw little of a son, said, 'You see my mother brought up my eldest after my husband died. He worked for her for a time.'

More often the tie had weakened after marriage. Once a mother had helped the elder children over marriage and childbirth she turned her attentions to the younger children. The eldest could move away with less compunction because brothers and sisters were still living with or near their parents. This explains part of the difference between eldest and youngest, but there is more to it than this. The eldest children were gradually attaining the status of grandparents. Sons and daughters who had reached their fifties were often grandparents themselves or had adult children. They had reached, or almost reached, the point of directing their own three-generation families. They saw much less of their parents than other eldest sons and daughters. They were not in the position of needing help from their parents or of being able to give it. The cycle of birth, marriage, and birth through the three generations had produced an off-shoot of the extended family ready to assume an identity of its own.

Nan and the Grandchildren

This difference between eldest and youngest partly depended on the changing relationship between grandparent and grandchild. Most people in Bethnal Green frequently saw some or all of their grandchildren. Altogether, there were 908 grandchildren, and ninety-three per cent of old people with children had at least one. Two-thirds of these had at least one grandchild living in the home district. Three features of their relationship are worth noting.

(i) *The first grandchild.* A grandparent, or rather a grandmother, attached special significance to the first grandchild, particularly the eldest child of the eldest daughter. The child embodied her right to the status of grandmother. From its birth she seemed to feel a special affection for it and their relationship was close, particularly when the child was aged from ten to fifteen. The grandmother took pride in preparing him or her for adult life, being able to give the adolescent child many attentions a mother, tied to work and small children, could not give.

> Mrs Shaldon said she paid a shilling a week for an endowment policy for her eldest granddaughter. 'Perhaps I can only do it up to the end of this year. I might need help myself then. It's for when Mary gets to be fifteen. You know with your first grandchild you give them more than you should give them. You spoil them.'

> Mrs Dominion's eldest grandson was with her at the time of the interview. 'He didn't go home last night. I thought it looked too bad [the weather]. I told him to stay here in the warm. My daughter didn't worry about him. She sent one of them to find out whether he was going back today.' The boy butted in to say, 'I'm the one who's up here the most. I'm the only one that's slept here lately.'

On average a woman was fifty-three when she became a grandmother (and a man fifty-five when he became a grandfather).

(ii) *Grandparents' leniency*. The grandparents were notably lenient towards grandchildren. The relationship of privileged disrespect between alternate generations has been reported from many other societies, and is a feature of anthropological literature. Something of the same kind existed in Bethnal Green. The grandchildren were expected to show greater respect for the authority of parents than for that of grandparents and the parents were expected to maintain authority in a way not expected of grandparents. Several old people said they had noticed changes in their attitude to young children as they got older. One woman said, 'I used to slosh my children. But I don't like to see my grandchildren walloped.' A man echoed this when he said, 'As a person gets older I definitely think he gets more love for children. He has more love and feeling for a child. I used not to mind when people hit their children, but I go crackers now if I see anyone hit a child.' Others referred more directly to the difference between parents and grandparents.

> Mrs Aylesbury was lenient with her grandsons. 'The grandmother

can be free and easy. She [her daughter] has to be fairly strict with them.'

Mrs George was talking about her mother. 'I paid her rent, and I paid my mother for doing things for my children. She was different to my children from what she was to us.'

(iii) *Bringing up the young*. The third and most important feature of the relationships between grandparents and grandchildren was one which largely explained why the bond with the children was maintained so long after the children's marriage. To many grandchildren in Bethnal Green the grandmother was much concerned with their care as the mother. Mother and grandmother were held together by the latter's continuing function in looking after young children. First they were concerned with the off-spring of the eldest and then of the youngest. Some widows had sole charge of grandchildren.

Mrs Soker lived in one large L-shaped room where there was a double-bed in which she and her small grandson slept. 'Bertie's company for me. She [her daughter] leaves him here and I enjoy him.' The grandson had lived with her for the past two years. She was seventy-one.

Sometimes the grandmother had main rather than sole charge of a child, as witnessed by one woman's small grandson who said, 'I've got two homes. I live with my Nan and go upstairs to my Mummy to sleep.'

Mrs Aiken's four-year-old grandson spent most of his time with her. Her daughter left him on her way to work in the morning. The daughter said, 'I don't know what she'll do when he has to go to school. He loves his Nan.' Mrs Aiken said, 'He follows me about like a dog. If I go out on the landing he has to come too.' For most of the interview the little boy sat on his grandmother's lap and when I went out with him and his mother he said, 'Nan, wave from the window.'

Until six months previously Mrs Hogmay had a grandson living with her. 'I brought up lots of my grandchildren. My eldest daughter was left by her husband with three young babies and I brought them all up. Then my youngest daughter was at home with me and I brought her children up.'

By the time they reached their mid sixties some grandparents were no longer responsible for the daily care of the younger generation, particularly if they were infirm or the grandchildren were children only in name. The child-rearing role of others persisted. What was so striking was how many women in Bethnal Green played a major role in rearing young children for as many as forty or fifty years of their lives. Because of this continuity of function, women's ties with children were maintained to the point when, in extreme old age, they needed far more help than they were able to give.

The Social Class of Children

Analysis of the relationship between people and their children as it progressed over life has given us an idea of the reasons why contacts with most children were maintained. The same reasons also help to explain why old people saw little of some children. Sons were drawn into their wives' families, which occasionally meant they made their homes far away. Eldest children were less dependent on their parents. Their children had grown up or they were grandparents themselves. If brothers and sisters remained in the parents' home district the obligation to maintain daily contact was weaker. 'My sons don't see so much of me. They know my daughter lives near. But if there was any trouble they'd come up sharp.'

Did old people see less of children who had a higher social status? Nearly all the people in the sample, or their husbands, were manual workers. Some of the children were in higher-status occupations. Altogether forty-two of the married children, or about eight per cent, had, or their husbands had, professional or intermediate occupations, styled as social classes I and II by the Registrar-General. A quarter of them lived within a mile, compared with nearly a half of other married children. As Table 15 shows, there was little difference in the frequency with which married sons in higher-status occupations, compared with those in manual occupations, saw their parents. On the other hand daughters married to men with higher-status occupations tended to see rather less of their parents. Significantly fewer of the daughters in the first two classes were seen than in the third. It would be unwise to draw too firm a conclusion. The data rests on information supplied by people who were sometimes vague about a child's occupation and numbers were small in the professional occupations, not to speak of the problems of defining social class.

The interviews gave a better idea of what happened when a child advanced, educationally or occupationally. A number of old people maintained that relationships with sons did not change much. A widow with two white-collar sons said, 'They wouldn't let the old girl go down the pan. . . . It doesn't affect family relationships if the children go up in the world.' Women often put this point of view; less so the men. They sensed a son's occupational

TABLE 15

MARRIED CHILDREN SEEN DAILY (AND WEEKLY), BY
SOCIAL CLASS OF CHILDREN

Social class	*Married sons*			*Married daughters*		
	% seen daily	% seen weekly	Number	% seen daily	% seen weekly	Number
Professional	15	58	26	0	31	16
Clerical	29	67	24	25	69	16
Manual	19	70	216	43	79	140
Not known	0	0	7	35	76	75
Total	19	66	273	36	74	247

NOTE: Widowed daughters and step-children are excluded from this analysis. Definition of the three social classes follows the Registrar-General's classification of occupations, combining classes I and II as 'Professional', class III manual and classes IV and V as 'Manual'; and styling III non-manual as 'Clerical'.

achievement as a reflection on their own, though usually they had the consolation that they had had fewer opportunities in their youth. 'They get so big-headed they won't take advice', was one man's remark. But, in general, parents, and particularly the mother, seemed to take pride in sons who did well. 'He's got a marvellous job. He only gets paid once a month.' One son who was a teacher-trainee thought the urge to get on in life and educate yourself was something which the parents did not obstruct 'because they're proud of you and what you do reflects on them. They like talking about you. If you have to move away because of your job the feeling might be just as strong as if you see them every day.'

Mrs Brink's three sons won scholarships to a grammar school. One was a chief statistician in a Whitehall Ministry. 'He came fifth out of 600 in the examinations. At first we wanted him to leave school at fifteen because his father was out of work. But then just as he was going to leave, my husband got a job after being out of work and he came to me and asked me, "Mum, do you think I can stay on?" I said, "What do you want to do, Charlie?" He said that he wanted to stay on and he wanted to go in for these exams but it cost 10s. I said I'd pay the 10s. entry fee. My three sons all took their matriculation. I thought if it was an advantage to them I'd struggle on to give them a good chance in life. If you've given them the chance, then they should look after you when you're getting on.' She saw her eldest son, who was thirty-seven, once a week. The youngest son was a university student and lived at home between terms. The middle son lived in the same street. 'I went and spoke for him and they got a flat in this street. I see him three or four times a week, he's a department manager now. I suppose I've really stood by him.'

The relationship between parent and son, particularly between mother and son, was largely maintained. Many mothers were widowed and this strengthened the relationship, preventing divided loyalties on the one side and cultivating a stronger sense of duty on the other. It was harder for a mother to take pride in a son-in-law, and she was uneasy in her relationship with a daughter who had 'gone up in the world'. The daughter often had a different view about house- and mother-craft, she had strange friends, and she usually lived in a completely different environment. There was not the same easy familiarity with a daughter as with a son who had a high-status occupation. The interviews suggested that in Bethnal Green differences in social class were more of a barrier between a parent and a child of like sex than between a parent and a child of different sex.

Decline in Contact with Children

Yet social class did not account for much falling-off in contacts between old people and children. Old people themselves laid more stress on two other things. First, those separated from one or all of their children often said both they and their children wished they could live nearer one another. Their complaints can be understood in the light of what was said earlier about housing. Despite great efforts to remain in Bethnal Green many children were obliged to

make their homes elsewhere and could not find a home there for
the parents. The consequences were many. The children had their
own homes and families to look after and were not able to visit
Bethnal Green as often as they wished. Their parents visited them,
but found they had to limit their visits because fares were so high
and because they were becoming more infirm. 'My eldest daughter
says to me, "I wish you lived a little nearer, Mum." But it's the
fares. It's 2s. 2d. to go and see her. It's this fare business what stops
you seeing your children.' 'I used to go and stay week-ends with
my daughter at Chingford but I can't do it any more. I just can't
get out.' There were many remarks of this kind.

Second, there were occasional complaints of a different nature
about children who neglected their parents. One man said he did
not think families did enough for their old folk. 'If you've got a son
they only acknowledge their parents. They don't do much. You
hear a man talking and saying he doesn't see his children. I know
it doesn't apply to everyone but the majority of cases the boys and
girls get married and want to look after themselves.' A widow said,
'When you're old you're not wanted. . . . . I kept on sighing. My
daughter just puts her head in the door when she's passing. She
doesn't do anything. It's very hurtful.' What was interesting about
such remarks was that they usually applied not to daughters, but
to sons who had left their wives or sons whose wives were un-
friendly. Of the two remarks above, the first was made by a man of
his only son living in a nearby flat; the second by a woman whose
daughter had the care of a husband with an amputated leg. A
rather unusual relationship usually lay behind the complaint.
Three children proved to be stepchildren or illegitimate, two had
separated from their wives, and two more were in the family of a
man who had married again after the mother's death. However,
it was not always possible to discover the reasons why some children saw little of their parents. It is necessary here to distinguish
between a specific complaint against a child and a general complaint against children. Old people often talked of children's
neglect of their parents, but hardly ever were these children their
own. They liked to believe the loyalty of their own family was
exceptional.

What is important in this context is the small proportion of
people who had little or no contact with *any* child. Whether the old

person had one or several children and whether he or she had sons *or* daughters, there was nearly always at least one remaining at home or nearby. As we found in Chapter 4, all but fifteen per cent of people with children had one living within a mile. All but seventeen per cent saw a child every day. Only six people, or four per cent, did not see one of their children at least once a week. Of these six, five had sons only. Their circumstances were unusual. One was a man separated from his wife and his two sons lived abroad; another was a woman with two illegitimate sons who had been reared by foster-mothers, and a third had only an elderly step-son.

Widowers saw less than married men of both sons and daughters, but widows, while seeing slightly less than married women of daughters, saw about the same of sons. As age advanced beyond the pensionable age there was a slight falling-off in contacts with children among the sample, but this was too small to be statistically significant. The numbers of old people in their seventies and eighties were perhaps too small to justify a firm conclusion and the question needs much further study. So far as it went, the evidence suggested people in their eighties did not see much less of children than those in their sixties. Considering the limitations on their mobility it would seem that children stepped up their visits to the home towards the end of the parent's life.

As, in this chapter, we have followed the relationship between child and parent in Bethnal Green over life, one outstanding conclusion has emerged. The strength of the relationship was founded on its continuity. It persisted through time and into marriage. In the interviews people continually spoke, if indirectly, of the social virtues of regularity, loyalty, constancy, and fidelity. Unmarried children rarely left home before marriage. The parents were usually in their late fifties or early sixties before the last child was of marriageable age, and if the father died one or more of the children sometimes delayed marriage. The old mother was the central figure in the kinship system. She stood by her children in their troubles and when they married she did not lose them, nor they her. Living near, they often provided, in effect, an extension of the old household. She helped her daughters rear their children; they worked for her and gave her company. It was her, rather than her husband, they visited and her they supported. Her children often saw her independently of their spouses, daughters while their husbands were at work and sons at midday, on their way home from work, or on Sunday mornings when their wives were preparing the Sunday dinner. Conflict between husband and wife due to such loyalties maintained outside the marriage was largely reduced or regulated by recognition of the force of the tie between grandmother, daughter, and grandchild and by a relationship of marked reserve or avoidance between in-laws. With the passing of time the eldest children were freer to move out of the home district because brothers and sisters remained there. Their own children were growing up; the grandmother was turning her attentions to the younger children's marriage and child-rearing, and they were reaching the point of becoming grandparental heads of new extended families. For such reasons the tie with youngest was often closer than with eldest children. But whether the old person had many children or not, one usually remained at home or nearby. This meant there was often an especially close relationship with an only child and that even in extreme old age a person who had had children was rarely short of company, help, and affection.

CHAPTER 8

Brothers and Sisters

IN the last chapter we saw how the extended family is built round mother, daughter, and grandchild, and how the grandmother begins to lose a major role in family life once all the grandchildren grow out of childhood. This is only one of the changes experienced with age. While the form of the family of three generations persists, its composition continually changes and individuals occupy different roles within it as they get older. New relationships substitute for old. A child looks to his parents, grandparents, and brothers and sisters for company and affection. After he grows up and marries he looks increasingly to his children, and then his grandchildren. What happens to his ties with brothers and sisters? This chapter suggests they weaken with age, especially after the death of parents, but they are often maintained by those who remain unmarried or childless.

Old people in Bethnal Green were born in a period (1865–95) when it was commonplace for a mother to give birth to a baby every two years or so between the date of her marriage and the onset of her menopause. People talked of 'steps and stairs' or 'ten on the trot'. It is clear, despite marginal uncertainty about the number of still-born siblings, that the parents of those interviewed produced an average of nearly eight live children each. Only seventeen per cent said their mothers had given birth to five or fewer children. A high proportion died in infancy or childhood but of the seven siblings born an average of 2·6 were still alive. One in six people had no surviving brother or sister but nearly one in four had at least five.

People in their sixties had more surviving brothers and sisters than those in their late seventies and eighties, but the fall with age was not sharp. This is because of the wide range in age between siblings. A woman aged sixty sometimes spoke of a sister in her eighties and vice versa. People in their sixties had an average of 3·1 brothers and sisters, those in their seventies 2·3 and those in their eighties 1·7.

Sisters outnumbered brothers by three to two. In the sample slightly more lived nearby; twenty-nine per cent lived with the old people or within a mile, compared with twenty-five per cent of brothers. (However, this difference was not statistically significant.) Over half of all siblings lived in the East London region. The proportion of surviving siblings whose whereabouts were known is probably underestimated in Table 16. Some people whose siblings emigrated to the Commonwealth thirty, forty, and fifty years previously, for example, had lost contact with them and, in a few cases, were unable to say whether they were alive or dead. Such doubtful cases are included in the category 'not known' in the Table.

TABLE 16

PROXIMITY OF ALL SIBLINGS

Proximity	Brothers %	Sisters %	Brothers and sisters %
Same dwelling	2	3	2
Within a mile	23	26	25
East London region	28	27	27
Elsewhere in London	17	16	17
Elsewhere in Great Britain or abroad	22	21	22
Not known	9	6	7
Total	100	100	100
Number	221	316	537

The Husband's Family

The relationship between brothers and sisters showed the consequences of the special bond between mother and daughter. After marriage a man tended to be drawn into his wife's family. Over time, and especially after the death of his parents, this became more marked and he had fewer contacts with his own brothers and sisters, seeing more of his wife's. This is shown in Table 17. The relationship between husband, wife, and their respective siblings was, however, complicated by whether or not siblings of both sexes existed on both sides of the marriage. In theory both man and wife could be regarded as having at least one brother *and* one sister. In fact this may not happen. Less than one in four of the married old people interviewed had siblings of both sexes. This influenced family activities.

When both had surviving brothers and sisters the wife often regarded her husband's relatives with hostility and he acquiesced, suffering her relatives more gladly.

> Mr Booth said, 'We don't bother about any of them. It's one of those family affairs where you all dwindle. Two of my sisters have got a bit of money but they wouldn't give you anything. They'd help the church sooner than their own. They wouldn't give you a slice if you asked for it.' One sister lived a few doors away. 'We don't have anything to do with her. She had three girls and a boy but we never see them.' His wife interjected several times in a disgusted tone, '*His* family!' She added. 'My sisters are different.'

> Mr Boulder said, 'I don't mix up with my brothers and sisters much. When we were younger we mixed up with my wife's family. Me and the wife was one. We never mixed up.'

Instances of quarrels with the husband's siblings were often given. These quarrels usually resulted in loss of contact and served to define and delimit family groupings. They symbolized the customary maintenance of the links between mother, daughter, and grandchild within the extended family. Alignment with the wife's siblings was sometimes complete. Several people said a husband's brother or sister lived in a neighbouring street but was not seen, except by chance. One woman said she had never had much to do with her husband's family even though one of his sisters lived in the next street. 'I don't bother. I never have.' Another woman's daughter heard her mother remark that the father's niece lived two minutes' walk away and she exclaimed, 'Fancy that. I didn't know they were there.' Some men admitted they had not seen a nearby sibling for months. Others met siblings occasionally but sometimes unbeknown to their wives. Such meetings were perhaps a carry-over into old age of the independent visits to the parental home. One man remarked he had met his brother in a pub a week previously and his wife expressed surprise. This was just after she had stated flatly, 'We don't see any of his family.'

The wife sometimes had no siblings or she had brothers but not sisters. Occasionally her siblings died before her husband's, or they moved far away. This permitted a relaxation of the usual rule or custom of avoiding, or being reserved with, the husband's family, and associations became particularly close with his *widowed* sisters, if he had any. The women met each other when the husband was out. This explains why married women, while seeing most of their own siblings, often saw more of their husbands' siblings than the husbands did. Table 17 suggests the trends in contacts. There was one noteworthy exception to the rule that wives had little to do with their husband's brothers and sisters unless their own were dead or far away. At least ten people gave instances of two sisters marrying two brothers. Thus a few wives saw their husband's brothers largely because they saw their own sisters at the same time. The two families of origin were intertwined.

TABLE 17

MARRIED OLD PEOPLE SEEING SIBLINGS DAILY (AND WEEKLY)

Old people	Spouse's siblings			Own siblings		
	% seen daily	% seen weekly	Total	% seen daily	% seen weekly	Total
Married men	3	15	99	1	2	122
Married women	6	16	146	5	27	159

The death of husbands or wives had many repercussions for old people. Usually they lost any remaining contacts with the husband's or wife's siblings, particularly if they were of the opposite sex. One woman said, 'When the husband's gone they don't know you any more. My husband had two brothers and four sisters. I haven't seen them for years.' Widows and widowers were asked for information about their dead spouse's brothers and sisters. In some cases they had been widowed many years previously and had lost all touch with their in-laws. So far as could be ascertained they had no contact whatever with two in three of the surviving members of the husband's or wife's family and very little contact with the remainder.

The Weakening Tie

People recognized as inevitable the gradual redirection of an individual's interests away from his family of origin and towards his children and grandchildren. One woman thought the relationship with brothers and sisters 'dies out you see. When you've got children of your own they're your own.' A man said, 'When you're single, when you're young, you go and see the cousins living with aunties but when you go and get married you lose touch. You have your own family to look to.'

Sometimes differences in social class appeared to have caused siblings to lose touch. One man said of his sisters, 'We hardly ever see them. It's because they've all got selected jobs. One of them's a school-teacher.' There were a number of such references to brothers and sisters who had raised their status. Old people thought of themselves as the 'poor relations' and talked of the 'posh houses of the swells'. One or two said they would not dream of seeking help from high-status siblings even when ill. They were self-conscious about their homes and, though their attitude to their siblings was sometimes tinged with envy and bitterness, their main concern appeared to be fear of being treated as inferiors.

> Mr Meek saw little of his brother and four sisters. One sister was doing well in Australia and he had not heard from her for years. The others were, or had married, bank or insurance officials and lived in 'posh houses. I like to be independent. I wouldn't like them to come up if anything was wrong. We have got ourselves and don't like them interfering. They have their own telephones and sometimes I go round to the box to ring one of them up.' One sister would not see him 'because she thinks she's above you'.

Such sensitivity about status may be due in part to a sense of failure. Siblings share childhood together. There is a natural equality, but also a basis for competition, between them. If one achieves more than the others in adult life the competitiveness is likely to be stressed. In Bethnal Green people considered siblings who had improved their status to be disloyal or they ridiculed them for their superior ways. One man said, 'They used to live opposite her mother. But his place wasn't classy enough for him. He couldn't invite his associates there. He's some bloke, a proper swell. I could tell you some tales about him. If his nibs goes and picks something off the floor he goes and washes his hands.' Status differences rarely disrupted the relationship between parent and child, as we saw in the last chapter, but more often that between siblings.

The death of parents, particularly of the mother, was a major cause of siblings losing touch with one another. Married sisters and brothers who had been accustomed to meeting one another at the old home were suddenly left without a natural meeting place. There was no longer a pivotal figure holding them together.

Mrs Wyler said, 'When parents go I think the family breaks up. We used to go down when the old girl was alive. You used to see your brothers and sisters then. But when they died we lost touch. When she died they went north, south, east, and west.'

Mrs Mill linked the death of her mother with the war. 'It's the mother who everyone comes to. The war drifted them all apart. When you lost the parents, they [brothers and sisters] don't want you. They can't get together again. I don't think they do it intentionally, but it happened with the war too.'

The death of parents sometimes led to disputes between the children over the inheritance of the tenancy or of possessions and speeded their separation.

Mr Nipperton said his mother left a will to his younger brother 'which wasn't right. She had a big family too. And he got everything. None of them [brothers and sisters] wanted to speak to him. Yes, mother made bad friends.'

Miss Rowntree saw nothing of her eldest brother. 'You see,' she explained, 'he wanted to know what money my mother had left. She hadn't left any but I don't know whether he believed it.'

Infirmity or ill-health weakened further the relationship with siblings. Many old people were unable to leave their homes or journey far afield and some of their brothers and sisters were similarly handicapped. Visits made weekly became irregular or stopped altogether. One widow left her home only to go twice a week to a shop a few doors away. Her sister, herself widowed and infirm, lived a few minutes' walk away. Until a few months previously they had been able to meet two or three times a week, but now scarcely ever met.

Other old people who could get about fairly well in their own locality could not travel far or could not afford the fares. They often expressed their affection for distant brothers and sisters through intermediary relatives or by writing letters. This was one striking way in which affections were reinforced. It even applied to brothers and sisters who had emigrated many years previously. There were just under forty of these, most of them being the eldest in the family. Although one widow's brother had been in Canada for over forty years 'not a week passes but that he doesn't write to me. There must have been a hold-up in the post a short time back because last week I had four letters.' A man kept up a regular correspondence with his brother and two sisters in America. During the war he saw a lot of their sons and when on leave they used to stay with him or his youngest sister.

There were sometimes special reasons for the weaker relationship. Some women did not visit their brothers much because they did not like their wives. One man did not see his brother because, it seemed, he was 'a past grand master of the Ancient Order of Druids'. Some brothers and sisters had been separated from an early age because of the death of their parents, when they were brought up in orphanages or entered domestic service. This does not happen so often today.[1]

Although ties with brothers and sisters were generally less close than they had been and were much less close than those with children and grandchildren old people felt they could often be depended on. In times of stress they knew they could fall back on them. One woman said of her sisters, 'We don't see much of them, but we all know where to find them when we want them.' Others gave instances of mutual aid during the war, when brothers and sisters provided a temporary home for each other when they were evacuated or bombed out.

Maintaining the Tie

For a number of reasons, then, the relationship between many people and their siblings had weakened over time. But a close relationship was in fact maintained with some and regular visits were still made to others, if less frequently. Nearly one-fifth of those with siblings saw at least one every day, and another quarter saw at

1. In 1931 there were 1·3 million female domestic servants (indoor) in England and Wales, or eight per cent of the female population over fifteen. This proportion had remained fairly steady since the early part of the century. In 1951 there were only 703,000, or less than four per cent of the female population.

least one every week. This is, however, a generalized statement about associations between relatives which, as so often, becomes more revealing when broken down into statements about people of different sex, marital status, and social situation.

First, men saw less of both brothers and sisters than women. They saw three per cent of their brothers and nine per cent of their sisters at least once a week, while women saw sixteen per cent and thirty-four per cent respectively as often as this. Although, proportionately, nearly as many brothers as sisters lived within a mile, the latter were seen more often. This adds to the evidence of the predominance of women in kinship affairs.

Second, widowed people saw more than married people of their brothers and sisters, though the difference was not marked. They saw twenty-one per cent of their siblings every week, and married people seventeen per cent. After the death of a husband or wife people seemed to seek consolation in the company of another relative, often a son or daughter but sometimes a sister. Occasionally a widower looked on his sister as partly replacing his wife.

Third, single and childless people saw most of siblings. As Table 18 shows, a third of the brothers and over half the sisters of both single and married or widowed but childless old people were seen every week, many of them every day. People with children had fewer contacts. Close relations with siblings had been maintained by those who had no husband or wife or children to occupy the centre of their affections and whose parents had died. This adds to the evidence of the way substitutes and replacements are found within the family circle for non-existent or lost relatives.

In the sample there were eighteen spinsters and bachelors, four of whom had no siblings. Half of the remainder lived with, and others near, a brother or sister. A special twenty per cent sample of the household schedules completed at the time of the 1951 Census in Bethnal Green confirmed this result. Only one per cent of married women over the age of sixty but thirty-nine per cent of single women of the same age were living with brothers and sisters. This is a noteworthy fact.

Single old people often lived with or near an *unmarried* brother or sister. As many as six of the fourteen single people with siblings were in this situation. (Another had previously lived with a sister after the parents' death. 'But she tried to make me join her down

the slippery slope, going off to sleep with men, and we quarrelled.')
It seemed that two unmarried children who lost their parents
when they themselves were adult often remained together. A
brother or sister may partly substitute for a husband or wife. One

TABLE 18

OLD PEOPLE SEEING BROTHERS AND SISTERS DAILY (AND
WEEKLY)

Old people	Brothers			Sisters		
	% seen daily	% seen weekly	Total	% seen daily	% seen weekly	Total
Single	10	29	21	28	56	25
Married or widowed but no surviving child(ren)	13	33	15	33	54	24
Married or widowed but with surviving child(ren)	2	9	185	4	20	267
Total	4	13	221	9	25	316

spinster said, 'I don't tell anyone this. Even my sister doesn't
know. But I could have married my brother-in-law when our
other sister died. He asked me to but he had his daughter and I
didn't like to leave my sister on her own. I've always been happy
and I wasn't one of those what they say chase men. We've always
had the chapel to go to and we've had our work.'

Married and widowed people in the sample showed special concern for their unmarried brothers and sisters. Occasionally married
women gave them a home but this caused difficulties with husbands.
'Relations are best apart. When it's single relations it's different,
but not married ones.' 'It's best to wait until you can get a place of
your own. It's best to live apart from relations. If it's only one
room, a creep and a crawl.' More often the unmarried brother or
sister lived on in the parents' old home, and their married sisters
kept a watchful eye over them. One married woman had an unmarried brother living nearby. He was in ill health and she cleaned
his flat and took him meals every day. 'I couldn't leave my

brother to look after himself. You can't leave your family when they need you.' Another woman said, 'If you're the same temperament you can't live together. It depends how you get on. If you're near one another you can lend a helping hand.'

The role of women in setting themselves up as guardian angels over unmarried brothers and sisters was an important one. Some old people would otherwise have lacked care and companionship, especially when ill and feeble. The tenacity of the sibling relationship sometimes disclosed was extreme. A widow of sixty-five lived alone in a flat adjoining another occupied by her single sister. On one visit to the home the latter was seen. She had wild, staring eyes, a croaky voice, wiry grey hair sticking out from her head like a brush, and one yellow tooth in an otherwise toothless mouth. The widow said her sister was 'funny in the head' and she assumed the role of protector, getting the shopping, helping with the cleaning, and keeping her company. 'She spends an evening with me. We talk about our home life when we were children and have a good laugh, remembering things.'

Many single and childless people gave much more help to their relatives than they received. A woman, in particular, often acted as family nurse and bottlewasher.

> Mrs Munnally was a widow with no children. 'I've always been the one in my family who has looked after them in illness. I looked after my brother [who was bedridden] for fifteen years. I suppose it's me not having children.' She said she had also looked after her mother and father when they were frail and before they died in their mid eighties. She had also nursed an elder widowed sister. Years previously, after another sister died in a flu epidemic, she had reared a niece. She now saw this niece and a sister nearly every day.

This is a good example of the way childless and single people found substitutes for husbands or wives and children within the kinship network. Through siblings they were often drawn into a three-generation family and took on functions similar to those of breadwinner, mother, grandmother, or housewife. As a consequence they had closer relationships than others with siblings and nephews and nieces in old age. One old widower without children had been living with his mother and a dead sister's single daughter until the recent death of his mother. He continued to live with the niece, and a sister living nearby called every morning to do his shopping. Her children called to see him nearly every day. A married man lived with his crippled wife. They had no children and no surviving brothers or sisters but a niece looked after his wife every day while he was at work and spent several hours in his home. These are instances of the urge or need to belong to a three-generation family when lacking descendants.

The Second Mother

After the death of the mother the eldest sister sometimes prevented or delayed the disintegration of the sibling group. She protected its unity. Her role was of particular importance if the mother died before all the children were married or when some of them were separated from their wives, or were widowed, crippled, infirm, or mentally backward. She partly assumed her mother's role and looked after the interests of the family, taking responsibility for the family problems and continuing its traditions. One woman repeatedly mentioned her 'Samaritan sister', the eldest, who, in emergencies, had stood by each member of the family.

The eldest sister's responsibility in adult life derived partly from her experience in childhood. A mother with several children in Bethnal Green expected her eldest daughter to look after some of the younger children in the day and help bath them and put them to bed. There were many references to the 'little mother' of from ten to fifteen who was almost as efficient as the mother in attending to the home and to young children. Indeed, some old people gave instances of the eldest daughter bringing up the children after the early death of the mother. Some, who *were* eldest sisters, talked of their siblings as if they were their children.

> Talking about her brothers and sisters Mrs Duckworth said, 'When Mum died I sort of took her place. Me being the eldest I'd like to know how they all are. I'm the eldest, so I'm entitled to know. They all pop along to me.'

> Mr Hawthorn said of his eldest sister, 'She was the only one who stayed single. She was like my second mother.'

Some married women had given a home to younger unmarried brothers and sisters and a few still had them in their homes. Their role as second mother was strengthened because they were so much older. In many of the larger families of origin in Bethnal Green the eldest was often twenty and sometimes nearly thirty years older than the youngest. One woman had brought up and now lived near her youngest sister, eighteen years her junior. Such age-differences reinforced the eldest sister's authority.

The part she played in caring for her siblings, if the mother died young, sometimes resulted in a close relationship between sibling and niece or nephew or cousin. The youngest in the family was sometimes of the same age as his eldest sister's children. A widow aged seventy-eight had almost a courtship relationship with a nephew of seventy, who lived on the other side of London. 'I meet Albert at 2.45 every Saturday at Marble Arch. We go in one of the parks or sit in Lyons Corner House and then go to a show.' They spent their holidays together and 'he gets me over a lot of my worries. He tells me not to go worrying and stops me being lonely.' The widow's mother died at an early age and she was brought up by her eldest sister, fifteen years older, along with his sister's children, the oldest of whom was Albert.

The eldest sister, like the mother, often refused to discriminate in her affections for different brothers and sisters. She said it was a rule not to have favourites (though, as with the mother, this ideal was not always practised). Her attitude differed from that of most old people, who expressed a particular affection for one brother or sister, usually one nearest them in age. One woman remarked that her siblings had always gone about in pairs of those nearest in age. Generally, with the exception of 'second mother' relationships, the greater the difference in age between siblings, the less they saw each other in old age.

In this chapter we have followed the relationship between siblings over the latter part of the life cycle just as, in the previous chapter, we did the same with the relationship between parent and child. The main conclusion is that as people became older and had children and grandchildren they saw less of siblings. This trend became more marked after the death of the parents and when differences in status developed. But unmarried, childless, and widowed people usually maintained or renewed close contact. Old people saw more of their sisters than of their brothers, and married people saw more of the wife's than of the husband's siblings.

CHAPTER 9

The Extended Family and the Kinship Network

SPARING use has been made of the term 'the extended family' in previous chapters. Its meaning has been implied rather than stated. Yet evidence gradually built up shows some such term is needed to describe the family group of which most old people (and others) in Bethnal Green were in fact members. Their lives, and their problems, could be understood only against this background. This chapter will first describe how often people belonged to such a family and will go on to summarize its main features and show its place within the kinship network.

The *immediate family* may be said to consist of one or both parents and their unmarried children living in one household. Any two of its members stand in one of three relationships to each other: wife/husband, parent/unmarried child, unmarried sibling/unmarried sibling. A single person, two unmarried siblings, or a married couple living in a single household are not described as a family. The *extended family* may be said to consist of a group of relatives, comprising more than an immediate family, who live in one, two, or more households, usually in a single locality, *and who see each other every day, or nearly every day*. At least two of its members stand in a relationship other than the three possible relationships of the immediate family described above. Most commonly, as we have seen, the extended family consists of three generations of relatives – grandparents, married children, and grandchildren – in contrast to the immediate family of two generations. Sometimes, however, when the grandparents, say, are dead, a group consisting of two or more immediate families – such as two married sisters, husbands, and children – can also be treated as an extended family. When the members live in two, three, or more households not all may be in daily association but only the 'connecting' members of each household.

Normally the individual benefits from the domestic, social, and economic services implied in his membership. As we have seen, there is great range and variety in the functions of the family. We can in practice rely on an index of frequency of contact with relatives as a guide to the extent of interchange of services, such as shopping, washing, cleaning, looking after children, nursing in illness, and so on.

Thus, in Bethnal Green fifty-eight per cent of the old people, as shown in Table 19, belonged to a *three-generation* extended family in the sense that they saw relatives of the two succeeding generations every day or nearly every day and shared much of their lives with them. The group of relatives varied in size from six to over twenty. Generally it was built around grandmother, daughter, and grandchild, but variations were introduced by the sex and number of surviving children, the marital status and degree of incapacity of old people, and the distances at which the relatives lived.

> Mrs Knock, aged sixty-four, lived with her husband, a single son, and a granddaughter of eight years old. Her eldest daughter lived in the next street and her youngest daughter in the same street. She saw them and their children every day. They helped her with the shopping and she looked after the grandchildren when they were at work. Money was exchanged for these services. Her youngest son, recently married, lived two streets away and called every evening. Her two daughters had the midday meal with her and she sent a meal to her youngest son because his wife was at work in the day.

Most other people belonged to family groupings of two generations (twenty-five per cent of the sample) or one (six per cent). Some of these people, it should be remembered, had no children or grandchildren. Usually these family groups were extended families, as already defined, but for convenience a few immediate families, composed, say, of a widow and two middle-aged unmarried daughters, and a few groups of two or three unmarried siblings, have been included.

> Mr Erskine, aged sixty-nine, lived with his wife and two single sons. He had four married children, two living twelve miles away, one in an adjoining borough and one, the youngest daughter, in the same street. This daughter had married recently and she had no children. She visited the home every day. One of the other three children was seen one evening a week but the other two only about once a month. They could not be said to be part of a group dependent on one

another day by day. No grandchild lived near and none was seen more than once a month. Mr Erskine had a blind sister he visited every week. The married daughter living nearby helped his wife with the shopping and various other jobs and she and another daughter recently cared for her during an illness.

Miss Dingley, a spinster aged sixty-five, lived alone. A single sister lived next door and cooperated with her in many household tasks. They had an evening meal and week-end meals together and looked after one another in illness. There were no other relatives nearby. They had one married sister and one married brother, both living outside London, whom they had not seen for years. But they talked affectionately of a nephew and his family living in Kent whom they saw fairly often. Miss Dingley stayed with him at Christmas and Easter and had spent her summer holiday at his home. His children sometimes stayed with her sister next door during school holidays.

Some married couples and single old people saw no relative daily. Some of them saw little of their kin; others had none to see. They formed eleven per cent of the sample.

Mr Craddell, seventy-four, lived alone in one room. He was unmarried and had only one sibling, a brother living several miles away who had four children. Both brothers had served in the merchant navy and had rarely met throughout their lives. Mr Craddell had not seen his brother and his nephews and nieces for two years. 'It's like swans turning on their elders. I don't know one perfect family. I suppose I'm the black sheep of mine. I'm one of the relics of the past. I don't mix in no company.'

TABLE 19

VARIOUS FAMILY GROUPS TO WHICH OLD PEOPLE BELONGED

Family situation*	Old people %
Member of extended family of three generations	58
Member of family group of two generations	25
Member of family group of one generation	6
With spouse only	5
Entirely alone	6
Total	100
Number	203

* Determined strictly in terms of the relatives seen every day or nearly every day.

The definitions which mark off the different groups give a rough picture, but only a rough picture, of the reality. Associations with different relatives, as the examples testify, shade imperceptibly from those where relatives play an intimate role in daily life to those where they are seen, say, one evening a week. The dividing line is blurred. Even among the minority of married couples and single old people in Bethnal Green who saw no relative daily, some saw several relatives weekly. But in attempting to draw a fairly precise line on the basis of daily contacts between relatives the importance of the three-generation family as a major social institution providing daily care for old and young emerges more clearly. What seem to be its major features? In summing up these we can draw upon the evidence of earlier chapters.

Features of the Extended Family

Most of an individual's basic rights, obligations, and needs are expressed and satisfied, if present assumptions are correct, in the extended family of three generations. This is as true of children as of old people. After all, they usually belong to this family from birth to death and are continually schooled in behaviour which can be reconciled with the interests of the three generations. This is where they first learn about arbitration between selfish interests, about loyalty to a group and duty to others, and about the control and management of the problems of daily life. This is where they first see what it will mean to be husband or wife, parent, and grand-parent. Childhood ties with grandparents, parents, and brothers and sisters are only gradually replaced and supplemented by others with husbands, wives, children, and grandchildren. For all kinds of reasons, as we saw in Chapter 7, the bond between parent and child often does not weaken much after the child's marriage. It is this *continuity* of relationships with the extended family throughout individual life which is so striking.

The relatives in the extended family are distributed over a number of households held together by the common services and activities that go on among and between them. Quite apart from obligations which may exist there is much of mutual advantage until the last ebbing of life. The grandmother may be of as much value to her daughter in looking after the grandchildren as the daughter is of value in looking after her mother in illness and old age. The balancing of interests, needs, and satisfactions between the generations is largely a result of the *reciprocation* of services between individual members of the family, which helps to explain its strength.

The family is continually regenerating itself through the cycle of birth, marriage, and death, enrolling new members as old members die. As time passes, an individual marries and so gains a new set of kindred. As he gets older children and grandchildren begin to take the place of parents and siblings as intimate companions. Wife takes the place of mother, and (in some respects) daughter of wife. Even when there are no children there are usually nephews or nieces or cousins, if not siblings, who partly compensate. An orphan brought up by his mother's sister calls her 'Mum'. One thing brought out time and again in the course of the previous analysis is the way an individual's relationships adjust to variations in family composition. Childless and single people see more of siblings than people with children. Those with sons but not daughters see more of daughters-in-law than other people. Those with fewest relatives seem often to intensify their contacts with them. Even the unmarried or childless are often drawn into a three-generation family. One of the chief functions of kinship associations is to provide replacements for intimate kin lost by death or migration. A second function is to compensate for the absence of children, grandchildren, or siblings by providing substitutes or preserving into old age some of the ties of childhood and adolescence. There may be substitutes for siblings and children as well as parents. In one meaningful sense the extended family of three generations is a self-balancing or self-correcting institution to which the principles of *replacement* and *compensation* are fundamental.

If the family of three generations frequently exists then particular rules, consciously or unconsciously defined, must be applied to limit its membership. When two people marry there is potential conflict between them in their loyalties to their respective families of origin. As we have seen, the conflict seems to be resolved or regulated by acknowledgement of the precedence of the claim of the wife's mother and therefore of the *special unity between grandmother, daughter, and daughter's child*. The family system of care is largely built round these three. One thing reinforcing its unity and the general predominance of women in affairs of kinship is the fact that men generally die before their wives, particularly now that so few women die in childbirth.

There are certain consequences. Since there is a close bond between grandmother, daughter, and grandchild there is also an implicit, if not explicit, rule of *reserve between parent and child-in-law*, which sometimes takes the form of avoidance. This reserve is found especially in the relationship between mother and daughter-in-law, though it enters into most relationships between parents and children-in-law and, indeed, between affinal relatives of other kinds. The fact that hostility is more often expressed between mother and son-in-law is partly the consequence of men tending to join their wives' family groups. Proximity makes contact, and hence friction, almost inevitable. They usually see more of their wives' brothers and sisters than their own. But man and wife can still practise a measure of avoidance, by maintaining separate associations with blood relatives. Wife's mother, wife, and wife's child meet in the day when the men are at work. The husband visits his parents by himself.

The maintenance of these separate associations helps to produce *segregation between man and wife in their financial, domestic, and family roles*. When a family system of care is organized by female relatives living near one another there is less need for a man to play a part. And because they have separate occupations and their own loyalties outside marriage, their relationship is more contractual. They are more likely to be interrupted in their moments alone together and less likely to accompany each other on evenings out.

Support from Outside

The extended family is buttressed by being in touch with other similar groups which lend it strength and cohesion. Each individual and each family is at the centre of a complex network of relationships. Through a sister a person knows the sister's family, through the mother, the mother's sisters and their children. A few 'connecting' relatives make acquaintance with scores of relatives easy. Individuals usually know something about fifty relatives, sometimes hundreds. Once, when the matter was pursued at length, 260 relatives were traced, covering six generations. A great-grandmother of eighty said proudly, 'My grandfather's mother owned a rag shop in Hoxton, on the bridge there.' A man claimed French ancestry dating back to 1646. However, these examples were rare: few people claimed knowledge of relatives further removed than their grandparents or great-grandparents, and sometimes not even as far away as that. Generally speaking, more relatives were traced on the mother's than on the father's side. Nearly always a wife knew more about both sets of relatives than did her husband. One man confessed, 'I don't know much about my relatives, to tell you the truth'; he was not unusual.

The same Christian names were often repeated through three, four, and five generations. The eldest son was usually called after the father and the eldest daughter after the mother. 'You used to cause jealousy, if you didn't name children after the grandparents and aunts and uncles.' Many people still felt some identity with older relatives because they shared the same Christian name. One woman said this did not cause confusion. Relatives could talk about 'little Rose' and 'big Rose'. The custom of naming people after their ancestors has lost much of its force in recent years.

Even distant relationships produced strong feelings of obligation. People said, 'We've always been brought up to be united. It's in the blood. We've always stuck together.' They mentioned distant cousins, never seen before, who suddenly appeared on their doorsteps. This happened frequently during the war, when servicemen from the Commonwealth were stationed in Britain. Always they were welcomed and given a meal, and a bed for the night if they wanted it. The occasion, sometimes never repeated, was remembered with a clarity and a warmth rarely equalled in memories of meetings with non-related people.

As people got older they usually lost touch with collateral relatives, especially cousins. The young children of two sisters meeting at the grandmother's house may see a great deal of each other but when they grow up and the grandmother dies, and afterwards their own two mothers, they meet less and less frequently. In general old people in Bethnal Green possessed knowledge of most of their first cousins, especially on the mother's side, but rarely did they see them, except by chance. What Mr Fairly had to say about cousins was typical.

'Of course I see them. I see them walking about in Bethnal Green. We often bump into one or the other of them. No, we don't visit one another, it's just if we happen to see one another in the street. Of course I treat them all better because I know this is my cousin. Only a fortnight ago when I was having a drink up the Bethnal Green Road I saw a fellow and he said to me, "It's years since I saw you. Your name Fairly? So's mine. Aren't you Henry Fairly's boy? I'm Alf's." Then we had a good drink and a chat. When I was younger I used to see more of my cousins. Yes, when my father and his brothers were alive. Me and my father used to go over there. Even now there's at least fourteen cousins living up the Bethnal Green Road.'

The discovery of a relative in need often made people uncomfortable and anxious to do something to help. Cousins or aged uncles and aunts who had no support from close relatives tended to be given support by distant ones. The familial principles of replacement or compensation, based on a deep-seated sense of obligation to kin, drew them together. A sixty-five-year-old woman, herself fifteen years a widow, continued to visit her husband's ninety-year old aunt, who was unmarried and lived alone in a neighbouring street. Twice a week she took a meal, fetched the shopping, and helped to clean the home. A married woman visited an unmarried first cousin once removed 'to give her company' two or three afternoons a week, although she had a full programme of family activities. This meant there were exceptions to the general rule that first or second cousins and other distant relatives rarely met in old age. It also meant many people placed confidence in relatives they seldom met. They mentioned cousins or nephews or widowed sisters-in-law whom they had known intimately at some stage in their lives or who were the children or wives of near relatives they had loved. Perhaps they had stayed in their homes during the war when they were evacuated, or they had worked, or spent holidays together. For many reasons these were people to fall back upon in time of trouble, a comforting line of reserves. Knowledge of this support system of relatives gave people a sense of security. They were not anonymous; they were known and could, if necessary, realize a claim on someone outside the extended family.

Ceremonial and Holidays

The kinship network was sustained in various ways, one of the most important being through ritual or ceremonial. There were engagement parties, weddings, golden weddings, churchings, christenings, birthdays, and funerals at which varying numbers of relatives gathered. Weddings involved careful preparations and provided something to talk about for long afterwards. Sometimes a hundred but more commonly between twenty and fifty relatives attended. Old people often played a part, sometimes a major one. A woman of seventy remarked in April that she had been to five weddings already that year. Another in her mid sixties said, 'I think they have a lot of big weddings these days. My son had a big wedding and we had to have two sittings. I didn't get back here till five the next morning. I was coming back down this street singing at the top of my voice "I can't find my way home".' The ceremony renewed bonds between distant kin and symbolized the start of a relationship between the husband's and the wife's family which formerly did not exist. It sometimes allowed the primacy of the bride's mother's claim on the newly-married couple to be acknowledged publicly. It also served as an outlet for hostility between one group and another within the kinship network, which helped to preserve and express the solidarity of each.

One woman's daughter said:

'There were eighty at my wedding, nearly all relatives. All the husband's and wife's families, aunts, and cousins too. We had the reception here. The place was crowded out. We took all the furniture out Saturday night and it went on till the early hours of the next morning. We didn't have a honeymoon because we'd had our holidays before. When you have a wedding in your own home, there's more clinging together. In these halls, and I've been to lots of them, the wife's family and the husband's family get together at either end of the hall. They just stand and look at one another. My husband's mother was a bit off-hand with Mum, but that's all. When you're in your own home, you kind of muck in more.'

Funerals were also elaborate affairs, but usually limited to smaller numbers. Children under ten were rarely allowed to take part. Old people approved strongly of the ceremony and liked to think that when their turn came they would be accorded the same respect. It gave them comfort to think their departure from life would be recognized in this way and not passed over as something uneventful. Often there were between ten and twenty-five 'followers', and other relatives went to the 'grounds'. The various features of the ritual demanded by custom, such as wearing of black, the drawn curtains, the black-coated men with top-hats walking before the hearse when it first leaves the precincts of the home, the expensive wreaths covering the coffin, the gleaming Rolls-Royces, the gravestone, the service, the tea following the return from the funeral, even the weeping of the widow or widower, publicly symbolized the bereavement of the individual and the family and expressed its unity. Proper respect was paid to a departed member of the family; the bonds between the remaining members were renewed or were adjusted, sometimes through quarrels, to new family patterns; and the extended family closed its ranks.

> Mrs Thackeray had been to a number of funerals in recent years. 'My husband was the youngest of sixteen, we were always going to funerals. We got to know Manor Park so well that we got browned off. One year we went to about four or five of them. That's the only time we saw some relatives. My husband's sister-in-law said to me at one of them "Isn't it terrible we have to meet on these times?" Well, it wasn't our fault we didn't meet at other times. You have your own families to attend to. It isn't as if they asked you over. Her and me nearly had a bit of a bundle over that. What a cheek, coming saying things like that.'

Quarrels sometimes broke out over the inheritance of money and possessions. A few people mentioned sums of £100, £150, or £400 they had been left by uncles or aunts or parents. More often possessions other than money were involved. 'There's generally a shareout,' said one woman. 'When my Mum and Dad died I had the wringer. Someone else had the figures with shades. Someone else had the armchairs.' The possessions were not divided like this between the children when one was unmarried. The unmarried one had everything. 'My single sister had all my mother's things.'

Many family parties were arranged for engagements, birthdays, christenings, and so on. One grandmother said, 'I made room for fifteen [including a first cousin once removed] when my granddaughter got engaged last week.' Others told of their own birthdays.

> Mrs Renfrew, a widow of seventy-six who lived alone, spoke of her birthday a fortnight earlier. 'I've never had such a birthday. I didn't know about it rather [beforehand]. My eldest son took a place in

Brest Street. They got the room done up and then we all went along. All the family. There were more than thirty of us. We had a nice tea and a lovely cake and a good booze-up at night time. We made our own amusement. And I sung like blazes. My eldest son arranged it all and the wives helped. Some of us were under the table, I can tell you, at the end.'

On birthdays most people received cards, sometimes just a few but occasionally as many as fifty, nearly all from relatives. The exchange of cards was greater at Christmas. People said they were 'never forgotten' and, except for those with few relatives, they had at least twenty cards. At one interview carried out just before Christmas a total of over sixty cards was counted. This festival was one to which people looked forward for months and put money aside each week. On Christmas Eve it was common to receive visits from more distant relatives and on Christmas Day and Boxing Day to have dinner and tea in a family gathering usually numbering from six to fifteen, but sometimes as many as twenty or thirty, and people spoke of 'eating in relays'. The following extract from a tape-recording with a woman in her early sixties provides a rather extreme example:

Q: You mentioned to me before, something that interested me about Christmas. You said you always used to gather together.

A: Every year, I think it's about forty years.

Q: At your mother-in-law's? How many used to be there?

A: Well, it started with about twelve of us and ended up with fifty of us.

Q: Well, how did you ever get in?

A: We didn't get in, we had to squeeze in.

Q: Was it for Christmas dinner, or just in the evening, or what do you mean when you gathered there?

A: Well, we always went Christmas tea-time. We used to have our Boxing Day dinner round there and tea, and we used to come home Boxing night. We always stayed round there, always. Then Boxing afternoon we'd play cards, you know, like that, but we've always been round there.

Q: But who managed it all? Did your mother-in-law cook?

A: Yes, she done the dinner with a couple of the girls. You see our children was little then. Well, the little ones didn't used to count much. When they're grown up they take more room. Well, there's eleven children and eleven husbands and their children. Well, now there's the children grown up, the children's married and got their children. Well, that makes the family bigger still.

Gatherings of a large number of relatives were not confined to special occasions only. References were made to other meetings of kin involving a larger circle than those relatives who were in daily contact. Family teas were sometimes held on Saturday or Sunday afternoons, and these sometimes turned into evening sing-songs or parties. One woman said some twenty to thirty relatives met every week-end in a pub. She spoke of the previous Saturday. 'There was a big table of men and a big table of women. Our husbands buy our beer and all the men treat one another. One has a call and then another has a call. They all have a jaw, you know. The women all sit round.' Another said, 'Only last month fifteen of us got together when my niece came over from Southend. By the time we sat down to tea together I suppose with all the children there must have been twenty-four of us. Sometimes on a Saturday we're sitting here and someone comes and I start getting tea and before I know where I am the place is crowded out.' Of course, infirm old people tended to play less part in such family activities, but even a few of these mentioned a striking number of family gatherings in the home.

> Mrs Cheevers was an infirm married woman in her early seventies. 'At Christmas, that's when they all come round. That's the time when the family really gathers together. That's the time the family meets.' She celebrated her golden wedding three weeks previously. 'The children clubbed together for a tea-party for us. You can see all the cards up there now. I still have them up. My husband says I ought to take them down but I like them there. [There were over twenty cards, many with gilt ribbon and padded red hearts, strung on a piece of string in one corner of the room.] There were twenty-four of us here [children, in-laws, grandchildren, nephews, and nieces] and Albert played the piano. It was a good party. They used to gather here Saturday evenings and they still do sometimes.'

Holidays were sometimes spent at the homes of distant relatives, or mention was made of a large group going on holiday to a seaside resort together. A few told of a week or fortnight spent in a holiday camp with eight or ten, or even fifteen, relatives. One woman said her family had a bungalow 'hut' outside London where they spent week-ends. 'There's usually seven or eight of us there. I sleep in the single bed with my grandson. He says, "Nan, mind you don't kick." My daughter and her husband must come where Nan goes. . . . The holiday I like best is Easter. It's what I call a sacred holiday and we usually spend it at the hut.' A few people said they went regularly in family groups to the Kent hopfields for a month.

In these different ways – to sum up – the individual and the extended family maintained links with scores of people. Many were the children or husbands of siblings and of parents' siblings. Through common or 'connecting' near-relatives people were brought into touch with other individuals and other families. Often they were invited to the same family gatherings and so could renew a relationship. Through ritual and through help in time of trouble group solidarity could be sustained. To feel an obligation to a sister was, at one remove, to feel an obligation to the sister's child. The network of kinship and the support system of reciprocal obligations spread outwards. Within the network the extended family was, to the individual, the most important group. As members of this family most old people in Bethnal Green found security, occupation, and interest day by day.

CHAPTER 10

Family and Community

AFTER so much discussion of family life one troubling question is inevitably raised. Has the importance of the family to old people in Bethnal Green been exaggerated? How important were people and activities outside? This chapter attempts to put the previous data, at least to some extent, into perspective. It considers some of the relationships between family and community, and shows how many people had contact with neighbours and friends and went to churches, clubs, and cinemas.

Associations with neighbours and friends proved difficult to explore. In the first place relatives often lived next door or in the same street and care had to be taken not to confuse them with non-relatives. At one interview a woman appeared to spend most of her day with her next-door neighbour and only by chance at the end did it turn out that the neighbour was in fact a sister-in-law. In the same way people sometimes talked about 'friends' who were later found to be relatives. These were usually cousins or in-laws of the same generation. A more awkward problem was the different meanings given to the terms 'neighbour' and 'friend'. Often a neighbour with whom there was a close relationship was no longer thought to be a neighbour but a friend. Thus a question about neighbours was interpreted by many people to apply only to those non-relatives living around them who were not friends. This partly explained some puzzling experiences in the early interviews, when people at first said, in complete honesty and good faith, they had nothing to do with their neighbours but later, in discussion, revealed they had a fairly close association with one or two of them. Apart from the ambiguity of the terms 'neighbour' and 'friend' other difficulties arose because people expressed as social norms general views about others living around them which differed widely from their actual behaviour.

Ideally, it would have been desirable to ask questions about each of the neighbours in turn, using the term 'neighbour' as little as possible. This was not practicable in an inquiry directed chiefly towards gaining knowledge of family life. Instead, a number of questions were designed to find whether each old person had regular contact with a neighbour or friend. Operationally, 'neighbour' was defined as an unrelated person living in the same street or block, and 'friend' as an unrelated person not living in the same street or block, with whom there was customary or pre-arranged contact at least once a month on average.

Altogether sixty-six per cent of the old people had regular contact with unrelated persons (compared with ninety-seven per cent with relatives). They visited, or were visited by, at least one neighbour or friend (or met a friend outside) once a month or more on average. Few people, however, had regular contacts as much as once or twice a week with more than one or two persons unrelated to them, whereas most saw several relatives every day or nearly every day. Unless this is remembered the general comparison between relatives and non-relatives will be misleading.

Restraint with Neighbours

About their neighbours old people were usually emphatic. 'We very seldom see anything of them. We keep ourselves to ourselves.' 'I talk to the neighbours but we don't go into each other's places.' 'We keep ourselves quiet. They want to know too much of your business.' 'We just say good morning on the stairs but we don't *see* them.' 'I never go in to see them and they don't come in here. My mother was like that and I suppose I'm the same. I never do such a thing. Mind you, they're friendly neighbours and I chat with them out in the street.' 'So we are now,' said one man, waving his hand towards his wife and married daughters, 'that's how we keep.' People made plain that their loyalties were to their families first.

They also made plain the characteristics of the good neighbour. He, or rather she, was someone who did not expect to spend time in your home or pry into your life, who exchanged a civil word in the street or over the back-yard fence, who did not make a great deal of noise, who could supply a drop of vinegar or a pinch of salt if you ran short, and who fetched your relatives or the doctor in emergencies. The good neighbour's role was that of an *intermediary*, in the direct as well as indirect sense. In illness the neighbour might be asked to pass a message to relatives or to the doctor. If you lived alone you could tap on the wall, or the neighbour came in if she saw your bottle of milk still on the doorstep at midday. Sometimes she was asked to give a message to a caller – an insurance or rent collector or a coalman. But she also provided street-corner news or gossip about the neighbourhood, about other families, and about the community. She was the go-between, passing news from one family to another, one household to another. Her role was a communicative but not an intimate one.

Mr Hinch, a widower, said his wife used to give unwanted food and other things to a woman next door. In return the neighbour had offered to help Mr Hinch whenever she could. I asked whether she was a good friend. He said, 'No, she's not a friend. That suggests intimacy. There's no association. What she is is what my daughter calls a good neighbour.'

A married daughter living in the same house as her mother, Mrs Talcott, confirmed what had been said about neighbours, 'We both pass the time of day, that's all. They'd help if we were in any trouble. When I was away with John in hospital the woman's husband next door popped in to mend the pipes [which had burst after a cold spell]. And if either of us run out of anything we pop in to one another. But we don't like people coming in. We never have.'

A wife was expected by her husband to give nearly all her attentions to home and family. Both men and women often referred to this. He looked indulgently on her gossiping but did not like her being in the homes of others.

Mr Witham asserted, 'It's just good afternoon, good night. We don't associate. We don't stand and have gossiping.' And his wife added, 'My husband's never found anyone in my home for fifty-five years I've been married. There's no running into one another's houses.'

Mrs Reason said, 'We keep ourselves to ourselves. They generally catch me at the door. When the weather's warmer. They don't like coming in when they know he's here [her husband]. We stand and have a little jaw.'

Nearly two-thirds of the old people claimed they did not go regularly into the home of a neighbour and a neighbour did not visit them. Such marked reserve was, perhaps, largely a means of preserving marital and family relationships but also a means of avoiding personal antagonisms. Loyalties between neighbours are not so deep as family loyalties. After a change of circumstance or a minor quarrel a former bond may prove to be an embarrassment or a handicap in continuing to live in enforced proximity. Relationships between neighbours are therefore more likely to be ephemeral or impermanent and cannot be relied on so surely. Women who had no husbands more often sought the company of neighbours. Fewer men than women had contact with neighbours and fewer married women than widows and spinsters.

Although fewer men than women had contact with neighbours more met friends. Generally they met outside the home. Women, and especially widows and spinsters, again did most visiting in the home. Men often met a friend at a pub, in a park, or at a football match. Friends who were visited in their homes were usually people who had been known at work or even in childhood. 'To tell you the truth I've known her all my life. Her aunt lived next to my mother and her nieces minded my children.' 'I go to see Mrs Cork every week. I met her when I was at school.' 'She used to live in the street where I lived.' 'My husband got to know him through fire-watching in the war and we've been friends ever since. We go to one another's homes sometimes. We usually meet on Saturday nights.'

Sometimes man and wife had formed a friendship with another couple and went out together or visited each other's homes. More often the wife was absorbed with her home and family and her husband was, as one woman put it, 'a lone wolf'. He went to a pub by himself, or met some of his friends in the park. 'My husband likes to have a drink and see a friend. He'd chat and make friends with anybody, but I'm not like that – only perhaps with one or two of the old neighbours.' The wife was more cautious about friendships. 'I've never had a woman friend. We've always been our own family. We're never going visiting people's houses. Well, it's only natural. When a man comes home he wouldn't like another woman in the house, would he?'

Church- and Chapelgoing

Some made friends through the church. Three-quarters gave their religion as Church of England. The remainder were mostly Roman Catholics, Methodists, or Jews, or had no religion. Only twenty-seven, or thirteen per cent, said they went to church as much as once a month. Most of these were people belonging to religions other than the Church of England. Widows without children and spinsters were the most frequent attenders. Few men, and few married women, went to church or chapel. It seemed that to some women (but not to men) churchgoing was a consolation for a solitary life.

> Mrs Fisk was a widow who had no children. She lived on her own. She was a Methodist and occasionally went to chapel. 'I go when I've got time. It saves being on my own.'

> Miss Curry was a Catholic and went to Mass frequently in the week. 'I go on outings. I perhaps go with the children to a couple of tea parties and theatres.' She explained that she was strongly attached to the Church. 'I'm what they call a Virgin of the Church. I have to do whatever they want. People come to me and I tell them where the Father is.'

Thus a number of people without children made friends through their religion. But most people rarely, if ever, went to church. They often expressed guilt at not going. When asked whether they went to church they often said, 'We've got to tell the truth. We don't.' 'We don't go but you can be just as good as those that do.' 'No, but it's the way you live that matters.' 'We're not church-goers but we're not heathens. If people were only to take a little of their Christianity to heart instead of thinking only about going to church the world would be a better place.' For many the church was a place to be visited only for weddings, churchings, or funerals, though they were often anxious to record that 'We went to Sunday school when we were small. My mother always made us do that.'

Men sometimes regarded the Church with suspicion or hostility. 'You don't see the Vicar these days. You only see him coming along the road with his wife after an evening out.' 'The Church is lazy. I blame the clergy of today for fewer people going to them. Them churches are for rejoicing, not for the poker-faced clergy what's around nowadays.' 'I don't believe in it. I think it's a matter of trade. Religion's only trade for archbishops and deacons.'

Clubs

Other people made friends through clubs. Altogether in the borough there were, in 1955, just under 8,000 people of pensionable age. Of these about 860, or eleven per cent, were members of the nine old people's clubs under the general control of the Bethnal Green Old People's Welfare Committee. Of the sample interviewed twenty-five, or twelve per cent, were members of these clubs. The clubs played a considerable role in the lives of this minority, with meetings at least once a week, annual outings, and dinners, and some took the chance of staying at a holiday centre outside London. Proportionately more women than men belonged to these clubs. Over half the members were widows. Wives sometimes belonged to them but, when they did, rarely their husbands also.

Those who were not members fell into three groups. First were those unable to attend because they were at work, or because they were infirm or had infirm relatives to look after. They numbered fifty-three, or thirty per cent of non-members. Second were those who, though they expressed interest, had not yet bothered to join. They numbered sixteen, or nine per cent. Third were those not interested in belonging. They did not take kindly to such associations or felt they were too absorbed with their families. Perhaps the clubs reminded them too forcefully of their age. People mixed only with those of their own generation and not, as in their families, with those of all ages. They numbered 109, or sixty-one per cent of non-members. One woman said, 'I don't want to join an old people's club. I've never been to anything like that – no mothers' meetings or anything. A lot of old hypocrites go along to those places to get what they can.' And a man said, 'There's something about it I don't like. Only ten bob the whole trip, dinner and all. I don't like the idea I'm getting something for nothing. You get pushed on a bus at such and such time. You get pushed into dinner and tea. It's like a Sunday-school outing. I like to know, if I *want* to go to Brighton, it's *my* day out. I'm free and I've got my money in my pocket and I can do what I like.'

In addition to the people who attended old people's clubs once or twice a week there were a further twenty-four, or twelve per cent of the sample, who attended other clubs or societies of various kinds, sometimes infrequently. These ranged from the British Legion, Working Man's Club, and L.C.C. Evening Institutes to church and chapel socials of various kinds. Altogether fewer than one in four of the sample attended clubs and socials. Some men, about one in

four, attended sports matches fairly often on a Saturday or Sunday.
A few people went to a local variety theatre or to theatres in central
London but films provided the most common afternoon or evening
entertainment. Even so, only forty-five per cent of the old people
said they went to the cinema as much as once a month. A small
minority said they had never seen a film or had not seen one since,
for example, a silent Lillian Gish film in 1922.

Community as Family

This account gives some idea of the extent of people's interests and
relationships (except those connected with paid employment) outside the family. Yet the facts are hard to assess. The importance of
neighbours and friends to old people is not just a matter of
establishing how many they meet regularly in their homes or
outside. Neither is the importance of clubs or the church solely a
matter of finding how many people attend for how long. In the
last chapter distant relatives were likened to a 'support' system
which could be called on in emergencies. Some such support and
security, although less easy to define, is provided by the existence
of casual acquaintances in the neighbourhood and of people who
were friends once, if not now. To people in Bethnal Green the
neighbours were there, they were heard and they were seen. Their
activities, demeanour, and dress were scrutinized and discussed in
the privacy of the home although most contacts with them were
fleeting. They rarely entered the home, even at such times as
Christmas. Yet these were people who recognized you and bade
you a cheery 'good morning' and whose lives were vaguely bound
up with yours because they shared the same scene, the same kind of
houses, the same political representatives, and the same shortages.
They formed part of the familiar environment which was, at one
remove, 'home'.

Out of this seemed to grow a strong sense of community which
personalized 'Bethnal Green' and 'East End'. One woman said, 'I
like Bethnal Green people. They say they're rough but they've a
kind nature to help. I always have had help from the neighbours. I
want to stop here in Bethnal Green and die. My roots are here. I
want to be carried out of here.' A man said, 'There's no place on
earth like the East End. There isn't that feeling anywhere else.' A
number of things conditioned such attachments, which were very

common. Both men and women had lived at their present addresses, on average, for twenty-four years. Some had moved within the previous few years, but usually from one home to another in the same district. No fewer than fifty-four per cent had been born in the borough and a further twenty-four per cent in adjoining boroughs. Many talked of going to school, to work, and bringing up their children, all in the surrounding few streets. They talked of parents and grandparents who had lived there. Through the localized network of relatives they had developed some knowledge of a large number of people. A mother's neighbour was, in a sense, your neighbour. A brother's friend in the market was your friend. The brother of your sister's husband knew all about housing applications or how to repair a radio or where to get anything from an egg-whisk to a secondhand gas stove.

Solidarity with relatives, neighbours, and friends was strongest in some of the oldest streets, despite the marked restraint that was still said to characterize relations between neighbours. People then talked, though very generally, of the community as a family. One woman said of life in a street which had been destroyed in the war. 'We was all one family. I think they are like that in these little turnings.' In such streets, where most people had known each other for many years, the strongest sanctions were imposed on individuals to conform with established practices. One person's son described how neighbours respected each other's family loyalties and how one man had been ostracized because he had neglected his wife and children. He went on, 'If an old person had children living round about and they didn't go and visit her, that would be the talk of the neighbourhood.' Continuity of residence within a local network of workplaces, shops, markets, and clubs and particularly a network of kinship had produced in old people a strong identification with the local community. Their social activities expressed their attachments not only to family but also to community, as the following illustration suggests.

An Old People's Outing

About 400 old people from Bethnal Green went in eleven coaches to Brighton for a day. The day was grey and cold. Everyone appeared to be early. One woman of seventy-five had been ill the day before and had passed a sleepless night. This did not prevent her coming on the outing. En route the coaches hummed with talk, large and small. At Brighton the 400 made their way, in slow-moving groups, to the end of the central pier, where they were to have lunch in one of the large, showy pavilions. Bystanders were told, 'We're from good old Bethnal Green.' There was much teasing and flirting, mutual sympathizing over infirmity and health and the inadequacy of pensions, and proud stories were told about children.

'You thought I was going to run after you, didn't you?'

'You don't want to put your very best things on when you go lark-ing about in Brighton. I've got my old whistle and flute [suit].'

'I told 'em my daughter doesn't keep me. I go halves, I told 'em, halves with the rent and the coal and everything. . . . It's terrible, isn't it, the cost of food? All your money has to go on the table, doesn't it?'

'Aren't you staying with your wife?' – 'She can keep herself com-pany.'

'If *I* was eighty *I'd* find it hard climbing about, poor soul.'

'If we hadn't a smile for one another we wouldn't be much good.'

'Such nice company. That's what matters, doesn't it, when you can come out like this with good company. We're all one happy family.'

The men, many of them in white silk scarves and caps, mostly gathered together in groups away from the women, partly, perhaps, because they seemed to be outnumbered. One had a box camera and was trying to take good photographs. During the midday meal only the nearest score of people or so could hear the speeches and the great majority continued eating or talking in complete innocence of the words of welcome. After the meal a long queue formed outside a sweet-shop and great quantities of rock were bought for grandchildren, grandnieces and nephews. The afternoon was free and the old people seemed to do much the same as any other group of people let loose in a seaside resort, except that they did it a good deal more slowly. They tried the promenade railway, the slot machines in the amusement arcades, the shelters and deckchairs along the front, the souvenirs, the ice-cream, and the postcards depicting little red-nosed men with droop-ing moustaches and fat women with large buttocks. People accompanied and talked to each other because they were sisters or cousins, or neighbours or children's neighbours or friends from schooldays.

A dozen of the women joined arms in one of the arcades and danced riotously up and down to the tune of 'Oh, Susanna, don't you cry for me, for I come from Alabama with a banjo on my knee'. At the centre of one of the larger groups was a white-haired, thin woman carrying a paper umbrella and wearing one bright red and one bright blue stocking, a multicoloured dress under her coat, and a Robin Hood cap. A final hour or two was spent on the pier during which vast quantities of fish and chips were consumed in the pavilion. On the way home the eleven coaches stopped at a wayside pub. Some bought flowers for their daughters from a man outside and many thronged the bar. Several of the women danced to an accordion, one of them capering about with a large ostrich feather trembling from her head and deliberately raising the hem of her skirt to reveal a pair of long, white frilly bloomers stitched with blue ribbon. In general the women seemed to have far more bounce and energy than the men. Throughout the journey the coaches bulged with a roar of Victorian and Edwardian music-hall songs. The words voiced the preoccupations and interests of working-class families. Most people seemed to know by heart scores of these songs. There were snatches of, 'We all came in the world with nothing and we can't take nothing out', 'You can get a sweet-heart any day but not another mother', 'When Grannie left him the old armchair', 'Mother I love you. You've worked for me and now I must work for you.' During one song a woman leaned across and said, 'I remember my mother singing that to my brothers.' It was, 'If there ain't no work about, what's the use of rowing.'

Consequence of Age

Despite their identification with, and attachment to, the local community old people nevertheless depended most on their families for their day-to-day interests. Such occasions as an outing to the seaside were rare. There was not, comparatively speaking, a lot of contact with non-relatives. The network of kinship provided an introduction to a large circle of associates but allowed few close friends. It demanded the prior loyalties of its members and was, to a large extent, a self-contained social unit. All the evidence about neighbours, friends, church-going, hobbies, entertainment, and club activities pointed to this. Indeed, in old age the family, compared with relationships outside the family, became more important, not less.

There were two chief reasons for this. One was retirement and the related fall in income; the other was growing infirmity. No longer was there work and the companionship of work; no longer was there enough money to entertain and treat friends and no longer was it easy to get about. People found it hard to make new friendships to replace those they had lost. 'They've all withered away. I don't know where they are now. I used to have friends at work.' 'Nothing is ever like it used to be. I used to be a member of the Free Church Sick Club. I used to like going up to see some of the old brothers. I had a letter the other day saying they'd like me to go . . . but I can't do it any more.' Money was short and this made it harder to reciprocate gestures of friendship. 'There's no such things as friends now,' said one man, 'no money no friends.' Neighbours moved away or died and newcomers 'don't want to have anything to do with old people. They talk to you in the street but they shun you. You can notice it. People just don't seem to be so friendly. These youngsters have got no time for old people.' People bemoaned the loss of familiar faces.

Mr Mayne said at one time he was known throughout the area. 'All the people round about here had a cheery word for me. Jack, the dustman, they all knew me. But they've grown out of knowledge now. When they see you're an old age pensioner they think you want something off them. I don't see much of them now.' He had one old friend aged eighty, whom he occasionally met at the top of the street. 'We have one brown ale each. That's all we can afford. I see him about twice a week.'

Mr Bowness said, 'In my younger days, your neighbour would see you were down and they'd do what they could to help you. But they don't do that now. . . . They can't agree, that's what it is. You're situated better than me – I'm not going in there. Too fussy. But in my younger days we were all on the level, you see. You were like me, I was like you. You were poor, I was poor.'

Experience seemed to have taught most people that friends and neighbours drift away, that things possessed in common at school, at work, and at the football ground do not last throughout life.

They had come to recognize this, with acquiescence and sometimes bitterness. To some extent their remarks may have represented social change rather than change with age. Whatever the reason, most insisted they had experienced a falling-off in the number and quality of their friendships and non-family activities. This was confirmed in tests of information they supplied. Fewer people in their seventies and eighties than in their sixties were able to leave the house or the immediate locality unaided. Fewer met friends or visited neighbours as much as once a month (sixty-two per cent compared with seventy per cent). Fewer went to the cinema (thirty-nine per cent compared with fifty-one per cent).

Substitutes for Relatives

The fact that most old people had many associates but few, if any, close friends has been stressed. Yet some were on intimate or fairly intimate terms with non-relatives and depended on them for help. Was this because they had no available relatives?

It is hard to devise a satisfactory test of the extent to which neighbours and friends substituted for relatives, because of the great variety in the number and kind of available relatives, in personal circumstances, and in people's associations with non-relatives. One crude test is to see how far the presence of a daughter at home or nearby affected visits and the exchange of services between non-relatives. It was found that fewer old people exchanged visits with neighbours and friends when a daughter lived at home or nearby than when no daughter lived in the immediate vicinity. Fewer, too, had any kind of help from non-relatives. Only twenty-four per cent with daughters at hand mentioned even one minor service often performed by a non-relative (such as passing on messages or fetching a paper), whereas some service was mentioned by forty-one per cent of those with a daughter living elsewhere and fifty-one per cent of those with no daughter. A few of these people received major help, such as the greater part of their shopping, washing, and cleaning or care during illness. They formed about five per cent of the whole sample.[1] Only one person among them had a daughter in the vicinity.

Detailed study of individual circumstances provided some con-

1. Excluding the small proportion assisted by the Home Help or District Nursing Services.

firmation of the suggestion that, when members of old people's families are not available, neighbours and friends partly take their place.

Mr and Mrs Harold were in their mid sixties and had no children. Mrs Harold had never had any brothers or sisters and though her husband had several, none of these lived in the locality. The most striking feature of their life was their close relationship with a Jewish woman and her family who used to live in a flat above. This woman sought their help in bringing up her five children when her mother died. The children, now grown up, still called Mrs Harold 'Nanny' or 'Aunt Elsie'. 'They were more often here than upstairs.' One lived nearby, virtually with them. The rest of this family was scattered in East London but continued to exchange visits regularly. One was seen two or three times a week and at least seven or eight others from once a week to once a fortnight. They seemed to look on each other as part of one family.

Mrs Singer was a deaf widow of nearly eighty, with no children. A married sister did her shopping, and called morning and evening to keep her company. A widower living on the next floor of the house looked on her rather as an aunt or grandmother. He said, 'I've been seventeen years here and my wife used to come and look after her, and this lady in here too [he pointed at a woman living next door who called for a few minutes]. If it wasn't for people like that, Mrs Singer wouldn't be able to carry on. I've seen them bring salt beef for her. It's not enough for their family but it makes Mrs Singer a meal. And we all buy her things. Her sister bought her a skirt at Christmas and I gave her something. I always give her a bit of money on her birthdays and at Christmas. And she shows you what your money's bought. She went out and she showed me what she'd got. Knickers and two vests. Georgina, that's the woman living the other side, she comes in of a night time to give her a cup of tea and if she sees that the place is a bit smudge she does it. She misses these things if you don't do them. If I don't bring her down a cup of tea first thing in the morning, I'm for it, I can tell you.' Asked who would help her when she was ill, Mrs Singer said, 'My sister and all these', waving at her two neighbours and indicating the houses to left and right. The widower living upstairs said, 'She's not really been in bed for about three or four months, and then for a fortnight. Her sister came round twice a day and the lady next door was in and out. And last thing at night when I came in I'd get her a cup of tea. When she's queer, you know what old people are like. She's a bloody old nuisance [he said this almost in terms of endearment]. I know she's a nuisance and we all do, but then that's what we all get like when we're old. Georgina still wouldn't leave her. She's just a working woman but she's an angel to her. She never fails to come in. And if the place needs a bit of doing up she doesn't say a word but gets down to it. I suppose it's just good nature, because she can't get anything out of it, can she?' This woman had no mother.

People without relatives intensified other associations. They exchanged visits more often with neighbours and friends and, partly through mutual services, found a means of satisfying personal or social needs. A few widowers had found widows living in the same street to take on some of the functions of their wives by providing meals and cleaning for them. Some widows sought the company of others of the same age. A few women without daughters had made friends with young women nearby, behaving, in some respects, like mother and daughter. A person without children or grandchildren tended to attach himself not only, as we have seen, to a sibling's family but also, if he had no available siblings, to a neighbour's or friend's family. These substitute relationships provided company and help even if they could not wholly replace family relationships.

The evidence was not decisive, however. There were some people with a rich family life who also met friends or visited neighbours. And there were a few with no relatives or little contact with them who nevertheless had little contact with non-relatives. These few, as we shall see in Chapter 14, were isolated and yet fairly contented people who had not experienced much change in their social relationships in later life. What friendships there are in old age appear to be sought more from loneliness than from social isolation. Perhaps this is why so many widows, and so few spinsters, for example, joined old people's clubs.

So far as it goes, then, this analysis of information about neighbours, friends, membership of clubs, and so on suggests that the importance to people in Bethnal Green of the family has not been over-weighted. Most people were very restrained in their relationships with neighbours; not many had even one close friend outside the family; and the minority affected by church and club activities was small. The network of kinship provided many links with the community and many associates, but allowed few close friends.

Moreover, in old age family life became more important, not less. Non-family activities diminished. Friends and neighbours died or passed out of knowledge, money was shorter, and it became more difficult to get about. Yet some people without relatives at hand, particularly widows, seemed to find part-substitutes in non-relatives. Those without a family sought one.

PART TWO

*The Family and the Social Problems of
Old Age*

CHAPTER 11

Retirement

THE first part of this book gave the main facts about the family and social life of the old people interviewed in Bethnal Green. This part discusses some of the social problems of old age against this background. One of these social problems is retirement from work, which is considered in this chapter. The chief theme is that retirement is a tragic event for many men, which has great repercussions on most aspects of their lives, not least their individual happiness and their security in home and family.

Men interviewed fell into two rough categories: those who were still in part- or full-time employment and those who had retired from all work. The numbers were not large, being twenty-five and thirty-nine respectively. The information was supplemented at many points, however, from that concerning the fifty-seven husbands of the married women who were interviewed. First I shall discuss the circumstances of men remaining in full-time work. They had a wage of rather less than £7 a week on average,[1] of which just under £4 10s. was given to a wife for housekeeping, rent, food, insurances, and sundries. The husband was usually responsible for holidays and entertainment and for occasional expensive purchases, such as curtains or oil-cloth. The wife rarely had more than the vaguest idea what her husband earned and often he did not know what the grown-up children gave her. Each had little detailed knowledge of the other's expenditure. The belief ran deep that 'What he does with his money is his affair'; 'What she does with her money is her affair.' As we found in Chapter 6, man and wife carried on many activities not so much as joint members of the same social groups as individual members of separate social groups.

The man played a relatively small part in family affairs. His wife

1. Other personal income, such as disability pensions, retirement pensions of those over seventy but still working, wife's earnings, and so on, is not, of course, included.

saw a great deal of the children, grandchildren, and other relatives while he was at work, and in the evenings and at week-ends it was she who made most visits to members of the family. Sometimes even the visits of the married children to the home at the week-end were described by the man in such terms as, 'They come up every Saturday and Sunday to see their mother'; 'They come up here and Mum gives them all a talking to.' He often passed questions about kinship to his wife as the obvious authority on the subject. Sometimes he became impatient if a discussion about family life became protracted, even if his wife was still following it with zest.

Men talked at greater length and with more interest about their employment and sporting experiences. Many of their activities and interests, in contrast to those of their wives, were shared with workmates and acquaintances in the locality (though these sometimes included relatives). A joke could be shared over a glass of beer in a pub, friends could be treated, and the respective merits of workplaces, football teams, and political parties thrashed out among those who had much in common. The workplace, the trade union, the local pub, and the football ground were all, in a sense, home from home. A man took pride in his own strength, skill, and know-how as a member with a contribution to make.

These men, all in their late sixties or early seventies, viewed approaching retirement with uneasiness and ill-concealed fear. Most agreed with the sentiments of one man who said, 'I'll retire when someone pole-axes me.' Many said they would miss being at work and would have nothing to do. They felt work kept them in good health and enabled them to preserve a standard of living they would otherwise have to surrender. The emphasis was on occupation. One man said, 'Work fills a gap when you get older. There was a time when I was waiting for the time I could get away, but now I'm glad, because it fills a gap.'

Mr Selwyn was seventy-two and was worried about his job as a railway labourer. 'I'm only hanging on, just hanging on, like this bit of paper.' And he shook a flimsy bit of paper under my nose. 'I'd sooner be at work but if they retire me I suppose I will have to, then I will have to grin and bear it. I don't want to stand at the corner and watch the other people do it, but I suppose it will come to that.' He recollected with pride the remarks of a foreman who had complimented him on wielding a pick and shovel 'like a young man. He said to

me, "If we had some more like you we'd make the railroad go."'
He was keen to go on working as long as he could because there was
not much for him in life beyond it. 'My father wasn't lazy and I'm
not. I want to do a good day's work as long as I can. I want to go on.
I don't want to stand on a street corner. What would I do but that?
I'd be worse off in every way if I had to sit at home and look at the
old girl all day long. I'd have nothing to do and no money.'

The wife recognized the strength of the husband's desire to
remain at work and she supported him. She thought he was happier
at work and feared he would deteriorate quickly once he was not.
She also preferred to have the home to herself. One said, 'There's
nothing for them to do when they stop work in places like these. It's
not as if there's a garden. As soon as they're down they're gone. . . .
I don't want him here.'

Many men preferred to remain at work even though it was
arduous and they had experienced recent spells of disability or
sickness. A third of the men worked irregular hours, in the sense
they did shiftwork by night or day or worked by night. One man
of seventy had just been ill for twelve weeks and he had to have his
spine supported by a corset. He worked as a night guard. Another,
also of seventy, had been at home because of illness for six months
but returned to his work in a warehouse, where he lifted heavy
weights. A third, in his late sixties, had gone back to work loading
beer barrels after a severe operation. And a fourth, aged sixty-five,
left home at 6.45 in the morning to go to his work as a labourer at
Woolwich Arsenal, returning at 6.45 at night. Other men were
employed as wood-machinists, cement-bag fillers, and powder-
mixers in environments which aggravated bronchial and similar
complaints. One man who had to handle soda ash said he was
unable to use a hood with a visor while he worked because he
could not get his breath and instead sucked a match to prevent him
opening his mouth and to stop his lips from becoming too dry.

Men in their sixties had noticed a falling off in their physical
capacity and their speed of work. This could often be masked for a
long time by exerting what was known from long experience to be
the minimum effort required to perform certain tasks satisfactorily, and could be counteracted by reliability and regularity of
performance. Experience acquired over the years substituted,
although not indefinitely, for the loss of physical capacity.

Approaching retirement threatened many of the long-standing associations of their lives. It reminded them of their failing strength and skill and that their period of usefulness to others was coming to an end. Often a man preferred to step down into a job of inferior status rather than take the bigger step outside into retirement. Several of the men had full or part-time jobs as lavatory attendants, door-keepers, night-watchmen, or office messenger boys, which they had taken on in recent years. Both those who were at work and those who had retired were asked whether they had changed their job after the age of fifty-nine. The result was that forty-two per cent of those at work and thirty-six per cent of those who had retired had changed their occupation in their sixties or seventies. These facts are notable because most men had stayed in one occupation for most of their adult lives and they took great pride in saying they had worked for the same firm for thirty, forty, or fifty years. Such changes in later life implied how great were the problems of ill-health and retirement.

These changes were partly responsible for the fact that men of pensionable age had, on the whole, a lower social status than other adult men, as judged by their most recent occupation. Table 20 shows the difference in social class between men in the sample and all males over fifteen in Bethnal Green, as recorded by the Census of 1951. Half the old men were in social class V, compared with a quarter of men of all ages.

Accepting a lower-status job had two important consequences. First, the man's wage fell. It is impossible to say by how much with any precision because the figures obtained refer to different periods within a general era of inflation. Some men had only recently changed their jobs. Others, in their eighties, had done so fifteen or twenty years previously. Illustrations may give some idea of the fall. In 1954 one man in his mid sixties was forced to accept a job of inferior grade on the railway because of infirmity and his net earnings fell from £7 15s. to £6. Another man who had been earning between £6 and £7 as a railway porter took a job as a lavatory cleaner for £4 10s. A third man who had been a boiler-maker earning around £10 took a job as a messenger for £5 10s. These were changes of full-time job. Other men took on part-time jobs of lower status.

Second, the man's position in the home and family became less

secure. While the mother was continually renewing her bonds with
her children through seeing them frequently, advising and helping
in the rearing of their babies, and receiving, in her turn, help with
the household chores, for his position the father relied mainly on
his traditional authority in the home, derived largely from his role
as breadwinner, and from his experiences in his occupation and in

TABLE 20

SOCIAL CLASS OF OLD MEN COMPARED WITH ALL
ADULT MEN

Social class	Old men, present sample	Adult men, 1951 Census
	%	%
I Professional	0	1
II Intermediate	3	6
III Skilled	31	55
IV Partly skilled	14	13
V Unskilled	52	25
Total	100	100
Number	64	21,145

NOTE: The classification is that of the Registrar-General.

his outside sporting and social activities. This position was
weakened if he was forced to take a job with lower pay and status.
I remember in particular the laughter of a wife and her married
daughter when they said the husband had become a messenger boy
in his old age.

Even if he did not take a new job it was often apparent that his
authority and prestige had been weakened in other ways. The
father's role in the family had, over the years, been greatly affected
by the new educational opportunities, the raising of standards of
living, and the improvement in work techniques and organization.
Sometimes he felt humiliated at seeing his wife continue in employment outside the home. His sons were often in jobs of higher skill
and status. Even when the occupations had the same name the
methods and content of the work were often different. It was rare
to find any man conscious of handing on his job, like the coalman

who said, 'My father handed down this business to me and his father before that. I run it with my money and when I die my son Albert will have it, like his father and his grandfather and his great-grandfather.' Some sons, dockers, market porters, stall-holders, and cabinet-makers, had followed their fathers into similar jobs, but not many. This may be compared with Charles Booth's finding some sixty or seventy years ago in East London. 'As a rule the wives do not work, but the children all do: the boys commonly following the father (as is everywhere the case above the lowest classes), the girls taking to local trades, or going out to service.'[1] Where they did it was possible to observe the pleasure and security of the father in seeing his life continued by his son. But most fathers felt out of date, because their experiences were of no use to the sons, and not simply because they were old. Their advice was unheeded. 'But, Dad, things have changed since you were young.' They began to take refuge in spine-chilling accounts of the cruelty and harshness of the past and to talk like prophets of disaster to gain sympathy when they could no longer command respect. 'I remember,' said one man, 'when I was working for 23s. a week and bringing up a family. Not like these here fellows earning £15 a week nowadays twiddling a few nuts and bolts.'

After Retirement

Disability or sickness was a means of reconciling some men to retirement but the individual had to face up to a fundamental change in the pattern of his daily activities and his social relationships. What was its nature? I shall now draw briefly upon the evidence relating to the second group of men enumerated earlier, those who had retired from all work. A third had retired within the previous three years and nearly a half between four and ten years. Only one in six had been retired over ten years, some of these being crippled or disabled men who had done little work after middle age.

The first point to make is the great variety in the age of final retirement. One man had given up work because of disability at the age of forty-eight and three in their fifties. Another man had worked as a shop assistant up to the age of eighty. Most men, however, retired in their late sixties or early seventies. The popular idea that

1. *Life and Labour of the People in London*, Vol. 1, 1891, p. 50.

most men retire altogether from work around the age of sixty-five did not hold for this mainly working-class group.

In view of what was said earlier of the men remaining at work it is not surprising to find that nearly all the men had retired involuntarily. It was extremely difficult to determine precisely the causes of retirement. The reasons for leaving work were sometimes found to be other than those first stated. This was particularly true of those saying they had been laid off by their employers. One man, for example, had had two long spells off work followed by a medical examination. On a third occasion, when the industrial doctor found the man not fit to continue work, he received three months' notice.

TABLE 21

NUMBER OF MEN RETIRING FROM FULL-TIME AND
ALL WORK, BY AGE

Retired men	Age at retirement							Total number	Average age at retirement
	64 or under	65	66	67	68	69	70 and over		
Retired from full-time work	7	11	2	4	3	5	13	45	67·0
Retired from all work	7	4	2	4	4	5	13	39	67·7

Was the reason the employer's dismissal, or was it ill health or strain? When the reasons given for retirement were checked with evidence about health (through medical records as well as information supplied in the interview) and financial and social circumstances, it appeared that ill health or disability played a part in the retirement of nearly four-fifths of the men and was the main cause for nearly three-fifths. This is shown in Table 22, though the data, because of complications introduced by contributory causes, must be interpreted with caution. The experience of the husbands of married women in this sample suggested that ill health was even more important than this.

In a recent survey by the Ministry of Pensions of the reasons given for retiring or continuing at work, twenty eight per cent of the men taking their pension at sixty-five gave ill health or heaviness or strain of work as the chief cause. A further twenty-five per cent had retired because of chronic illness, having been ill for not less than six months before minimum pension age. Another twenty-eight per cent said they were retired by their employers and the remainder said they gave up work because they wanted a rest or because of other reasons.[1] It is difficult to know how reliable such figures are. For example, although men giving ill health as the cause of retirement had, in general, more incapacitating illness in the years before retirement than others, three in ten had no record of such illness. The present inquiry suggests ill health may be a bigger factor in retirement than has hitherto been supposed, but further inquiry needs to be made on a larger scale in contrasting areas.

It is worth considering in detail the small number retiring mainly from choice. One of the four was a tallyman who, though physically

TABLE 22

REASONS FOR MEN'S RETIREMENT FROM FULL-TIME WORK

*Reason for retirement**		Number	%
ILL HEALTH:			
Disability, etc.	4	} 26	58
Ill health only	22		
RETIRED BY EMPLOYER:			
Sole reason	6	} 12	27
Partly ill health also	6		
CHOICE:			
Sole reason	4	} 7	15
Partly ill health also	3		
Total		45	100

* As assessed from a range of information supplied by each man.

fit, chose to retire at sixty-three, when his business failed. The second was an old people's attendant who had had a spell of a year in hospital just after he retired at sixty-five, although no evidence of serious ill health before retirement was disclosed during the

1. *Reasons Given for Retiring or Continuing at Work*, 1954.

interview. The third was a bookmaker's clerk who 'retired' at sixty-eight but still gained a fair living from his bets. The fourth was a man of eighty-seven who had given up his work as shop assistant at the age of eighty.

A substantial proportion of the men laid off by their employers or retiring from ill health sought lighter jobs. Often they were told, 'You're too old'. Others did not do this, either because of their infirmity or because, having been in one occupation most of their lives, they did not find it easy to face such a change.

Mr Grundy was forced to give up his work drawing trolleys in a tobacco factory at sixty-five because of the strains involved. 'A day looked a week to me. I feared too much time on my hands.' He set about looking for work. He applied to thirty offices, businesses, and insurance companies in the City, without success. Sometimes he lied about his age. 'I told one man I was fifty-five. It was silly really, because they could have found out as soon as I started work from my insurance cards. He said, "Are you sure you're not sixty-five?" So I said, "Why ask all these questions – give a man a chance."'

The overwhelming evidence, therefore, was that voluntary retirement was rare in Bethnal Green. Among the retired there was scarcely a single person in favour of retirement. This was evident in the answers to the first question on the subject, 'When did you retire?' A number of the men gave the precise date, such as 'the 23rd of November, 1951'. Those who had retired within the previous year or two told the most vivid stories.

Mr Kite was sixty-five. He had been obliged by ill health to give up his work as a brewer's labourer two years before. 'I kept losing time. It was on account of my health. The work was too heavy. I went to my doctor and he said that I'd never be able to do any work again. The next week I got the sack.' His wife added, 'That was a day that was. There was him crying and the children up here crying too. They thought he'd done too much.' Mr Kite continued, 'I had the hump. I didn't know what to do. It was like being stuck in the Army in a detention camp. All I could see were these four walls. I used to go out and see the boys on Saturday evenings. I'd meet my sons-in-law and we'd go out to the pub. [He used to earn £8 of which he gave his wife £5.] Now I can't do it. It's like being a pauper. I had to turn away from that because I didn't have a pound like I did in my pocket. I couldn't stand anybody anything [drinks]. I couldn't do my share.'

It may be added that when he was asked some time later what had been the happiest time in his life he answered, 'When I was at work. When I was at work I was happy.'

Good health enabled a man to continue at work. Occasional illness and growing disability made a job insecure and, eventually, impossible to retain. Compared with women, men were much more preoccupied with their health. They took greater pride in talking about any good faculties they still possessed and they were more depressed by illness and infirmity. For them the difference between relatively good and relatively poor health did not mean a gradual adjustment in occupation and social activities, as it did for women; once across the boundary of retirement it meant an entirely different style of life. One man referred again and again to the good physique he had once possessed. 'I used to be good at all kinds of sport, but now I can't even walk properly. My feet seems to go flop, flop, flop. I feel miserable about it, yes, just like that, flop, flop, flop.'

Those who had retired gave a little more emphasis to loss of income as a reason for reluctance to retire than did men remaining at work but they gave as much emphasis to boredom and the related sense of uselessness. Two-thirds of the men made spontaneous remarks alluding to one or both of these reasons. They said it was a hardship to live on a retirement pension and that work sustained a man's interest in life and helped to maintain his health and spirits. Other complaints derived from these two. As a result of losing job and income some men felt unwanted. Most of them were clearly not as unwanted as they made out. They were preoccupied with the fear of burdening their children and other relatives, even when services were performed or repeatedly offered. To be independent was one of the remaining sources of pride.

What did the loss of income involve? It is difficult to give precise figures, partly because some men had retired several or many years previously when average earnings were much lower than in 1954–5, partly because some men had earnings from part-time jobs or their wives were still employed. The contributions of children living at home were an additional complication. A fairly accurate idea of the fall can be given by the figures of £8–£9 and £3 10s.–£4. The first figure was the approximate personal income of recently retired men before their retirement. It includes net wage, disability and other pensions, and, for some of those who were married, wife's earnings. The second figure was the approximate personal income of retired men. It includes retirement pension, national assistance, occupation pensions, and gratuities. Personal income ranged from £2, for a few widowers who relied partly on savings to supplement a pension of £2 or refused to apply for national assistance, to £8 14s., for one married man who had an occupational pension in addition to his retirement pension and whose wife earned £2. The evidence was that most men experienced a fall in income of over a half, some of them as much as, or more than, two-thirds.

This fall in income affected men much more than their wives. They no longer felt they had the status of breadwinners and they lost nearly all their accustomed pocket money. The pension went, as it was said, 'on the table', and unless they were among the few who also had a small occupational pension, they were dependent on wives or children for any pocket money they did get. The pensioner usually received from 2s. 6d. to 5s. back from his wife. She was the household cashier and manager and the effective if not the nominal head of the family. Several men remarked spontaneously that they were closer to their wives because they saw more of them and their children. 'When people get older they cling together more.' 'You get more matey together.' 'You get to know one another better. You never see enough of each other at work.' 'Where is a man without his wife?' But often, as we saw in Chapter 6, wives did not share this enthusiasm and within some marriages there were serious frictions. Although men were thrown back on their families they could not match in range or quality the wives' bonds with relatives, particularly daughters, and no longer could contribute much to their welfare. One man said, 'A couple of years ago when I had a bit of money in my pocket, I'd put my hand in my pocket and give my daughter a couple of pounds for the children. I can't do that now.'

Some men were able to take on some of the domestic chores, particularly if their wives were infirm and had no daughter available, but many found even this unnecessary. Competent wives and competent daughters did not need them in the home. 'The wife always used to have the place on her own. They get grumpy if you get in their way. "I want to do this," she'll say. "What you doing here?"

and you have to get out. . . . . You see some of the old 'uns. It's like penal servitude. They come out about nine in the morning and don't go home till five in the afternoon.'

Men pottered about in the home doing odd jobs and repairs, they went for a stroll to meet a few acquaintances in the park or stand with them at a street corner. Their chances of a holiday away from home were slight. Only six of the thirty-nine men who had given up work had had a holiday of from one to two weeks in the previous year, compared with twelve of the twenty-five still working full or part-time. Despite the cheap rates of admission for pensioners, they did not go more often to the cinema. Only two in five went as much as once a month, the same proportion as those remaining at work. In the early months after retirement men sometimes met former workmates but usually they soon found, with regret and often with bitterness, that old friendships could not be maintained. 'I saw a rare lot less of my friends. They don't want you when you're old. You remember the old song "When you're down, the world don't want you".' They felt a blow had been struck at their prestige and standing in both locality and family. In time they were more likely to reconcile themselves to the reality of being old age pensioners and were more likely to join an old people's club. Although family relationships and activities now became all-important they could not give men back the skills, experiences, and associations of youth and middle age.

If the pension had ensured a more comfortable standard of life men might not have had the depressing sense of having become 'poor relations' and might have held their heads higher among their children. Those with the highest incomes in retirement undoubtedly had a more confident outlook. Even so, they still preferred to be at work, because so few seemed to occupy their time in ways which gave satisfaction. Reading, walking in the park, visiting their children, listening to the radio, tending a few flowers, occasionally going to a club or cinema or on an outing to Southend – these seemed to be the common recreations of retired men. They did not give much opportunity for self-expression. Those unable to help their wives or female relatives in domestic and family activities were left without many ways of justifying their lives.

This was why so many men talked of retirement as a tragedy.

They were forced to recognize that it was not their working life which was over, it was their life. 'In the sweat of thy face shalt thou eat bread till thou return unto the ground.' Perhaps, unlike some professional men, most men in Bethnal Green had never laid plans for retirement. They had no cottage in the country, no book-list for old age and no opportunity to grow prize-winning roses, take the chair at committee meetings, write memoirs, or perfect their bridge. A few bred budgerigars or looked after rabbits, but most did not have opportunities of this kind and anyway wanted more than time-filling recreations. The inescapable conclusion was that after retirement most men in Bethnal Green could not occupy their time satisfactorily. Their life became a rather desperate search for pastimes or a gloomy contemplation of their own help-lessness, which, at its worst, was little better than waiting to die. They found no substitute for the companionship, absorption, and fulfilment of work. Their families gave them what sense of fulfil-ment they had left.

The Old Woman at Work

In contrast to men, women rarely experienced a drastic change in their way of life upon retirement. Over half the 139 women in the sample had been in full- or part-time occupations late in life. Four, all widows, actually had a full-time job and twenty a part-time job, giving a proportion at work of seventeen per cent or one in six. A further fifty-four, or thirty-nine per cent, had retired from full- or part-time occupations after the age of fifty. The variation in age of retirement was very wide, thirteen of the fifty-four retiring in their fifties, only seven at age sixty, and the remaining thirty-four at various ages from sixty-one to seventy-four.

Women remaining at work were mainly in occupations resemb-ling the ones they had at home. Fifteen of the twenty-four were cooks, canteen workers, office or domestic cleaners, and ward orderlies. Most of the rest had jobs as part-time machinists, wrappers, packers, or shop-assistants of one kind or another. The average wage of the four in full-time employment was just over £5, of the twenty in part-time employment £1 15s. The earn-ings of most supplemented their pensions. About half were in their early sixties and all but three of the remainder in their late sixties.

The occupations of retired women had been of much the same

kind. A half had been in jobs connected with cleaning, cooking, or similar duties. The reasons for retirement differed from those given by men in two important respects. First, women more frequently retired from choice; and second, no woman said she had been laid off by her employer. As many as a half said they retired because they were getting old, or because of ill health or accidents; most of the remainder said they had done so because they wanted to or because of family reasons. They had an ailing husband or other relative to look after. Even those who gave ill health as the main cause of retirement sometimes stopped work because of relatively minor ailments. There was much to occupy women at home and in their families. Spinsters and women with no children made more complaints about retirement than others but even they protested less strongly than most men.

> Mrs Breeze, a widow of seventy-two, had given up office cleaning three years previously. 'I'll tell you for why. It was all that fog. It got on my chest and I had to fight for my breath. And my daughter said, "Mum, you've had to fight hard in your life and there's help for you. I think you want a rest, Mum, and you should give it up." I think my children were right, and I had had a hard life, and I gave it up.'

> Miss Rowntree and her sister had worked at 'hand button-holing. We were what you call finishers. We were mainly in the gents' fancy vest trade. You were lucky if you got something over £2.' Her sister said she left as soon as she qualified for a pension. 'There was enough to do here – the cooking and cleaning and washing. We'd both been there forty years. We still keep in touch with one or two of them who work there. We were glad to leave really, there's such a lot of house-work to do.' Miss Rowntree had given up work two or three years later at sixty-six, because of the development of a cataract in one of her eyes. Both sisters said retirement had not meant a drastic problem. 'We found a lot to do here. When you get old you've got enough to do in the house. We've been spending what we've saved.'

Proportionately more single women and women without children had worked regularly in middle or old age. This was only to be expected. What was not expected was that, among the remaining women, who formed the great majority, those who were at the centre of a complex local network of relatives more often took up an occupation than those who had few or no relatives nearby. It is difficult to devise an adequate test of this from the small numbers in the sample. Fifteen out of thirty married women whose daughters lived within a mile had been at work after the age of fifty, but only five of twenty-two (having surviving children) who had no daughters nearby. A woman and her married daughters living nearby were able to organize domestic work and the care of children in such a way that each of them was able to maintain a part-time job. One grandmother went off to work as an office cleaner at six in the morning, returning home at 10 a.m. She then had the care of three grandchildren while two married daughters went out to work, one as a waitress and the other as a part-time newspaper wrapper. The daughters did her shopping on their way home from work. By contrast women with sons but no daughters living nearby or women whose children had moved out of Bethnal Green often said they had too much housework to find outside employment or their husbands did not 'like women who went out to work'. If women belonged to a localized family of three generations it was, in short, easier for them to take part-time employment.

Women thought of a job largely as a means of supplementing their housekeeping money and meeting other people and not, as men often did, as the main means of securing enough money, prestige, and associations to justify life itself. The household's standard of life fell when grown-up children left home to get married and, by taking an occupation for a few hours each day, a woman was able to supplement her housekeeping money. The extra was all the more useful when her husband was retired or accepted a lower-paid occupation. The work was often well within her capacities, because it resembled her work at home and because she could count on the support of her married daughters. In a borough adjoining the City of London, the demand for women cleaners and canteen workers was sufficiently great for her to find a job easily.

New Employment for the Old

The effect of retirement from work upon man and woman and upon the role of each within home and family has now been described in some detail. The conclusions most relevant to policy were first, that in Bethnal Green voluntary retirement was very rare indeed; second, that although a proportion of men was apparently laid off by employers at a fixed age, deeper inquiry often revealed ill health to be the underlying reason for retirement; third, that over a third of all the men over sixty-five had in fact changed their jobs in their sixties or seventies (and this figure accords with the findings of other studies); fourth, and most important, that the loss of an occupation was felt much more acutely by men than by women and often left them, because their womenfolk had the care of home and family, without a useful function in the last years of their lives. To many working-class men retirement is a social disaster.

The obvious implication for policy is that there is a major need for occupations for old men. In part the problem is one of encouraging employers to retain employees who do not wish to retire and of finding ways by which the employment of elderly workers can be made more feasible. But the other part of the problem is that whatever is done for the healthy there will still be many men, and also women, who are not fit enough to take full- or part-time employment at an economic wage. Much too little attention has been directed towards their needs.

In Bethnal Green there were many men who talked of their wish to return to work. They had insufficient means of occupying their time, had no money, and were acutely aware of their loss of status. Most of these were not fit to continue their previous employment but were not incapacitated. A careful examination of each interview-report was made to gain an approximate idea of the number of men retired from full-time work who were fit enough and willing to take a full- or part-time light job near their homes, *including those who could work at their own rate in fairly sheltered conditions*. Those in extreme ill health or infirmity, including the bedfast and the housebound, were ruled out, as were men over eighty.

The finding was that of men retired from full-time work between fifty per cent and fifty-five per cent might have been able to continue in an occupation of this kind. This, if applied to Bethnal Green as a whole, suggests there may be as many as from 700–900 men in the borough who would benefit from such occupation. This number excludes the 700–800 of the 2,500 men over the age of sixty-five in the borough who are in full-time work.

Making an estimate of the potential demand for a light occupation among old men does not reveal how their need for occupation can be met. One thing has to be faced. The problem cannot be solved by normal employment practices. Such men could not compete with other work-people in their output; many of them would require sheltered employment, and, in the final analysis, many of them would have to be partly subsidized. This suggests that much of the need can be met only by special employment centres for the elderly, run and subsidized by local authorities or by the State. These could be similar in some respects to the Remploy factories for disabled people.[1] They could be closely linked to the old people's welfare committees of local authorities. It would be no part of the purpose of such centres to employ people capable of undertaking ordinary part- or full-time jobs in industry. Their object would be to make some provision for occupational needs of elderly people who are not fit to re-enter *normal* employment.

There have in recent years been a number of experiments on these lines which give force to the proposal. In the London borough of Finsbury, for example, an experimental employment scheme for the elderly has been going on since 1951. The purpose is to help those who cannot continue in normal employment to keep well in body and mind. A new prefabricated building provides occupation for 110 people, only one in four of them men. The old people work two hours a morning or two hours an afternoon for five days a week. They do outwork for a variety of commercial firms – assembling electric-iron elements and special bottles, sorting and packing medical dressings and animal wool. They also make articles for direct sale – aprons, night-dresses, coat-hanger coverings. Each person is paid a flat rate of 10s. per week, said by the organizer to be more than he earned on average. Administrative and running costs are subsidized by the borough council and by voluntary organizations and contributors. A few other London boroughs have now started similar schemes.

An experiment not yet tried by local authorities or others is the provision of work for elderly people unable to leave their homes. Nearly one in ten old people in Bethnal Green were confined to

1. A strong plea for the development of local authority welfare services for handicapped and disabled people of normal working age has been made by a Government committee and this development could be associated with occupation centres for the old. (*Report by Committee of Inquiry on the Rehabilitation, Training and Resettlement of Disabled Persons*, 1956.)

their homes. This proportion is roughly the same as that indicated by surveys in other parts of the country. Perhaps three-quarters of a million old people in Britain rarely, if ever, leave their homes. Many bedfast and housebound people have nimble minds and hands and would welcome an occupation. The development of outwork for them may be one of the rewarding innovations of the future.

Further research would be needed to confirm the Bethnal Green results but they suggest, so far as they go, that there is a very real need for occupational provision for retired people, especially men. The need may be much greater than has been supposed hitherto, and it is social, rather than economic. There may be as many as three quarters of a million men and over a million women in Britain who could benefit from occupation centres of the kind suggested.

This chapter has moved from an analysis of the circumstances of men and women before and after retirement to the implications of the findings for social policy. The outstanding conclusion is that retirement is a tremendous blow to the man. It completely alters his life, lowers his prestige, thrusts him into poverty or near poverty, cuts him off from the friendships and associations formed at work, and leaves him with few opportunities of occupying his time. He is thrown back on his wife and family. Here he finds his wife has the dominant place. He is thus often deprived of a useful function and finds his life difficult to justify. The sudden degeneration in his physical health may be in part, as so many people thought in Bethnal Green, a consequence of retirement itself.

The effect on women is far less drastic. Rarely do they consider gainful employment to be more than a supplement to work within home and family, unless they are unmarried. Though the extra money is valued it is just one of the jobs which they can give up without disaster as they become older and more infirm. The localized extended family seems to play a part in helping mothers take part-time employment and sustains them when they give it up. These conclusions point to the importance of (*a*) enabling men to carry on longer in normal employment, (*b*) providing sheltered part-time employment for men (and, to a much smaller extent, women) incapable of earning an economic wage, and (*c*) providing outwork for housebound old people.

CHAPTER 12

Poverty

ONE of the possible consequences of retirement is poverty. Most studies of poverty in Britain over the past sixty years have concentrated only on the cost of maintaining some standard of subsistence needs and its relation, in chosen survey areas, to people's total income. Households were found to be so much below, or so much above, the 'poverty line'. Why research has been restricted to this approach is puzzling – although it probably explains why a philosophy of payments on a basis of subsistence has been written into the nation's social security scheme. The authors of such studies appear to have been too sanguine about the validity of definitions of 'subsistence'; human needs in modern society, with the possible exception of nutritive needs, are now generally acknowledged to be incapable of scientific measurement or of easily agreed social definition. They also failed to show how people spent their money and arranged their lives when their income was at or below the poverty line; if they had, perhaps more account might have been taken of the force of social custom and habit in determining certain kinds of expenditure in any community. And finally they failed to inquire into the effect of a change in income: a person who suffers a large reduction in his income, when, say, he becomes ill or unemployed or old, is likely to feel himself poor whatever the level to which his income has fallen and he may respond in different ways. This, in particular, seems to be a vital piece of information in understanding poverty and its causes.

The Fall in Income

Among retired people interviewed in Bethnal Green the fall in income on retirement explained many of their problems. Some social problems, involving role and status in home, family, and community, especially for men, have already been described. The most immediate problem was the sudden drop in the standard of living. People were very much worse off. Table 23 shows the average personal income of people still at work and those who were retired. The figures include any net earnings of man and wife, retirement and occupational pensions and gratuities, national assistance, and other State aid, but not the use of savings or board money or other income from relatives living at home or elsewhere. Changes in the rates of retirement pensions and national assistance came into force in the middle of the interviewing, early in 1955. Those previously interviewed were visited again and the figures given in Table 23 refer to the personal income of the people in the sample during the spring and summer of 1955.

TABLE 23

AVERAGE PERSONAL INCOME OF OLD PEOPLE IN FULL- AND
PART-TIME EMPLOYMENT AND RETIRED FROM WORK
(To nearest shilling)

	Full-time work		Part-time work		Retired from work	
	Average income per week	Number	Average income per week	Number	Average income per week	Number
	£ s.		£ s.		£ s.	
Single and widowed	7 16	8	3 8	12	2 10	85
Married couples	8 16	45*	6 8	9†	4 4	44
All	8 12	53	4 14	21	3 2	129

* Married people interviewed who were, or whose husbands were, in full-time employment.

† Man and/or wife in part-time but not full-time employment.

Judged from these figures the income of single and widowed people fell on average by sixty-eight per cent, that of married people fifty-two per cent, when they retired. Even these figures do not represent the full extent of the drop in the standard of living in the last years of life. The income of some people had already plunged before retirement, in that they had taken lighter and less well-paid jobs, such as messengers and lavatory cleaners earning £4 or £4 10s.

Comparable figures cannot be given for other parts of the country. All that can be said with certainty is that retirement pensions and national assistance payments are very small, when compared with average weekly earnings in the United Kingdom. As Table 24 shows, in 1955 the pension for a single person was eighteen per cent of average weekly earnings; for a married couple twenty-nine per cent.

TABLE 24

SOCIAL SECURITY BENEFITS, COMPARED WITH AVERAGE
WEEKLY EARNINGS IN THE UNITED KINGDOM

Old people	Retirement pension		National assistance†	
	Amount	% of average weekly earnings*	Amount	% of average weekly earnings*
	s. d.		s. d.	
Single or widowed person	40 0	18	49 0	22
Married couple	65 0	29	76 0	34

* £11 2s. 11d. in October 1955, for all men twenty-one years and over.
Source: Ministry of Labour Gazette, March 1956.

† Information supplied by the N.A.B. suggested that the average rent paid for an old person living alone was about 11s. 6d. in 1955, for a married couple about 13s. These two figures have been added to the ordinary scales of £1 17s. 6d. and £3 3s. to show the approximate total sums which can be claimed through the N.A.B.

Among those interviewed a fall in income of over a half and often as much as two-thirds was certainly *felt* as poverty. Some tried to conceal it and did not like people living around them to know how much poorer they were. One couple said their income was exactly £4. 'When we were both working we had £10 a week coming in. If we wanted to buy something for dinner, we went out and got it. Now anything a bit tasty is out. But it's when you're getting on you need it. I'm telling you this in confidence. People think we're comfortable and I wouldn't have them know otherwise. But we're not.' Expenditure was reduced not only on such things as cakes, newspapers and periodicals, betting and drink,

T – G

but also on meat, milk, fruit, and clothing. Reduced spending on some form of entertainment or pleasure, such as radio rental, gifts for grandchildren, occasional drinks or cigarettes, was usually regarded as 'essential'. No one, however poor, spent money only on what are conventionally regarded as necessaries.[1]

Mr and Mrs Treasure used to live on a personal income of £9–£10. Now they had just over £4, from which £1 1s. 6d. had to be paid for rent. 'I used to have two pints of milk a day, and I said to the milkman, "I don't like to owe you money," so after that I'd only have one pint. We used to have eggs for supper, or a kipper, but not now. We have p'rhaps a bit of toast. But we always have dinner. We always have something hot. We had to cut down on everything, I can tell you. He [her husband] doesn't even smoke now. And he doesn't drink. But I like a drink when I can, I don't mind admitting. And he has to put his shilling on the pools.'

Mr Preeley was a cripple in his late seventies and he lived alone in a small two-room flat. He was unmarried and socially isolated. He was very deaf. He lived on a non-contributory pension and supplementary assistance of £2 10s. 6d. per week. His rent was 10s. 6d., coal about 6s. ('I use about three-quarters cwt. a week.') No money, Christmas or other club. Insurances – an endowment policy costing him 2s. 0½d. a week. 'It covers everything and every now and then I can draw on it. When the man called he said I could draw on it again in June. It's an all-in. I had it [the sum of money] three years ago when I drew £1 for the radio licence.' Radio rental 2s. 3d. No pets. Apart from the tobacco he got free with his coupons 'I get another half ounce in the middle of the week'. It was quite clear he was living in poverty. The outgoings mentioned amounted to about £1 2s. to which must be added a few shillings for electricity and gas. He had no more than £1 4s. a week left for his food, clothing, household sundries, and everything else. 'I don't have any breakfast. I mostly have boiled beef when I get meat, and with it I have carrots or parsnips or brussels sprouts and potatoes. Sometimes I make myself a pease pudding. Oh yes, I'm a great one for tea. I can't do less than a quarter lb. every week. I drink more of that than I ought to. I used to like a drink, I used to be terrible for drinking – especially when I was in the musical line, you had a lot of that in those days. But I can't afford it now.'

Mrs Docker was a widow living with a single daughter. She had a

1. A survey of unemployment in Lancashire cotton towns came to a similar result (P.E.P., *Social Security and Unemployment in Lancashire*, 1952).

retirement pension of £2 plus assistance of 5s. [Her daughter had a
low wage and contributed £1 10s. for her keep.] Rent was 12s. 1d.,
coal 8s. (7s. 6d. – 'You've got to give a tip, haven't you?') Her daughter usually bought a bag of coalite for 1s. 6d. each week. No subscription clubs. Radio rental, 2s. 3d. She used her tobacco vouchers
worth 2s. 4d. a week. She had a 'free' insurance policy. 'If it isn't
enough to bury me, somebody else will have to bury me.' She had
trouble with her feet and could not get out to have them treated. 'I
have a lady who comes to do them every two months. It's 2s. 6d. a
foot.' She had to buy a stick recently to help her get to the corner of
the street for errands. She had a mongrel dog, costing a few shillings
a week, and a budgerigar. 'My son bought it. I think it was 15s. I get
a bag of sand every three or four weeks. That's 9d. And then I get
half a pint of budgie seed – that's 7d. about every week.' She added,
'The money goes like anything. It costs me a £1 for my rations. Last
Saturday our joint was 7s. 6d. and it was only a little one, but we spun
it out till Monday. . . . We can't afford luxuries. I just have a bit of
toast for breakfast and a cup of tea. I can't afford eggs.' Her daughter came in from work for a midday meal, and in the evening, 'I
usually just have a bit of toast and tea and then we have a cup of
cocoa before we go to bed. Sometimes she might bring in a bit of
haddock.'

All details about expenditure were not sought. Information was
systematically gained only for rent, subscriptions, life insurances,
coal and regular payments for radios, furniture, and pets. Other
information was acquired haphazardly. Of the 203 interviewed
179, or eighty-eight per cent were still paying life insurance
premiums, ranging from 2d. to £1 per week, the average being
2s. 9d.[1] In a locality where the funerals demanded by tradition

1. It is possible the conditions under which the old are privately insured
may need inquiry. Several felt they had been talked into starting new policies
or continuing old ones. One man explained that after his wife died he wanted
to give up policies on himself but was persuaded instead to start two further
ones. A number of people were bewildered by the difficulties of being guaran-
teed what they had paid to a company and what they imagined they had a
right to when forced to discontinue payments. Many said they had 'free'
policies. One remarked, 'You can get a free policy after eighteen or twenty-
five years. But you don't get so much. It's reduced. That's how these insurance companies go with their policies. We had my mother insured for £30
and when the man came along to me and I asked whether I need go on paying, he offered me £15 if I didn't pay any more. No wonder these insurance
companies have these big new buildings. They do well out of their policies.'

cost anything from £40 to £60 these payments were a necessity. Over fifty per cent were also paying weekly sums for rental of radios, for sick, social, holiday, or clothing clubs, and for furniture averaging 3s. 6d. per week. Fifty-six per cent had pets of various kinds which ranged in cost from a few pence a week for budgerigars to several shillings for dogs and cats.

Many people remarked on their need for more 'firing' now they were old and they spent more on coal. Some found deaf aids purchased privately more satisfactory than those provided through the National Health Service. Some, anxious to conceal incontinence, bore the labours and heavy cost of the washing involved. Others had to have outside windows cleaned; a common charge was 2s. 6d. once a fortnight or once a month. A striking impression was of the variety and regularity of purchases from the local chemist. Some people did not like to bother doctors for medicine when prescriptions cost a shilling, or walk as far as their surgeries, or they found doctors would not prescribe their favourite medicines. There were also fares to visit relatives, cups of tea for married children, Saturday pocket-money for grandchildren, Christmas to prepare for, and birthday cards. (One woman's daughter said her mother had so many grandchildren she bought a birthday card every other week.)

Special Needs and the Level of Income

Two things were evident. First, as members of families and of society old people felt compelled, so far as they were able, to continue the traditions of working life: buying birthday and Christmas presents, treating grandchildren, paying fares to visit relatives, providing for a socially approved funeral, contributing a share towards holidays, clubs, churches, coronation parties, wreaths for a neighbour, and outings with friends and so on. These were genuine needs on which money had to be spent. Many pre-retirement spending habits and customs were difficult to change, despite the sharp fall in income. Small wonder that cuts in expendi-

---

The 'free' policies I was shown by some people gave the following kind of facts: a man had been paying 2d. a week from 1924 to 1948, when he gave up his payments; originally the sum for which he had been assured was £13 16s. but now it had been reduced to £8 11s. 7d.

ture were first made where no one else would notice. Second, in old age there were personal needs of a special kind: medicines and appliances to buy which could not necessarily be provided through the National Health Service, extra sheets and clothing for the incontinent, extra coal, electricity, and gas as well as compensatory things such as radios, house pets, newspapers, and periodicals, for the housebound and infirm. These special family, social, and personal needs were expressed as priority claims on the income of the old. Some had existed before retirement; others were the consequence of ageing and replaced the needs of working life. Money saved on fares to work and wear and tear on clothes, for example, was now needed for extra visits to the doctor and extra comforts at home.

While more detailed studies of such needs must be made there is little doubt that the needs are there. There is virtually no provision for them in 'subsistence' payments to the old. The object of national assistance is largely to make up income, on test of means, to a subsistence level. (The retirement pension, originally intended to provide for subsistence needs irrespective of other resources, is now officially regarded as providing a minimum income below such needs.) A general definition of need is incorporated in its scale rates, and these are applied to individual circumstances, with certain discretionary disregards and allowances. The sums are intended to cover food, fuel and light, clothing, and household sundries, besides rent, and sometimes, after investigation, small additions are made for laundry, domestic help, or special diet. This definition of 'subsistence', on such evidence as exists, appears to be completely unrealistic.

Nevertheless, retired people in Bethnal Green had, on average, little more than this subsistence income. Table 25 shows that the total personal income of the 129 retired people in the sample was only a little higher, after deducting rent, than the national assistance scales. Twelve per cent of the retired had, or their husbands or wives had, occupational pensions or gratuities ranging from a few shillings to £3. These sums are included in the averages. Thirty-three per cent had savings, only thirteen per cent £100 or more. Eighty-five per cent of the men entitled to tobacco vouchers were using them, and nearly sixty per cent of the women.

Some, of course, had a smaller personal income than the national

TABLE 25

PERSONAL INCOME OF RETIRED OLD PEOPLE, COMPARED WITH
NATIONAL ASSISTANCE SCALES

Old people	Average personal income		Average rent*		Personal income less rent		National assistance scales 1955†		Total number
	s.	d.	s.	d.	s.	d.	s.	d.	
Single and widowed	49	7	10	9	38	10	37	6	85
Married couples	84	2	15	0	69	2	63	0	44

* When an old person shared housekeeping arrangements with unmarried or married children or others he was asked what contribution they or he made to the rent. When no fixed contribution was made he or she was assumed to be paying half the total rent.

† As from 7 February 1955. These sums are payable in addition to rent.

assistance scales. Altogether forty-two per cent of the 129 had assistance grants, ranging from 1s. 6d. to 30s. 6d. a week, which supplemented retirement pensions, and a further eleven per cent other assistance grants, such as non-contributory old age pensions. These were higher proportions than in the country as a whole, probably because most people were working-class.[1] Yet inquiry into each individual case showed a further substantial proportion had not applied for assistance when they would have been entitled to it.

Of the retired, forty-six, or thirty-six per cent, had a personal income lower than the National Assistance Board's ordinary scales. Thirty-two of these were single or widowed. Taking into

1. It should be noted that the group of retired people, as defined, did not include all retirement *pensioners*. Three men in their seventies, for example, had a full-time wage as well as a pension; a few others were in part-time employment. Some of the retired depended not on a retirement pension, but on non-contributory pensions, or a widow's pension or allowance and so on. In the country as a whole, in 1955, there were about 4½ million people receiving retirement pensions, or about sixty-four per cent of those of pensionable age. Of these pensioners about a quarter had supplementary assistance grants. Altogether, of all retirement pensioners interviewed in Bethnal Green, thirty-seven per cent had supplementary grants.

account savings, the presence of other members of the household and infirmities meriting discretionary additions to the sum fixed for meeting their needs, it was calculated that from twenty to twenty-five per cent of the retired would have been entitled to supplementary assistance grants, usually between a shilling and 15s. a week, had they applied.[1]

Personal Rights and Family Support

This is a high proportion. Why had they not applied? The answer lies partly in their unwillingness, partly in their unawareness of qualifying conditions, but largely in the support given them by their families. Many were unwilling to seek State aid. Those who would have qualified for supplementary assistance made remarks of the following kind:

'It would be worth it if a person wasn't like me. I've never liked to cadge. I'm not a one to go running for help. I don't spend money. I manage on what I've got. I don't smoke, don't drink, and I've never been used to eating much. I've never been used to it. I'm not a cadger. I've never been that way brought up.' This was a spinster living alone who had a retirement pension of £2 and savings amounting to less than £100. Her rent was 8s. 5d.

'I don't want to tell people all my affairs. They ask too many questions. I'm proud I suppose.' This was a married woman living with her husband and each had a retirement pension of £2. Their rent was £1 7s. 10d. They had £75 savings, from which they were drawing at the rate of £1 a week, and felt they would be obliged to apply for assistance once these were exhausted.

'I'm a bad one for pleading. I've got my son. They wouldn't allow me anything. I'm awful about asking for anything. I'd starve rather than ask for a penny.' This was a widow living with a single son. She had a pension of £2, but no savings. Her rent was 15s. 3d.

1. The method of assessing needs followed that outlined in the National Assistance Board's Explanatory Leaflet A.L.18. Thus the resources of old people who were householders were regarded as including a contribution of 7s. a week from members of the household who were not dependent on them, but if these, usually married children, had dependants of their own they were not regarded as contributing more than an appropriate share of the rent. Some small resources (as described in the leaflet), such as a few shillings superannuation or small amounts of savings, were disregarded.

Such people were proud. They liked to be independent. They felt a pension, but not assistance, was their right. However presented to them, they thought of supplementary assistance as charity. They depended, for as long as possible, on their own resources and on their children. One man said, 'I don't like the idea of going to ask for it. Your pension, now, you have a right to that. You know what I mean. The supplementary benefit is not like something you're entitled to.' Another man said, 'They should give people enough so they don't have to apply for assistance. The pension's not near enough. I reckon you should pay in more [for a pension] to get more. I think it's a good idea.' A woman said, 'Some people are much tougher about it. They say they'll get everything they're entitled to. But I can't think of it like that. The pension is different, everyone has a right to that, but the other, they have to come round every six months or so asking questions.'

Their unwillingness to seek aid was rarely based on experience of harsh or unfair treatment. This should be made plain. By and large the evidence was that national assistance officials were sympathetic. Their 'fairness' was generally acknowledged. One man said, 'It's a wise idea. It's very fair indeed.' But he had not applied. One case is perhaps worth quoting in full, to underline the importance of this point.

Explaining how she got supplementary assistance two years before, Mrs Jameson said, 'I met a friend of mine, a widow, with several children like myself. She said, "Do you get any national assistance?" She advised me to apply for it. I had a young lady to come to see me and she said,"However do you manage?" She said, "Why didn't you come up before?" I took her in the front room and I said I had a piano and she said, "Don't worry about that." I didn't like taking the lady in the kitchen, what with the tellie there. But it's not like it used to be. The lady said, "But we don't put things outside." She was really very nice.' She compared her experience with poor relief before the war. 'When I got married I went up for relief and told them I was working. I went up to the Assistance. I'll never forget it. I said I didn't have enough money. I told them I went out and started work at six o'clock and came back at nine o'clock. And they said, "What do you do then?" And I said I did the washing and the housework and got the kids their dinner. They said, "What do you do then?" I told them that I tried to get out in the afternoons to do another hour or two. They said to me, "Couldn't you do work in between?" I said,

"You want black women to go out to work, that's what you want, you don't want white women."'

Old people usually put off applying for national assistance while they had savings, however small. At least half of those getting assistance had not sought it for months, or even years, after retirement. One woman said she had applied nine months after retirement, when she had used up her savings. 'I was jawed by my sisters and brothers because I didn't like to go. I like to be independent. I thought I was asking for charity. When the man came, he was a gentleman. He told me I should have applied before.' Some put off applying for aid even when they knew the N.A.B. disregarded certain amounts of savings. Others did not know they qualified even when they had a few savings or other small resources, such as a few shillings earnings or superannuation. Many could not be expected to understand all the complex conditions under which assistance is granted. 'I've got a daughter living with me. They wouldn't give me money.' 'When the pension goes up [early in 1955] I'll be able to get that little bit extra so that I can pay for a wireless each week. Would they [the N.A.B.] interfere if I did that?' 'I don't think the public assistance would let me go on a week's holiday. But they [her daughter and son-in-law] paid for it. I don't think the public assistance would like it.' Others could not understand why the grants varied so much. 'She's getting more than me. Yet she's just a widow, like me, on her own.'

Desire for independence and unawareness of qualifying conditions partly explained why retired people had not sought assistance or postponed application. Support by relatives provided the rest of the explanation. Two-thirds of those who would have qualified for assistance grants, but had not applied, were sharing housekeeping arrangements with unmarried or married children or other relatives. They were, in effect, subsidized by relatives. In Chapter 6 the economy of the home was described in detail. There, attention was drawn to the extent and variety of transfers of income within the localized extended family and to the fact that people often received money and gifts from children at home or elsewhere, partly for the services they performed in providing meals and caring for grandchildren. But the size of the subsidy, as we saw, was sometimes small. The conclusion is that retired people living within a localized extended family generally enjoyed a higher standard of living than others. Many of them would otherwise have been in poverty.

Implications for Policy

The chief facts described in this chapter about the standard of living of old people are therefore these:

(i) The very great fall in personal income upon retirement, a fall of over two-thirds for single and widowed and over a half for married people.

(ii) The existence of special money needs, for health, comfort, and security in family and community, which are not taken into account in subsistence standards (such as that of the National Assistance Board).

(iii) The low *personal* income of the retired; a third had a personal income below the National Assistance Board's subsistence minimum and between a fifth and a quarter were not receiving assistance but would have qualified for it had they applied. As many as seventy-five per cent in fact had an income low enough to qualify for assistance.

(iv) The way in which the contributions of children and other relatives, living at home and elsewhere, prevented many people falling into poverty or applying for aid to the State.

These facts require further investigation. The last deserves some comment, for it is open to misinterpretation. It does not mean there were no financial worries. Some of the retired did not have families or had become separated from them; the relatives of others could not always afford to give much help because they had dependent children, or were disabled or sick. Thus there was a small minority of people in dire poverty, as examples above testify, and a much larger number who were poor rather than very poor only because of small contributions from relatives. The circumstances of these people were a disturbing commentary on the provisions of the Welfare State.

Neither does it mean that bigger pensions or allowances would diminish the sense of family responsibility and so help to destroy family life. There was no evidence to suggest that the financial dependence of the old upon the young enhanced family relationships or was liked by either party. Indeed, old people themselves seemed to prefer financial and household independence, so long as support from relatives nearby was available if required. There was no evidence of people with larger incomes being neglected by their families. Quite the contrary. One woman, for example, whose husband had a small occupational pension as well as a retirement pension amounting to £5 7s. 6d. altogether, saw two of her three children every day and one every week. She said of pensions, 'It's a wonderful thing since they came in. It makes you not have to worry where the next meal's coming from. When you're old you don't have to be a burden on your children.' To be financially independent meant people could hold their heads higher and did not have to become supplicants of their children. This was particularly true of men. It meant they could contribute a share towards the cost of family activities and be more indulgent towards grandchildren and others. It meant their children were free of financial obligations which sometimes caused resentment. The strength of the family was partly built on reciprocal services being freely performed. Both old and young liked to think they could give to one another without feeling compelled to do so.

This was the principle on which old people wanted family life to be built. The evidence suggested that the present fall in income on retirement is much too sharp to allow past relationships and interests to be adequately maintained and special needs met. It also suggested that people endure hardships rather than apply for national assistance to which they would be entitled. To follow these conclusions to the point of making suggestions for policy, it seems that officers of the National Assistance Board should at least visit all new retirement pensioners to see whether they qualify for assistance. More important, it seems that efforts should be made to prevent the old experiencing so sharp a fall in their standard of living on retirement. This is not the place to argue how,[1] but it is obvious that previous ideas of 'subsistence' have been wholly unrealistic. If the pension were enough to preserve personal pride and identity the old would fit more happily into family and society.

1. For general discussion see Titmuss, R.M., 'Pension Systems and Population Change', 1955; Abel-Smith, B., and Townsend, P., *New Pensions for the Old*, 1955.

CHAPTER 13

Isolation, Loneliness, and the Hold on Life

THE poorest people, socially as well as financially, were those most isolated from family life. The questions of social isolation and loneliness in old age have not so far been examined in this book and will be discussed here. A distinction is made between the two: to be socially isolated is to have few contacts with family and community; to be lonely is to have an unwelcome *feeling* of lack or loss of companionship. The one is objective, the other subjective and, as we shall see, the two do not coincide.

Social isolation needs to be measured by reference to objective criteria. The problem is rather like that of measuring poverty. 'Poverty' is essentially a relative rather than an absolute term, and discovering its extent in a population is usually divided into two stages. Most people agree on the first stage, which is to place individuals on a scale according to their income; they often disagree about the second, which involves deciding how far up the scale the poverty 'line' should be drawn. The task of measuring isolation can also be divided in this way by placing individuals on a scale according to their degree of isolation and by drawing a line at some point on the scale so that those below the line would, by common consent, be called 'the isolated'.

It is no easy task. One man works in a factory, lives with his wife and children, goes to the cinema and the pub regularly each week, and is secretary to a poultry club which meets each week-end. Another man lives alone because his wife is dead, has retired from work, visits a married daughter every day, spends his week-ends with a son, and meets his friends in the park. How can these two men be placed on a common scale? The method suggested here is crude and tentative; but perhaps it can be developed into something more systematic.

It is based on information about old people's social contacts, particularly their contacts with relatives. By 'contact', as stated earlier, is meant a meeting with another person, usually pre-arranged or customary at home or outside, which involves more than a casual exchange of greetings between, say, two neighbours in the street. The first step for each person in the Bethnal Green sample was to add together the average number of contacts a week with each relative, some of whom, of course, were seen together; the second was to add on contacts with non-relatives, mainly neighbours and friends but also, for example, district nurses, home helps, and doctors; the third was to add on an arbitrarily-chosen score for other social activities in the week. Thus a weekly visit to a club, to the cinema or to church was given a score of 2; a full-time occupation was given a weekly score of 20, a part-time occupation 10. The following is an example:

Widow living alone	*Number of social contacts per week*
One married and one widowed daughter seen daily	14
Two grandchildren seen daily	14
Son-in-law seen once a week	1
Sister seen once a week	1
Two married sons, their wives and three children seen once a week	7
Brother and wife seen every fortnight ($\frac{1}{2}+\frac{1}{2}$)	1
Twelve other relatives seen from once to six times a year	1
Part-time occupation as school-cleaner	10
Visit to old people's club once a week	2
Neighbour exchanging visits twice a week	2
Irregular social activities (doctor, monthly visit to cinema, etc.)	1
Total score	54

The difficulties of applying this method must not be underrated. For one thing, no account was taken of the function, intensity, or duration of the contact: the score for a visit to another person, for example, was the same whether it lasted five minutes or three hours. A relative or non-relative living at home was given twice the score of a person seen daily, i.e., 14. Irregular contacts, such as annual holidays with distant relatives, were averaged out on a weekly basis for the year as a whole. Such contacts were generally of small importance, compared with the number occurring regularly, every day or every week. This is largely why, on balance, this method of scoring social contacts seemed to be feasible, at least in this district. Day-by-day contacts with relatives formed the major part of the social world of these old people. Many of them, in any case, had a limited range of social activities because of infirmity.

TABLE 26

SOCIAL ISOLATION OF OLD PEOPLE

Degree of isolation	Old people		Social contacts in week	
	%	Number	Mean	Median
Not isolated	77	156	72·9	67
Rather isolated*	13	27	29·1	28
Isolated†	10	20	14·6	17
Total	100	203	61·3	52

* 22–35 contacts per week (or between 3 and 5 per day).
† 21 contacts or fewer per week (or 3 or less per day).

The weekly social contact score for each individual represented the extent of an individual's isolation from, or involvement in, family and society. The scores of the 203 people in the sample were listed on a continuous scale, the highest, 208, being at the top and the lowest, 2, at the bottom. Examples will show the variations in social activities underlying these scores.

A married woman of sixty-four lived with her husband, a single son, and a granddaughter. She had a part-time occupation as an office cleaner. Three married daughters lived nearby and she saw them and four of their children every day. She saw two of their husbands nearly every day and one once a week. Her eldest son and his wife called once a week and her youngest son every day, his wife only once or twice a week. The surviving members of the husband's family were not seen but two of the wife's nieces called every fortnight. She had a widowed friend living alone whom she visited once a fortnight but she took pride in not having any regular association with a neighbour. She went to the cinema once or twice a month. *Total score 124.*

A married man of sixty-nine lived with his wife. He had a full-time job as a nightwatchman. He attended a club once a week, went to the cinema once a fortnight, and met two friends in a local pub two or three times a week. His only child, a daughter, lived nearby with her husband and child and he saw the three of them every day. Most of his surviving brothers and sisters lived abroad but he saw two of them and their children a few times each year. He saw three of his wife's brothers and their families from once a month to once a fortnight at week-ends. *Total score 69.*

A widow aged seventy-eight lived alone in a tenement flat. She had no children, had lost touch with her husband's family after his death fifteen years previously, and had not seen her surviving brother for some years. Two of a dead sister's three children lived nearby. Seeing them was her chief social activity. One married niece had two children and her household included her unmarried brother. The widow visited them two afternoons a week and the unmarried nephew also called on her once or twice a week. Another niece lived in South London and the widow visited her every other week-end for an afternoon. Otherwise she had no regular associations with friends, neighbours, or relatives. She did not go to church or to a club, but went to a cinema two or three times a week, alone. *Total score 18.*

The people at the bottom of the scale merit close attention. They were usually living alone, older than average, without children or other relatives living nearby, retired from work, and infirm. It was the combination of three or more of these factors that produced social isolation rather than any single one. Many of the oldest and most infirm people in the sample had a secure and rich family life. Many living alone saw a great deal of relatives and friends nearby. Some with no children were at work and had close relationships with brothers and sisters and nephews and nieces.

The Isolated

There were twenty people, as shown in Table 26, who had a social contact score of twenty-one per week (three per day) or less. Relatively to the rest these were the very isolated. Their ages ranged from sixty-four to eighty-three. They comprised two married women, two widowers, eight widows, five spinsters, and three bachelors. Thirteen of them lived alone; twelve had no children and half of the rest had sons only. It is worth examining their circumstances, taking first those with children.

Four of the eight with surviving children had daughters. One was a widow living with her only daughter, unmarried; she had few other relatives and all lived outside London. The second was a widow who had come with her only daughter from Scotland after the war, leaving friends and relatives behind. They were together until the housing authorities gave them two separate homes, several miles apart; now one of her daughter's children lived with her but she saw the rest of the family once a week or less. The third was a very infirm widow whose only daughter was married to a naval officer, obliged to live near Portsmouth; she lived in the same house as a widowed and childless sister and saw her every day but infirmity prevented other social contacts. The fourth was a widower of eighty who said his daughter and son living in Bethnal Green visited him twice a week to see he was all right but did not spend much time with him, now his wife was dead; he had a drink with a friend twice a week but infirmity precluded other activities.

The other four very isolated people with children had sons only. One was a married woman whose only son had moved into his wife's home district outside London; she and her husband had only one relative in Bethnal Green, the wife's unmarried sister, who was seen each week, and they had no friends or outside social activities, largely because the husband could not walk. Another was a widower, living with an unmarried son, who saw two married sons about once a week; he had no other surviving relatives. The two remaining people were both widows living alone. One had three sons living outside London, two of them visited her once a week; she saw a sister and two aged aunts in Bethnal Green every week but she spent much of her time on her own. The other had two illegitimate sons but no other relatives; she saw these sons occasionally.

There remain the childless and the unmarried. Most were in a worse position. The ten most isolated people of the 203 interviewed were all unmarried or childless. The circumstances of two are summarized below.[1]

Miss Paley, aged sixty-seven, lived in a one-room tenement flat. It was a large airless room with dismal orange-brown wallpaper peeling off in huge strips. Two or three mats, ingrained with dirt, covered the

1. One of the two most isolated people of all those interviewed is reported on at length in Appendix 2, p. 272 (Interview Report 2).

floor. There was an old iron bedstead propped up in the middle by two strips of wood and on this was a heap of grey and brown blankets. An ancient iron mangle stood in a corner and there was a gas stove, a gas mantle for lighting, three or four wooden chairs, and a table with a flat-iron propping up one of its legs. Miss Paley wore a pair of stockings, extensively patched and tied around her knees, and a ramshackle navy-blue skirt and slip. Her skin had the whiteness of someone who rarely went out and she was very shy of her appearance, particularly the open sores on her face. She said she suffered from blood poisoning, but had not seen her doctor since the war. (This was confirmed by the doctor.) She was the only child of parents who had been street traders and who had died when she was young, in the 1880s. 'I was with my aunt until I was nearly forty. She was eighty-five when she died. I had cousins in the street but they were my aunt's children. In the war they got scattered. They all had families to bring up and I haven't met them since the war. I don't know where they are. They had to leave me behind. I don't want them people. I do my work in my own way. They wouldn't have the patience with me.' Persistent questioning failed to reveal a single relative with whom she had any contact. She did not go to the cinema, to a club, or to church, and had no radio. She had spent Christmas on her own and had never had a holiday away from home. She sometimes made conversation with her neighbours in the street but because of her appearance did not go into their homes or they into hers. She had only one friend, a young woman who 'used to live in the street where I lived', and they visited one another about once a week. Her answer to a question about membership of a club was typical of much she said. 'No, I can't be shut in. I don't go to those clubs. They'd be too much excitement for me.' At one point she said she went to bed about 8 p.m. and got up between 10 and 11 the next day. I also found she had an hour or two in bed in the afternoons.

Mr Fortune, aged seventy-six, lived alone in a two-room council flat. There were two wooden chairs, an orange-box converted into a cupboard, a gas stove, a table covered with newspaper, a battered old pram with tins and boxes inside, a pair of wooden steps, and little else in the sitting-room. There was no fire, although the interview took place on a cold February morning. Mr Fortune had been a cripple from birth and he was partly deaf. He was unmarried and his five siblings were dead. An older widowed sister-in-law lived about a mile away with an unmarried son and daughter. These three and two married nieces living in another East London borough were seen from once a month to a few times a year. Asked how often he saw his sister-in-law Mr Fortune said, 'Only when I go there. It's a hard job to walk down there in winter time and I haven't seen her for three or four months.' Asked about an old people's club he said, 'No. I'm simply as I am now. I shouldn't like to join. Walking is such a painful job for me. I can't get any amusement out of it.' He spoke to one or two of the neighbours outside his flat but he had no regular contact with any of them. He had one regular friend, living a few blocks away, who came over to see him on a Sunday about once a month, 'more when there's fine weather'. He was not a churchgoer, never went to a cinema, rarely went to a pub because he could not afford a drink, had never had a holiday in his life, and spent Christmas on his own. 'My nephew came down for an hour. He gave me a little present, 2s. 6d. No, I didn't get any cards.' He received a non-contributory pension and supplementary assistance through the National Assistance Board, which recently arranged for him to have a woman home help for two hours a week. Her regular call was the main event of the week. 'I sit here messing about. Last week I was making an indoor aerial. I made those steps over there. I like listening to the wireless and making all manner of things. My time's taken up, I can tell you, with that and cooking and tidying-up.'

The most striking fact about the most isolated people was that they had few surviving relatives, particularly near-relatives of their own or of succeeding generations. This lent special significance to familiar references to fathers having weaker ties with children than mothers, to sons being drawn into their wives' families, and to distant relatives being lost sight of after the death of 'connecting' relatives. The isolated included a comparatively high number of unmarried and childless people, of those possessing sons but not daughters, and of those without siblings. Rarely did they have friends, become members of clubs, or otherwise participate in outside social activities in compensation. Nearly all of them were retired and most were infirm; some were shy of revealing to others how ill or poverty-stricken they were or how they had 'let themselves go'. They had little or no means of regular contact with the younger generation, and for one reason or another could not be brought into club activities.

Loneliness in Old Age

So far the circumstances of isolated people have been described without indicating how far they experienced feelings of loneliness.

One of the most striking results of the whole inquiry was that those living in relative isolation from family and community did not always say they were lonely.

Particular importance was attached during the interviews to 'loneliness'. The question was not asked until most of an individual's activities had been discussed and care was taken to ensure as serious and as considered a response as possible. One difficulty had to be overcome. A few people liked to let their children think they were lonely so the latter would visit them as much as possible. This meant they were not inclined to give an honest answer if children were present. In an early interview one married woman, asked whether she ever got lonely, said, 'Sometimes I do when they are all at work.' But she hesitated before answering and looked at two married daughters, who were in the room. On a subsequent call, when this woman was alone, she told me she was 'never lonely really, but I like my children to call'. A widow, who was alone when interviewed, said she was never lonely. In fascinating contrast to this was a statement of one of her married daughters, who was interviewed independently. 'She's not too badly off. The most she complains of is loneliness. She's always wanting us to go up there.' Care was therefore taken to ask about loneliness so far as possible when the old person was alone and to check any answer which seemed doubtful.

Some people living at the centre of a large family complained of loneliness and some who were living in extreme isolation repeated several times with vigour that they were never lonely – like Miss Paley and Mr Fortune, described above. The relation between isolation and loneliness is shown in Table 27. Despite there being a significant association about a half of the isolated and rather isolated said they were not lonely; over a fifth of the first group said they were.

What is the explanation? Previous investigations have pointed to the multiplicity of causes of loneliness. In his Wolverhampton study Sheldon showed that those experiencing loneliness tended to be widowed and single people, to be living alone, to be in their eighties rather than in their sixties, to be men rather than women, and to be the relatively infirm. There seemed to be no single cause of severe loneliness in old people. He concluded, 'Loneliness cannot be regarded as the simple direct result of social circumstances,

TABLE 27

SOCIAL ISOLATION AND LONELINESS

Old people saying they were	Old people who were			All old people
	Not isolated	Rather isolated*	Isolated*	
	%	%	%	
Very lonely	3	15	10	5
Sometimes lonely	18	41	30	22
Not lonely	79	44	60	72
Total	100	100	100	100
Number	156	27	20	203

* As defined in the previous table.

but is rather an individual response to an external situation to which other old people may react quite differently.' He added, in parenthesis, that the main exception to this statement was when the death of a spouse was recent.

In several respects the present inquiry reached similar results. Forty-six per cent of widowed people said they were very or sometimes lonely, forty-two per cent of those living alone, fifty-three per cent of those in their late seventies and eighties, and forty-three per cent of those who were infirm, compared with twenty-seven per cent in the sample as a whole. But it is possible that less emphasis should be given to personal differences and to a multiplicity of causes. The results also suggested that a single social factor may be fundamental to loneliness. This is the recent deprivation of the company of a close relative, usually a husband or wife or a child, through death, illness, or migration.

Recent Bereavement

Examination of individual interview-reports showed that of the fifty-six people saying they were very or sometimes lonely, twenty-eight had been recently bereaved and seventeen separated from children. This seemed to be the chief cause of their loneliness. A further eleven had experienced other drastic changes in family circumstances. It is necessary to consider these lonely people.

All but four of the twenty-eight who had been recently bereaved had lost a husband or wife within the previous ten years. 'No one knows what loneliness is till your partner happens to go.' 'You don't realize it until you know it. But loneliness is the worst thing you can suffer in life.' The men in particular talked about their bereavement with very deep feeling. 'I miss her. Every time I look over there – that's her seat. People kept telling me to have someone to look after me but I said to myself, there'll never be another woman who will take her place.' Three of them did not talk, they wept.

Mr Heart had lost his wife seven years earlier. He lived with an un-married son but he had no daughter. 'Sometimes I get lonely. I think of her. There's not a day passes but she's in my mind. When she died I don't know how I stood on my feet. You don't know what it is when you don't have a wife. . . . I wish I had a daughter. If you had a daughter it would put you in mind of your wife. Sometimes I think I hear her calling in the next room. She was what you call exceptional, exceptional good. You never had to run round any public house for her. My son still goes and puts flowers on her grave. . . . You can't tell how you miss someone until they go. Death's a terrible thing, to lose someone you love.'

One of the major consequences of a wife's death was that the man saw less of his children. He acknowledged it was the mother who held the family together. 'When my missus was alive I had to come and have tea in the bedroom because there wasn't room in here. The place was crowded out with them [married children and their families on Saturdays and Sundays.]' 'My daughters used to come round often when my wife was alive, but I don't see so much of them now. But they like to know I'm comfortable and being looked after.' Widowers in fact saw less of their children, particu-larly of their sons, than married men and married or widowed women, as judged by average frequency of contact. But this falling-off did not apply to all a widower's children. A close relationship with one child was usually maintained. Several lived with a single married daughter, or visited a married daughter daily, and then described the pleasure grandchildren gave them.[1] 'My young

1. Two of the diaries in Appendix 3 (James and Tulier) give a good idea of the activities of many retired widowers.

granddaughter likes swinging and I pick her up and she swings between my legs. And then she climbs up on me. Playing with my grandchildren is my greatest pleasure.' They found some consolation here. 'I'm a grandfather,' said one man, 'and that's the only goodness I get out of life.'

The loss of the marriage partner was not such a disaster for women. They had always depended less on husbands than husbands on them, and they found it easier to console themselves with their families. Nevertheless, many of them were lonely, particularly if their husbands had died recently and particularly if infirmity or shortage of relatives prevented them from finding comfort readily in the companionship of others. One woman's husband had died eight years previously. She had no children. 'I get so lonely I could fill up the teapot with tears.'

> Mrs Pridy was very infirm and her husband had died only a year previously, when she was eighty. She lived with a daughter and grandchildren. 'I sit here for hours and hours sometimes thinking about it. I get depressed and I start crying. We was always together. I can remember even his laughing. "Come on, girl," he'd say, "don't get sitting about. Let's liven 'em up." They say what is to be will be. I never thought he'd . . . But we've all got to go. A good many of them don't even know he's gone [neighbours]. I sit here for hours thinking about him. I can't get over it.'

Almost every man and woman whose husband or wife had died within the previous five years, compared with a half between five and ten years and a quarter over that limit, felt lonely. The shorter the period since the death the more likely were people to complain of loneliness. Although practically everyone felt lonely at first after about five or six years the presence or not of an affectionate family seemed to determine how long such feelings persisted.

Four people had lost a child and not a husband recently. Three were women widowed in the 1914 war who said a son had died in the previous few years. One had lost two sons in the 1939 war and another three years previously. 'I could cry my heart out sometimes when I sit here.' There was also a married woman whose only son had been killed at Arnhem in 1944. 'He's never out of my mind. I always see him in my mind and they're still talking about wars.' In speaking of the loss of children and other relatives it was notable how long people felt grief and how indelible was the memory of these people. The 'In Memoriam' column of a local East London newspaper provides many examples of the feelings of relatives for those who have died, some of them several years previously. In the following three illustrations, printed in 1955, only the names have been changed.

HOWARD – To the beautiful memory of my beloved daughter, Alice, who fell asleep June 17th, 1949.

> Time takes away the edge of grief,
> But memories turn back every leaf.
> Ever in our thoughts – Mum and all.

TALEWILL – In treasured memory of our dear Mum, who fell asleep June 7th, 1945.

> Not a day do we forget you, Mum,
> In our hearts you are ever near,
> Loved, remembered, longed for always,
> Bringing many a silent tear.
>> Sadly missed – Loving sons and daughters.

HUGGINS – In loving memory of a dear nephew who passed away June 6th, 1953.

> Sad and sudden was the call,
> To one so dearly loved by all,
> This month of June comes with regret,
> It brings back a tragedy we shall never forget.
>> – From Aunt Caroline, Uncle Bill, Uncle Herbert, Uncle Steve, and cousins Mary, Alice, and children.

Recent Separation

After bereavement, recent separation from children and grand-children was the most important reason for loneliness, affecting seventeen of the fifty-six people. Eleven of the seventeen had no contact with a child living in the district although recently at least one child had been there. What happened was that, if the last child to get married moved out of the district or was unable to find a home in it and there were no other children living nearby, the old person greatly missed their daily companionship, particularly if widowed. A further three old persons had a son living nearby but the daughters had recently moved away. And three widows who had been living with married children now lived alone, although some of their children still lived in the same district.

Mrs Marvel was eighty and she lived alone in a new council flat. Her husband had been dead for thirty years. None of her six surviving children lived in Bethnal Green although five of the six visited her regularly once or twice a week. A married daughter lived with her until she obtained a council house outside London five years previously. Mrs Marvel wanted to stay in the district where she had lived nearly all her life. Speaking of her former home, which was recently demolished, she said, 'We went in ten and came out one.' Later she said, 'I'm sometimes lonely, especially as my children are away. Still, I count my blessings. They're all good children.'

Mrs Foreman had been a widow for over thirty years. She had no daughters and until twelve months previously had been living with her married son. He had now moved to a new housing estate. Although she stayed with him every week-end she was lonely at home. 'I don't like coming back here. I get the hump.'

There remained eleven whose loneliness seemed to be due to other causes. All had recently experienced a marked change in their social circumstances. The husband of one and the daughter of another were in hospital, and had been there for some months. A third complained bitterly about the new council flat to which she had been moved a year previously; she was among neighbours she did not know or like and she was further from two of her relatives. Two married men were infirm and could not leave the house; both had retired within the past three years. A married woman had experienced several drastic changes in the past few years and was one of the most lonely of all those interviewed. As an extreme example, she is worth noting.

Mrs Austin, in her late sixties, lived in a council flat with her husband. She said she missed not having her seven children around her and that she was 'very lonely. I can't account for it at all. I get so depressed.' Five of the seven had married within a space of three years around 1950 and had left home one after another. All but two had moved to housing estates outside London or in other East London boroughs. These two lived about a mile away. One son, to whom she was particularly attached, had been killed in an accident several years previously. Soon after the children had married Mr and Mrs Austin had to leave their home, because it was to be demolished. 'I can't

settle here. I'd been over forty years in one house. Since it's been
pulled down and we've come here I've hardly spoken to my next-door
neighbours. All the old neighbours have gone. You can't go in and
out like you used to.' She saw much less of her children than formerly,
although her two youngest visited her twice a week and three of the
others once a fortnight. Her only sister had died three years ago.
Because of headaches she could no longer read and because of a fall
which damaged her hand she could no longer knit. Her husband had
been in ill-health for several years and was on bad terms with some of
the children. Mrs Austin had made two attempts at suicide and had
recently spent six months in a mental hospital.

In this example nearly all the disturbing social changes that can
occur in the life of an old person had occurred. Close relatives had
died, the children had migrated, the old home and neighbourhood
had to be given up and many activities had to be abandoned
because of increasing infirmity. This was desolation with a
vengeance. Now to be *desolate*, as defined earlier, is to have been
deprived recently of the companionship of someone who is loved.
And the main conclusion of this analysis is that people saying they
were lonely were nearly all people who had been deprived recently
of the companionship of someone they loved. They were *desolates*
and not necessarily *isolates*. They were isolated only in the sense
that they had *become* isolated, relative to their previous situation.
Many were not short of company. Several widowed people, in
particular, lived with children and grandchildren and had many
social activities.

The Hold on Life

We have seen that desolation, or the loss of someone who is loved,
is more important than social isolation in explaining the loneliness
of old people. Such a change may explain much more than loneliness, for it affects a person's health and whole state of mind. The
problems of the physical and mental health of old people need to
be studied against their known social condition and the sudden
changes in that condition. In Bethnal Green many people talked
of the drastic effects of retirement on men and of bereavement on
both men and women. Remarks about people who had just
retired or who had been recently widowed suggested they had less
will to live and deteriorated quickly. 'He didn't want to live any

more.' 'Men break up when they give up work. They soon go.' 'He just went to pieces when she died.' 'She was left all alone in the world and didn't want to go on living.' 'I've got nothing left to live for.' 'He won't be long in following her.' These remarks deserve careful attention. They imply the possibility of sudden physical degeneration, after retirement, for men, and after bereavement, for men and women.

While this is a very complex matter which cannot be discussed in detail here, three separate points seem to be worth making. The first concerns widows and widowers. The difficulties of old people in adapting themselves to new situations are well known. It may be particularly difficult for them to adjust their lives to the fact of bereavement. This is strongly supported by what they say about loneliness. The mortality rates for widowed old people tend to be higher than the rates for single and married people. This is shown by the statistics issued by the Registrar General. The rates for those widowed in old age may also be higher than for those widowed in middle age or youth – but statistical confirmation for this hypothesis seems to be lacking. Of course, if it were true it could in part be due to certain infections being passed on more easily in old age. On the face of it, however, the influence of recent bereavement may be worth careful study.

The second point concerns the higher death rates for older men than for older women. The differences between men and women may not be explained entirely by biological and physiological differences. Social factors may play a significant part here too. It was shown earlier, for example, that the man in Bethnal Green, on retirement, had to change virtually his whole style of living; he was deserted by workmates and friends and while he was thrown back on his family, he could rarely do other than play second fiddle to his wife. On the other hand his wife, to whom the affairs of household and family had always been dominant, could usually go on to a ripe old age doing most of the things she had always done. Sheldon observed that fewer women than men were in extreme good or ill health and while more of them had sub-normal health their hold on life was tenacious. The present limited findings, so far as they go, confirm his observation. It is possible that the effect of retirement on men and the greater security of women in job and family may contribute to the woman's longer expectation of life.[1] This complicated question cannot be entered into here: a plea is made only for further study of these social influences.

The third point in this matter of the effect of social factors upon health concerns social isolation. The trials and tribulations of old age may be harder for isolated people to bear, because they are not sustained by family and friends. A crude hypothesis may be put forward. Those who are socially isolated in old age, particularly those with the fewest contacts with relatives, tend to make greater claims on hospital and other health and social services and to die earlier than others.

Information concerning the first part of this hypothesis, on the social characteristics of old people making claims on the social services, will be considered in the next chapter. There is little information which will help in refining or confirming the second part, except that concerning deaths of unmarried and of married or widowed but childless people. Proportionately more single and childless people were found to be socially isolated in Bethnal Green; this is likely to be true elsewhere. In old age the death rates for bachelors are higher than those for married men but lower than those for widowers. The differences between single and married women seem to be very slight, except at the oldest ages. The subject is, however, very complex because of the influence of physical selection for marriage and of diseases associated with child-bearing, to say nothing of the changes in patterns of marriage. There has been a rise in marriage rates since 1939. As those who marry are likely, on average, to be in better health than the unmarried it seems that as the number of spinsters becomes progressively smaller, a higher proportion will have inferior vitality. Recent evidence has shown that death rates of single women, relatively to married women, have increased in the last twenty years. Safer child-bearing has also contributed to the relative improvement in the death rates of married women.

1. One interesting fact is that suicide rates increase much more quickly with age for men than for women. Sainsbury suggests this is partly due to the greater susceptibility of men to change and economic stress. He also pointed out that 'during the war, for example, when elderly men were able to obtain useful employment, the suicide rate among them fell more than that of younger men' (Sainsbury, P., *Suicide in London*, 1955, p. 81).

Even so, in a long analysis comparing the mortality of single and married women before the war, the Registrar General stated, 'It is difficult to escape the conclusion that in the present state of society the married condition *per se* for women is more favourable to vitality than the single condition at ages up to sixty.'

Other data concern the once-married but childless. Since 1938 information has been obtained, at the registration of deaths of women who were or had at any time been married, as to whether they had had children. The number of such children, and whether they were live or still-born, is not recorded. Infertility rates, derived from such information, are published from time to time. The infertility rates for older deceased widows are lower than those for older deceased married women. This 'unexpected' relationship, as it is described in the Statistical Review, may be due to a number of factors. One is that women with children may live longer, or may more often outlive their husbands, than childless women because the company of children helps them to keep a hold on life. All the available information about death rates is, however, rather scanty. None of it – so far as the writer is aware – allows any exact test of an association between death and social isolation or, more generally, any systematic study of the relation between longevity and social circumstances.

Some of these speculations may deserve further inquiry. Here it is suggested that the social and especially the family circumstances of individuals are a major determinant of the rate of decline in the power of self-adjustment and self-defence in later life. Broadly speaking there may be a marked association between each of three social factors, these being social isolation, social desolation, and retirement, and the expectation of life of old people. Biological, physiological, and health factors aside, one would expect, on the rather limited evidence from the present study, that old women and, to a lesser extent, old men who are at the centre of a secure family live longer than those who are socially isolated or desolated, particularly the latter.

The chief purpose of this chapter has been to distinguish between *isolates* and *desolates* in old age and show the importance of the distinction. Those who are secluded from family and society, as objectively assessed on the basis of defined criteria, are the isolates. Those who have been recently deprived by death, illness, or migration of the company of someone they love – such as a husband or wife or child – are the desolates. A major conclusion of the present analysis is that, though the two are connected, the underlying reason for loneliness in old age is desolation rather than isolation. The method of defining the isolates described above was to place those interviewed on a scale according to the number of social contacts they had. About a tenth had an average of only three social contacts a day or less; these were the most isolated, and they included a relatively high number of unmarried and childless people. The problems of such people seem to be acute and it has been suggested they are likely to make by far the greatest claim on the social services. This suggestion will now be examined; if it is true the implications for social policy are many.

CHAPTER 14

Who Claim State Care?

THE social and family circumstances of old people helped by the social services, particularly those entering institutions, have been attracting much attention from doctors, administrators, and research workers in recent years. By some they are said to be much more important than physical and medical conditions in explaining admissions to hospitals. Yet study of them has rarely been pressed beyond very general inquiry. It is the aim of this chapter to show how closer study helps us to understand the problems of old age more clearly. In examining the social characteristics of those making claims on the State we begin to recognize the practical problems of isolation.

Studies of the social background of those entering institutions have certainly grown in number in the last few years. In one, Lewis and Goldschmidt argued that social circumstances were a main cause of admissions to a mental hospital and that the failure to retain a place in the community and to be a member of a family was strongly detrimental to mental health. Roth and Morrissey stated that the differences in the social and the economic status of the old in America and in Britain may account for a much sharper rise in admission rates to American mental hospitals. Amulree and others have emphasized the importance to hospital authorities of knowing about the home circumstances of older patients and the availability of relatives. Graham and others have said that a long stay in hospital is often necessary for social rather than medical reasons. In a survey of hospitals in the Bristol region Hughes and Pugmire stated, 'We cannot divorce the social problem from the hospital problem; experience shows that elderly patients are rarely admitted to hospital for clinical reasons only.' Howell in fact presented evidence showing that some ninety per cent of people on the waiting list of a chronic sick hospital in Croydon needed admission for social as well as medical reasons. The Standing Medical Advisory Committee for Scotland have stated in a report, 'The problems of the medical care of the elderly

. . . are more domiciliary than institutional, and are more problems of social medicine and of medical administration than of clinical medicine.'

Much of the interest in the social causes of admission to hospitals has been stimulated by recent evidence of the striking differences in marital status between the hospital and the general population. Following a number of local studies, Abel-Smith and Titmuss were able to present comprehensive material. At the time of the 1951 Census two-thirds of hospital beds for the elderly were occupied by single and widowed or divorced people. Nearly seven per cent of single men aged sixty-five to seventy-four were in National Health Service hospitals, compared with nearly two per cent of widowers and one per cent of married men. There were also nearly four per cent of single women of that age in hospital, compared with just over one per cent of married and widowed women. 'Marriage and its survival into old age appears to be a powerful safeguard against admission to hospitals in general and to mental and "chronic" hospitals in particular.'[1]

Such evidence, important as it is, gives no more than a broad idea of some social causes. All the factors contributing to the isolation of the elderly have yet to be examined to see what effect they have on admission rates, among which, as was shown in the last chapter, are childlessness, living alone, lack of near relatives, and separation from them. In their study Abel-Smith and Titmuss remarked that in any interpretation of the hospital statistics by marital status 'in relation to the role of the family (and particularly the part played by surviving children of elderly hospital patients) it has to be borne in mind that no information whatever is available to show what proportion of married, widowed, and divorced people have children to whom they can turn for support'. They suggested that perhaps over half the adults in all hospitals were either childless or had no surviving children. 'The existence or otherwise of surviving husbands, wives, and children is perhaps the most important single social factor governing the amount and distribution by age and sex of demand for hospital care – particularly from the older age groups in the population.'[2]

1. Abel-Smith, B., and Titmuss, R. M., *The Cost of The National Health Service in England and Wales*, 1956, p. 71.

2. Op. cit., pp. 146–7.

In Bethnal Green it was hoped that an examination of a random sample of old people in family and community would throw up reasons why some rather than others had recourse to the social services, but this was recognized to be only one part of the story. Confirmation would have to be sought in local hospitals and residential Homes and at the headquarters of domiciliary services. Accordingly, information was collected from a local geriatric hospital, from the records of the L.C.C. about residential Homes, and from the local home help service. The object was to compare people claiming help from the State with a cross-section of those in the general population.

Old People in Hospital

The records of 304 people in a geriatric hospital near Bethnal Green were studied in the summer of 1955.[1] All but twenty-four of these people were of pensionable age. It was possible to establish their age, age at admission, marital status, next of kin, whether or not they had surviving children, whether or not they had been living alone prior to admission to hospital, and what district they came from. One in six had lived in Bethnal Green and most of the remainder in the neighbouring boroughs of Shoreditch, Finsbury, and Islington.

Compared with the local population, there were significantly more single and widowed or separated people in hospital. The great majority of people were, however, in their seventies and eighties and this partly, but not wholly, explains why the percentage of widowed was so high. There were relatively more men in hospital – thirty-eight per cent compared with thirty-one per cent. Women were older at admission than men, and single and widowed people, for both sexes, older than married people. Men with children were older at admission than men without children but women with and without children entered hospital on average at about the same age. Over fifty per cent of those of pensionable

1. I am indebted to St Matthew's Hospital, Finsbury, for access to these records. A full analysis of the previous social circumstances of the elderly patients could not be made, partly because information in the records about relatives was usually restricted to the names and addresses of children (sometimes not all of them if there were several) and/or next of kin, and partly because a number of the old people had been transferred from other institutions and their case-histories were sometimes incomplete.

age in the hospital had been living alone before admission. This compares with twenty-one per cent living alone in the Bethnal Green sample of people of pensionable age. As many as twenty per cent had no next of kin, or rather none were recorded.

The most striking fact about the hospital population was, however, the proportion of people married or widowed who had no surviving children. This was fifteen per cent of men and thirty-three per cent of women. By comparison only ten per cent of the married and widowed men in the general sample, and nine per cent of the women, had no surviving children. The greater difference for women is probably attributable to the fact that women are more secure in their families than men and are more likely to be nursed in illness by their children. Thus, relatively fewer of those with children and more of the childless entered hospital.

A second striking fact about the hospital population was the proportion with surviving sons rather than daughters. Thirty-three per cent of those with children had at least one son but no daughters, which compares with fourteen per cent of those in the general sample. Daughters often, but sons rarely, nurse old people at home and this probably explains why relatively more people with sons only entered hospital.

Before admission to hospital at least one-third had none of their children recorded as living in the same borough as themselves; only fifteen per cent in the Bethnal Green sample were similarly placed. This suggests that geographical separation from children may be a strong factor making it more likely for an old person to enter hospital. The hospital records of people with children also showed that some of the children suffered from ill-health. A few were noted as being in mental hospitals, or as being disabled, or suffering from TB. The children of some people were old age pensioners themselves and could no longer do heavy nursing.

The conclusion is that those admitted to a local geriatric hospital differed markedly from the general population of old people in their family and social circumstances. Apart from differences in marital status, which broadly confirm previous findings, there were three significant features of the family circumstances of those in hospital: (1) The unmarried and the childless formed forty-three per cent of the people in hospital, compared with eighteen per cent of people in Bethnal Green. (2) Only thirty-nine per cent

T–H

of the hospital population had surviving daughters, compared with seventy-one per cent outside. (3) A higher proportion of those in hospital had been geographically isolated from children when living at home. These conclusions apply only to one hospital for the chronic sick and require confirmation elsewhere, but on this showing marriage and the availability of children, particularly of daughters, is a strong protection against admission to hospital.

Old People in Residential Homes

In addition to the small-scale study of a local hospital a study was made of the reasons why old people sought admission to residential Homes (previously called 'institutions'). The object was to explore further the social influences on demand for institutional care. By the courtesy of the Chief Officer of the L.C.C. Welfare Department a random sample was drawn of the records of 203 people, previously living in east and south-east London, who had died in residential Homes.[1] Of the 203, 188 were of pensionable age on first admission, and the following analysis is concerned with these. The most useful records were the Admitting Officers' reports, which usually gave a brief summary of physical and social conditions as well as the reasons for application to enter a Home. The reports were based on a visit to each person's address. Some consisted largely of vague phrases like 'in need of care and attention' and 'unable to look after himself', and usually concentrated only on the home environment. Admitting Officers are not required to establish the whereabouts of all the children of old people, other than the next of kin, or to see whether any alternative to admission to a Home could be arranged within the family. Thus, for the purposes of the study, while it was possible to ascertain some facts about children it was not possible to gain full information.[2]

1. A random selection was made from the records of those previously living in Bethnal Green and in neighbouring boroughs, who had died in L.C.C. residential Homes between 1948 and 1955. Homes for the blind and for mothers and babies, hostels, and reception centres were excluded, as were voluntary establishments. In intention at least, the large and small Homes from which the cases were drawn are now reserved for the old and infirm.

2. The records contain, however, much illuminating case-evidence about the problems of admitting old people to residential Homes and caring for them. They contain first-hand evidence of the changes in the method and administration of Homes after the introduction of the 1948 legislation.

The 'immediate' causes of admission to Homes, as indicated by the records, varied widely. The people could be grouped in the following broad categories. In each category infirmity usually played some part. There were (1) those who lived alone and had no resources to meet growing infirmity; (2) those who had lost former accommodation, because of eviction by an unsympathetic landlord, because relatives moved to a new home or needed more space for growing children or for nearer relatives, or because of quarrels with in-laws; (3) those who had lost relatives who supported them, usually by death but sometimes because prior claims had been placed on the relative; (4) those depending on a relative who was now infirm or ill.

The sample of people who had entered residential Homes contained more men than women and was made up largely of the unmarried and widowed. Thirty-five per cent of the men were single, compared with fourteen per cent of the women; but sixty-one per cent were widowed or separated, compared with eighty-three per cent. Nearly two-thirds of both men and women had been living alone before admission. As many as twenty-three per cent had no next of kin, or none recorded. Written across many records were the words: 'no relatives, no friends'. These old people had been living in extreme isolation. For example, there were several bachelors, disclaiming relatives or friends, who had spent the last part of their lives moving from one Salvation Army Hostel or Rowton House to another. Sometimes they had been refused admission to a hostel, because they were incapable of caring for themselves any longer.

A very high proportion of the married and widowed had no surviving children, twenty-eight per cent of men and forty-six per cent of women. As many as thirty-eight per cent of those with children, so far as could be ascertained from the records, had sons but not daughters. Many had become separated from their children before admission but the incompleteness of some records did not allow their number to be established precisely.

Before 1948, the test of admission was homelessness and destitution. But with the abolition of the Poor Law, the L.C.C. decided to admit people to public Homes mainly on grounds of infirmity and absence of adequate care, others being supported at home by a combination of national assistance and domiciliary services. On this account, it is possible the characteristics of those in old people's residential Homes are gradually changing.

It was the most solitary who first sought admission, particularly men. The average man was $77\frac{1}{2}$ upon admission, the woman $80\frac{1}{2}$. Single and childless people had a lower average age on admission than those with surviving children. The isolated bachelor had the fewest resources to meet the onset of infirmity. Men who had lost, or never had, or become separated from wives and children seemed to be less able to support an independent life than women in these circumstances. Even when men had children the tie seemed to be less strong than between a woman and her children. A much higher proportion of men than of women with children had entered residential Homes. The woman with children, particularly if she had daughters and if she lived with them or near them, ran the least risk of entering a public home in old age.

The conclusion is that, compared with the elderly patients in a local geriatric hospital, old people in residential Homes differed even more markedly from the general population in their family and former social characteristics. There were five significant features of this group: (1) there were relatively more men than women, even though infirmity is more prevalent among older women than among older men in the general population; (2) there was a particularly high proportion of single men; (3) fifty-four per cent were unmarried or childless, compared with eighteen per cent of the general population; (4) it seemed that thirty-eight per cent of those with children had sons but not daughters, compared with fourteen per cent outside; (5) many more people had been separated from their children before admission than was the case among people living at home in Bethnal Green.

One of the most important findings of this small-scale study of old people who had been in residential Homes was the early death of a large proportion. Over eight per cent had died within a month of admission, and forty-four per cent within a year. In the case-reports it was interesting to observe that on admission there was often no remark about people's ill health, yet they died shortly afterwards. The relationship between the hold on life and residence in a Home merits close study.

Old People Served by Home Helps

Finally, by courtesy of the L.C.C. Divisional Medical Officer, a survey was made of the records of all old people being visited by home helps in Bethnal Green in the winter of 1955–6.[1] Altogether 464 people of pensionable age were then being visited, or had been visited recently, by a home help.[2] This was just under six per cent of those of pensionable age in the borough.[3] All but a small minority were visited once a week, usually for two or three hours, and mainly to be helped with their cleaning. Fifty-four per cent lived alone, compared with twenty-one per cent of the random sample interviewed in the borough. Most of the others were married couples.

Single people made a demand roughly proportionate to their numbers in the population, but relatively more widowed and fewer married people claimed help. Thirty-five per cent of the men being helped, and sixty-seven per cent of the women, were widowed or separated, compared with twenty-six per cent and fifty-one per cent respectively in the local population. Probably because there were fewer single or widowed men in the population than women, relatively fewer men sought domestic help. Only twenty-seven per cent of those claiming such help were men, compared with thirty-one per cent in the borough population as a whole.

In other respects those aided by the domestic help service differed in their family characteristics from the general elderly population, though not so strikingly as those in hospital and in residential Homes. Twenty per cent of the married and widowed had no surviving children, compared with ten per cent in the Bethnal Green sample. Of those with children as many as twenty-three per cent had surviving sons but not daughters, compared with fourteen per cent in the general population. As many as forty-four per cent had no child in the borough, compared with

1. I am particularly indebted to Dr G. O. Mitchell and to Mrs Kenworthy, the area organizer, and her staff. Mrs Kenworthy went to great trouble to check the records.

2. It should be noted that the number of people stated as served by the home help service is higher than the number visited in any one week. Some people were still on the 'active' list although not being visited, because they were temporarily in hospital or on holiday or had found substitute help for a period. The figures are derived from this list.

3. In the country as a whole the proportion of old people served by the domestic help service is about two per cent. The service has developed much more quickly since 1948 in some areas than others, particularly urban areas.

fifteen per cent. Separation from children, particularly from daughters, obviously had a marked influence on applications for the services of a home help.

Family and State

The conclusions from this analysis fit in very well with some of the conclusions from the intensive Bethnal Green study, though it is important to make the reservation that they depend on information which is rather limited in extent and depth. They suggest a consistent picture. Old people who make claims on the institutional and domiciliary services of the State seem to form a very unrepresentative group. Compared with the population at large many more live alone; more of them are unmarried, more are childless, more have sons but not daughters, and more are separated from daughters when they have them.

The two inescapable conclusions seem to be that (1) old people, particularly women, with daughters and other female relatives living near them make least claim on the services of the State, and (2) isolated old people make disproportionately heavy claims. People who need help with their shopping and cleaning or need nursing because they are infirm or ill are most likely to get it at home if a daughter lives with them or nearby: if the daughter lives some distance away there is less chance of getting it. As the variations in family circumstances are followed through – to those with sons and daughters-in-law but not daughters, to the childless, and finally to the unmarried, especially those having no siblings – the availability of family help diminishes and claims on the social services increase. This is largely what one would expect from the interviews with people in their homes in Bethnal Green; and this is largely what the data about the social services seem to confirm. On the whole women are better off than men, but the picture is slightly confused. More of the men are married; up to a point their wives can look after them. This explains why fewer men, on the whole, are aided by the domiciliary services. But single or widowed men are less likely than women to get support from relatives once they become infirm, and widowers, at least, are less capable of maintaining an independent life. Proportionately more men than women, therefore, seek institutional care from local councils or the State.

CHAPTER 15

Keeping the Family Together

Two of the most important conclusions to emerge from the last two chapters are, first, that old people with daughters and other female relatives living near them make least claim on health and welfare services, and second, that isolated people make disproportionately heavy claims. There would be many consequences for social policy if these conclusions could be confirmed in detail elsewhere. About three per cent of old people in Great Britain are cared for in institutions, most of them being infirm or ill. It is likely that for every one of these there are a further three or four at home who, but for the care given them by relatives and friends living with them or nearby, would justify admission to a hospital or residential Home. Detailed investigation of the Bethnal Green sample suggested that between five per cent and ten per cent might have required hospital care but for the help of families and friends. A further five to ten per cent, while not justifying admission to hospital, might have justified admission to a residential Home because they could not have cared for themselves if relatives and friends had not been available.

Reference to domiciliary services tells much the same story. About two per cent of old people in the country are aided by the home help service. In many urban areas, where the service is better developed, the percentage is higher. Even so, although as much as six per cent of the Bethnal Green sample had their cleaning done by a home help, forty-three per cent were helped by relatives and another eight per cent by neighbours or friends.[1] This gives a rough indication of the relative importance of family and non-family. Much the same appears to be true of other services. Indeed the coverage of domiciliary services often tends to be exaggerated. For example, in a recent study in another London borough it was stated that 19,053 meals were served in the course of a year by the mobile meals services. This figure becomes less

1. See pp. 60-1.

impressive when one recognizes it is equivalent to one meal each day for fifty-two people.

While these comparative figures of the care of the old by family and community services are imprecise, they compel reflection. They remind us that the family has the care of a far larger number of the infirm aged and chronic sick than all our hospitals, residential Homes, and domiciliary services put together. They remind us of the need to maintain the family ties of those entering institutions so that they shall be able to return to their homes as soon as possible. And they remind us of the value, if only in terms of cost to the State, of keeping the family together or finding substitutes for it as a means of reducing demand on institutions. It would be ironical if the State, through housing and other policies, separated individuals from their kin and thus made more professional services necessary.

Housing Policy for Families

These general reflections require closer study. It is not enough to say it should be the object of policy to keep the family together, to give it practical help, and to find a substitute for it when necessary. What do these aims involve? In the first place they involve reconsideration of housing policy. Again and again in this report, in discussing the family system of care, the stresses of infirmity, and the problems of retirement, poverty and institutional care, we have seen the value to old people of relatives, particularly daughters, living close at hand. People made repeated references to housing problems during the interviews. This was even more of a preoccupation than income. Sometimes they spoke of peculiarly local conditions but more often of matters common to many parts of the country. Their main concern was to live near members of their families. The following examples illustrate the kind of things they said.

> Mr Bridger lived with his wife and single daughter in a terraced cottage. 'We don't want to move away from here. These building improvements split 'em all up [families]. We might have to move anywhere. We might have to go to Harlow and the sister round the corner to Hainault. That's what old people don't like, to be put down among people you don't know.'

> Mrs Shadrap lived with her husband in a terraced house adjoining

one occupied by her two sisters. 'We've got to move. These places are going to come down. They wrote to us a few months back and offered us Aveley. I wrote back the next day saying that we didn't want to go out of Bethnal Green. We'd like a little house and wouldn't like rooms but I suppose you can't get that now. I don't want to go out of Bethnal Green because I would miss my sisters. That's why. My sisters help in case of illness. When my girl was ill I don't know how I would have managed without them.'

Mrs Harrington now lived with her husband in a new L.C.C. flat. Only two of her ten surviving children were in Bethnal Green. She was moved because of demolition. 'My daughter got moved out to Chingford when we came here. I'd have liked to have gone with her – and I'd have been company for her. Her husband works in the docks and often he's not home till 9 or 10 at night. But the housing people just said my daughter wanted a place on her own and didn't ask us.' (The daughter's children used to spend most of the school holidays with their grandmother.)

Recent clearance schemes made it harder than ever for married children to find a home in the borough. Moreover, an extended family in one or more households was usually unable to move *en bloc* to a new district. Relatives often went to extraordinary lengths to live near one another, repeatedly visiting the local housing offices and arranging 'exchanges' with third parties.[1] In one way or another isolation from kin was often avoided. Nevertheless thirty examples of involuntary separation arose in the course of interviewing the 203 people in the sample.

People objected to present housing policy and, more specifically, housing clearance schemes, not only because they were often threatened with separation from their families but also because they were usually obliged to move from the district in which they had spent most or all of their lives and to leave a house or part of a house for a flat in a large block. 'They put you where they like to put you. It's not right. They take you away from the neighbourhood you're used to and put you in a neighbourhood you're not used to and where you can't settle down. We are comfortable here. I don't want to go out to Poplar or Higham's Park or somewhere. This L.C.C. is going a bit too far.'

Again and again people objected to flats, and some of the most

1. See p. 46.

forceful criticisms came from people who lived in the newest. One married woman living in a new L.C.C. flat with an unmarried daughter kept returning to the same theme, 'I get so depressed here. It's worse than illness, being shut up in these flats all day. I'll tell you for why. Everyone wants a certain amount of companionship. But here it's like a prison. There's no outlook. . . . When you look out all you see are those ruins opposite [the next block in the new estate]. There are people from all over the place here. From Wapping and Shadwell and all over. You couldn't even talk to them. . . . We came into here and thought we were going to be happy, but there's no happiness here.' Some argued that many of the houses being cleared were in good condition or could be put into good condition cheaply. Men in particular disliked the loss of a yard or garden. Others said that much open space around blocks of flats was quite wasted. They could not understand why so few houses were built. Significantly, of those living in council flats (mostly built just before or after the Second World War) thirty-three per cent said 'yes' in answer to the question 'do you want to move?', compared with fifteen per cent living in old terraced cottages. Thirty-nine people, or nineteen per cent of the whole sample, lived in the former, and seventy-one, or thirty-five per cent, in the latter.

Although some of the houses being demolished under clearance schemes are obviously unfit, many are in a reasonable state of repair or could be put into good repair at small cost. Were they in wealthier boroughs, such as Hampstead or Chelsea, there is little doubt they would be preserved and converted. While it is impossible here to discuss the complex issues which housing authorities have to face, it is, on the basis of experience in Bethnal Green, worth asking what seem to be the crucial questions. How much old housing could be economically preserved? How far are clearance schemes separating people involuntarily from their relatives and friends? How far could the movement out to new housing estates in the suburbs be *reduced* by making better use of space inside the city – building and converting small houses? And how far are more flats being built than need to be, in view of the overwhelming evidence of people's preference for small houses with yards or gardens?

Wherever possible, old people should, if they have to be moved at all, be moved near relatives. It is not enough to experiment with special housing for the old – by providing, for example, groups of bungalows or one-room self-contained flats at ground-floor level – if the people going to live there have no links with the community around them. The social group is more important than the physical surroundings and every effort should be made to preserve it. This is as important for young as for old. If children continue to be moved to new housing estates on their own we shall be depriving ourselves of the principal support for the elderly and inevitably producing grave new problems and incurring new costs of unknown dimensions.

Supporting the Family

The principle we have been developing is one of preventing old people from unnecessarily becoming wards of the State, by making it as easy as possible for them to be cared for in their own homes by their own relatives. We have seen that the most general method of putting this into effect is by means of housing policy. The more people can be rehoused near relatives and friends, the fewer social casualties there will be. But there are other means than prevention. The family itself needs direct support in various ways.

The bedfast and homebound suffer from lack of occupation and need work and interests in their own homes. As for physical discomfort, this can often be eased if people have sufficient money to pay for extra laundry, bed-linen, fuel and light, special meals, chemists' goods of various kinds, and domestic services.[1] Many of them, in particular, like to repay relatives and friends for kindnesses. The National Assistance Board sometimes makes discretionary additions of a few shillings for laundry, domestic help, or special diet but the amounts are usually very small and people not drawing assistance are not entitled to them. War and disablement pensioners with one hundred per cent disability allowances are allowed to claim a 'constant attendance allowance' from the Ministry of Pensions if they need regular personal attendance.[2]

1. See Chapter 12, pp. 177–83.
2. About 10,000 were paid in 1955 to war pensioners and 1,000 to disablement pensioners (*Report of the Ministry of Pensions and National Insurance for the year 1955*).

The amounts usually vary from about 10s. to 30s., though sometimes they are higher. This allowance might be extended to severely disabled or bedfast retirement pensioners to enable them to be more financially independent and secure. They would be better placed to repay a relative for the care given.

The relatives themselves may sometimes experience great strain. Earlier we saw that thirteen per cent of those in the sample of old people were imposing strain on their relatives, some of it severe.[1] Most of these were bedfast or housebound and some had only one person available to look after them. Lists of such infirm people are sometimes kept by local authorities but efforts to complete the lists and bring them up to date are rarely made. It should perhaps be one of the duties of each local home help service, working with local authorities, doctors, and others, to keep in being a full list of all housebound old people, whether or not they are aided by the social services. This might provide the basis for a comprehensive domiciliary service helping the family. People could be visited from time to time by welfare workers working in close cooperation with general practitioners. The link with the family doctor may well be essential to the success of such an enterprise. If mental or physical deterioration is to be fought effectively and without delay and if relatives are to be given as much assistance as possible before disability, incontinence, or eccentricity defeat them, then the more contacts with families undergoing strain the better. It could, for example, be a recognized object of the service to relieve hard-pressed relatives by providing substitute help for one evening a week or for a holiday period. Night-sitters could be provided at times of great stress and perhaps temporary accommodation could be found for relatives who want to help but live too far away. At present home help services can rarely provide for much more than two hours' cleaning a week.

The service could be of even greater value to people with no relatives or friends to depend on for help. As Sheldon says, these elderly isolates 'form the hard core of the nursing and domestic problem of old age. Their precise numbers are impossible to determine but they form a group of considerable size'.[2] Despite an expansion in local services, it is undoubtedly true that they do not

1. See p. 73.
2. Sheldon, J. H., 'The Social Philosophy of Old Age', 1954.

reach all the isolates; many have to manage on their own. For a variety of reasons, fear of being made to leave their homes, shyness, shame of their appearance and of their possessions, they put off visiting doctors or social workers and shrink from joining clubs. Day by day they deteriorate until maybe a neighbour sees a bottle of milk standing on the doorstep hours after it has been delivered, makes inquiries, and sends for an ambulance. In Bethnal Green, despite the work of local authority, National Assistance Board, and voluntary organizations, such people were found to be living in conditions of strain and misery with practically no aid from any quarter. They made no attempt to join a club.

Of all the aged, the isolates are most in need of regular visiting. An attempt to meet this need might well be the most rewarding measure that could be undertaken in preventive social medicine. The chief problem is one of locating the people, and the logical step may be to devise a means of compiling a full list of the isolated and handicapped old in each local community. This list might be maintained, as already indicated, by an expanded local home help service which undertook visiting.[1] In principle at least it should also be possible, in cooperation with the Ministry of Pensions, for each new widowed or unmarried pensioner to be visited. In an area the size of Bethnal Green, this would probably mean visiting 200–300 people in the course of a year. Of these perhaps eighty to ninety per cent would not need another visit for a year or two, because of their security in their families. In time a list of from ten to twenty per cent of the retired population would be built up. Such a list might comprise, again taking the example of Bethnal Green, some 600–1,200 old persons. The combined resources of local authorities and voluntary organizations would not be stretched unduly in ensuring that these people were regularly called upon and their needs met by the appropriate services. As we saw earlier in discussing the role of neighbours and friends, substitutes are sometimes accepted by those without families. With imagination the life of the elderly community could be greatly improved. One hopeful experiment is the boarding-out of isolated

1. A recent official inquiry into the role of Health Visitors recommended that their work for the aged should be widened in accordance with the National Health Service Act of 1948. This might be done in liaison with existing home help services. See *An Inquiry Into Health Visiting*, 1956.

people.[1] Another, already tried in many areas, is the conversion of a large house or a row of houses into one- and two-room flats with an elderly woman as warden or housekeeper on call.[2] Such measures might become more general.

Such a method of looking after the welfare of the old would require detailed investigation and experimentation. But we so keenly need services to prevent and not only to treat the sufferings of the old which are capable of adjusting flexibly to different social and physical requirements that it is hard to escape the conclusion that nothing less than a comprehensive family help service of such a kind will suffice.

Institutions without Walls

In developing these ideas about support for the family and finding a substitute for it when necessary, it is natural to ask at what stage people should be admitted to institutions. This question has become increasingly difficult to answer in recent years because we have begun to realize there is no natural division of the elderly into a home and an institutional population. The move of expert opinion towards smaller Homes with private rooms and hospitals with smaller wards, the continuing argument about who takes the responsibility for admissions, the gradual realization that the hospital problem is more social than clinical, even the greater variety of colour and setting and the more generous visiting hours – all these are perhaps indications of a fundamental change of outlook in recent years. It is increasingly realized that life in institutions cannot be separated from life outside. It is no longer (if ever it was) efficient or economical to keep the two distinct.

Only in this way can we explain many profitable experiments that have been going on in recent years, such as the day hospital at Oxford, the 'half-way' Homes in London and elsewhere, such as those financed by the King Edward's Hospital Fund, the consultative health centre at Rutherglen, and the integrated mental

1. A boarding-out scheme for elderly people in Exeter, supervised by the local Council of Social Service, has been running for several years (*Manchester Guardian*, 26 November 1954). Another has been running successfully in Hampshire.

2. Examples of particularly successful ones can be found in Salford and Liverpool (*The Times*, 12 March 1956). Also in Bermondsey, London (*Manchester Guardian*, 30 April 1956).

health service at Nottingham. Opinion is moving in favour of greater flexibility in provision for the elderly, more home-like surroundings in all kinds of institutions, more interchange between home and hospital, readier access by relatives, and more domiciliary services on call.

Yet despite the swing of opinion physical and administrative change is slow to follow. There are still too many large Homes built and maintained like barracks, and too many small ones with unjustifiably high standards of admission. As Vine says, for many welfare Homes 'the broad criteria of admission are "ambulant and able to manage stairs, of good behaviour, able to feed and dress themselves, and continent". It is rather like looking for the finer points at a cattle market.'[1] In too few hospitals do the staff make it their job to acquaint themselves fully with the social background of their patients, even though they agree that the hospital problem is as much social as clinical.

Lack of familiarity with the social background of residents or patients is probably the main reason why change is so slow and why there is not more flexibility in residential Homes as well as hospitals. In connexion with the present inquiry visits were paid to different hospitals and residential Homes in England which showed that, because of lack of recognition of the importance of family life, or because of oversights on the part of hard-pressed staff, or simply because of errors in recording next of kin, the existence of close relatives was sometimes unknown. Essential facts went unrecorded. It seemed to be too difficult to cope with people's families as well as people themselves. Some who were actually being visited by relatives were recorded as having none. This was not known to the staff, or only came to their attention months later, and even then some case-reports went uncorrected. It was said the existence of members of the family was not revealed for fear a charge would be levied upon them. Even if true this statement does not seem to suggest the old people had much confidence in the institutions they entered. On a few case-reports a relative was recorded as having paid for a funeral when all other entries reported 'no relatives'. One showed that three different officials had on three separate occasions visited a wrong address; the error had not been corrected.

1. Vine, S. M., 'Clinical Pitfalls in the Elderly', 1955.

All these instances arose only from a few scattered inquiries, but they suggest there may be a need for a searching investigation of the facts about admission to institutions. They may or may not be symptomatic of an important defect in institutional care, that people may be treated too often as cases in beds and not as being also members of a family and of a community. The failure to take proper account of a person's social and family background may sometimes have serious consequences, especially when people transfer from one institution to another within a short period. In the sample study of those entering L.C.C. residential Homes, described in the previous chapter, the number transferred from a hospital to such a residential Home, and then to another residential Home, was large; some had as many as five, six, or seven changes in two or three years. People in an advanced state of physical or mental infirmity may often reach institutions with case-reports which explain little about them and which often go unchecked because so little time elapses before their next move. One suspects that too many of the aged in institutions are unidentified; their ties with the community have been broken and it is no one's job to preserve or repair them. It is no surprise to read occasionally in the medical press of complaints of listless and degenerating residents of residential Homes who are 'content to sit thoughtless, despondent, and inactive all day long, the only interruption to their monotony being mealtimes'; or of hospitals which neglect the social problems of their patients.

What emerges from this brief discussion is the need for a consistent policy of maintaining old people's ties with family and community and of recreating in institutional life as much of the life of home and family as possible. There may be a need for a comprehensive family help service providing support and substitute help when necessary. One of its jobs would be to experiment with alternatives to institutional care – boarding-out the isolated, transforming old houses into self-contained one-room flats with housekeepers in charge, and finding nearby accommodation for relatives. Such a service could supply useful information to hospitals and residential Homes which admit elderly people and could provide an important link between hospital and family, facilitating an early return home. The institutions themselves need to take careful note of information about *all* the children and other near-relatives of the people they admit, to place people as near as possible to their home districts, and, by encouraging and acting through those who visit them, to preserve old people's contacts with relatives and friends.

The underlying assumption of this discussion is that the social services could not and should not replace the family. They could not, because, as we have seen, the burden they would have to carry would be impossibly large. They should not, because the deepest attachments of most people are to their families. This is particularly true of the old. The plain fact is that nearly all old people prefer to be looked after by members of their families even when seriously ill. During the interviews in Bethnal Green people repeatedly expressed the fixed desire to spend the final days of life at home. The widowed sometimes spoke of dying husbands or wives who had implored them not to fetch an ambulance. Many spoke of their relief at not having 'others' to look after them. One woman said, 'Nurses haven't the touch of your own'. Another needed nursing after a severe operation in hospital. For a few days a district nurse had called. 'I was really better off without her. I had my daughter and she's taken a month off work.' This sentiment was echoed by several other people who had been able to do without help from local services.

Neither is there much hard evidence of neglect on the part of old people's children. This is the conclusion of other field inquiries besides the present one. Following a survey of some 1,100 households assisted by the domestic help service in the London boroughs of Lewisham and Camberwell, themselves forming a special problem group, it was said that, 'In those instances where relatives existed but gave no assistance, inquiries were made as to the reason for this failure to help. Nearly one-third of these relatives lived too far away, one-tenth were too preoccupied with their own affairs, and one-twentieth were ill or too old. Only a dozen of them could but would not help.' Widespread fears of the breakdown of family loyalties and of married children's negligence seem to have no general basis in fact. Doctors, social workers, and others who express such fears may sometimes forget they are in danger of generalizing from an extremely untypical sub-section of the population or from a few extreme examples known personally to them. And the fact that these fears have been expressed by one generation after another inclines one to be sceptical. Helen Bosanquet wrote in 1906, 'Every generation, I suppose, has its complaint to make of the one which is to succeed it, and we must not attach too much weight to the grumblings of those who see a general falling-off since the days when *they* were young. But there is one complaint which is almost universal, and which does seem to touch a somewhat unlovely characteristic of the present day. I refer to the accusation that there is among the children a prevailing and increasing want of respect towards their elders, more especially, perhaps, towards their parents.'[1] In this context it is perhaps important to note Titmuss's finding, that so far as can be ascertained, 'the proportion of people aged over sixty-five accommodated in hospitals and institutions of all kinds is lower today than it was when the Royal Commission on the Poor Laws reported in 1909'.[2]

So far at least as the old are concerned, therefore, there is no justification for an attempt to supplant the family with State services. Their job is to support the family and provide substitute help when it no longer exists. This chapter has put forward a few suggestions of how this can be achieved and, in doing so, has gone somewhat further than previous parts of this report in discussing the general implications of the purely local findings of this study in East London. Giving priority to the wishes of relatives to live near one another in extended families when allocating housing; incorporating the existing home help service within a new, comprehensive family help service which has the special task of caring for the isolated and handicapped old and giving support to their families; providing 'constant attendance' allowances for the bedfast and housebound; and bringing institutions more into the life of the community, by varying their character and introducing more features of home and family life – these are the main suggestions put forward. The general principle we have developed has been to prevent old people from needlessly becoming wards of the State, by helping them to be cared for in their own homes and, wherever possible, by their families.

1. Bosanquet, H., *The Family*, 1906, p. 310.
2. Titmuss, R. M., 'Some Fundamental Assumptions', a paper in *Old Age in the Modern World*, London, 1955, p. 48.

CHAPTER 16

Conclusion

THE general conclusion of this book is that if many of the processes and problems of ageing are to be understood, old people must be studied as members of families (which usually means extended families of three generations); and, if this is true, those concerned with social and health administration must, at every stage, treat old people as an inseparable part of a family group, which is more than just a residential unit. They are not simply individuals, let alone 'cases' occupying beds or chairs. They are members of families and whether or not they are treated as such largely determines their security, their health, and their happiness.

In the first part of the book, which is wholly sociological, we saw how the extended family was the dominant interest of most old people in the London borough of Bethnal Green; in the second, we examined the social problems of old age in the light of this knowledge and considered, with extreme brevity, some of the implications for policy. The aim has been to derive practical recommendations for policy from sociological evidence. An attempt has been made to follow this principle explicitly, with the express reservation that a book like this which is largely a field report obviously cannot deal in any comprehensive way with all the various political, administrative, and legal questions involved in assessing policy.

We started by asking how far in fact old people were isolated from family life, and found that they often lived with relatives but preferred a 'supported' independence. Those not sharing their homes rarely lived alone in a literal sense. Three generations of relatives were generally distributed over two or more households near one another and old people had very close ties with their families. Those interviewed had an average of thirteen relatives within a mile and they saw three-quarters of all their children, both married and unmarried, once a week, as many as a third of them every day. We found old people getting a great deal of help, regularly and in emergencies, from their female relatives, particularly their daughters, living in neighbouring streets. The remarkable thing was how often this help was reciprocated – through provision of midday meals, care of grandchildren, and other services. The major function of the grandparent is perhaps the most important fact to emerge from this book. If confirmed elsewhere we may have to re-examine many of our ideas about the family, child-rearing, parenthood, and old age.

An individual's loyalties to the closely-knit group of relatives of three generations were potentially in conflict with those to his or her spouse. We found, in discussing first the economy of the home, and then the relationships with married children, how such conflict was reduced or regulated by marked segregation between man and wife in their financial and domestic roles, and by individual, rather than joint, associations with blood relatives. It was also reduced by acknowledgement of the special bond between grandmother, daughter, and daughter's child and of the pre-eminent place of the old 'Mum' in the family. All this helped to explain how the extended family was kept in being through time. Finally, in discussing relationships between parent and child, grandparent and grandchild, and one sibling and another over the course of individual life we saw the importance of the principles of replacement and compensation as applied to the family. An individual's relationships adjusted to variations in family composition. Sons took over part of the role of the father after the mother was widowed. When people had sons but not daughters they saw more of daughters-in-law, and when they had no children they saw more of siblings and nephews and nieces. Some without families tended to attach themselves to a friend's family. The functional or structural principles on which the extended family was based could therefore be summed up as those of continuity of membership through individual life; unity between grandmother, daughter, and grandchild; reciprocation of domestic and personal services between members; replacement of, or compensation for, lost or non-existent members; segregation between man and wife in financial, domestic, and family roles, and reserve between parent and child-in-law. Application of these principles allowed different interests, needs, and satisfactions to be judiciously composed.

The three-generation extended family, then, provided the normal environment for old people. By comparison with its ties of blood, duty, affection, common interest, and daily acquaintance we found that the ties of friendship, neighbourliness, and club and church membership were neither so enduring nor so indissoluble. Most people were very restrained in their relationships with neighbours; not many had even one close friend outside the family. The network of kinship supplied many links with the community but allowed few close friends. Moreover, in old age non-family activities diminished. Friends died or passed out of knowledge, money was shorter, and it was more difficult to get about.

These findings do not mean the course of ageing always ran smooth. They rather provided a frame of reference for assessing the problems of age. As Part Two showed, the fact that the old grandmother was usually such a dominant figure helped to explain why retirement was a particularly tragic event for most men, because they could not find much to justify their existence. The adjustment was all the greater because of the sharp fall in income which most people suffered upon giving up work – a fall of over two-thirds for single people and a half for married people. Even this does not take account of wives themselves giving up work or men taking a lighter job at lower pay in the years immediately preceding final retirement. Previous customs of life were hard to maintain, especially for the men, despite help from children and payments for family services.

The poorest people, not only financially, were those without an active family life. They had fewest resources in time of need. Yet many of them denied they were lonely, and in examining the reasons for this, a distinction was drawn between *isolates* and *desolates*. The hypothesis put forward was that desolation rather than isolation was the fundamental cause of loneliness in old age. Elderly isolates seemed likely to make disproportionately heavy claims on health and welfare services. A supplementary investigation of a geriatric hospital, of residential Homes, and of a local domiciliary service in fact showed this to be so. People with daughters at hand made least claim of all.

But for the care given by female relatives the number of old people seeking admission to hospitals and residential Homes would have been from three to five times greater. This estimate gives some idea of the extent of care undertaken by the family; it also reminds us of the amount of incapacity and ill health among the old. Two-fifths of the sample were infirm (or bedfast) or living with a husband or wife who was infirm. A third had had a spell as a hospital in-patient within the previous five years. One in eight were imposing strains on their relatives at the time of interview. Yet the evidence of the burden the institutional services would otherwise bear, as well as the statements of people themselves, revealed the need to help old people to be cared for in their own homes by their relatives.

Housing policy is one general means of meeting this need; if people were rehoused near relatives and friends there would be many fewer social casualties. There are also a number of specific means, which we considered briefly, such as constant attendance allowances for the bedfast and housebound, substitute help one evening a week or for a holiday period, and the provision of temporary accommodation for relatives living far away.

What, in addition, should be done for people with no relatives? In considering what means there were of meeting their needs and at the same time taking account of the trend towards more home-like surroundings in all kinds of institutions, more interchange be-tween home and hospital, and readier access by relatives, we came to the conclusion that a comprehensive family help service, built on to the existing home help service and closely connected with the work of family doctors, may be the best – and in the long run perhaps the inescapable – means of dealing with the lack of coordination and inadequacy of existing welfare services. The effectiveness of such a service would, however, depend upon meet-ing the two most urgent needs – for a higher personal income in retirement and for occupation for the infirm and housebound, especially men.

How far are the findings from the working-class area of Bethnal Green applicable to the rest of the country? And how far do they apply to patterns of life fast disappearing? Questions such as these, which can be asked about most reports on field research, are as harassing as they are important. No clear answer can be given. Although there are general sociological and anthropological studies of urban and rural areas, and even studies of old people, which suggest, or hint, that in many respects family life may be very similar in other parts of Britain, they are not exactly comparable to this one. Moreover, neither this nor other studies tell us much about the patterns of life in specifically middle- or upper-class families or in suburban populations as a whole. So much is conjecture.

It may, however, be worth referring again to some of the facts about Bethnal Green which do and do not distinguish it from other areas. It is a long-settled working-class borough. Local industry is very mixed and, compared, for example, with some Yorkshire mining or Lancashire cotton towns, the same habits of work and daily routine do not spread through the length and breadth of the community. Roughly the same proportion of the population (fourteen per cent) as in London, and as in England and Wales as a whole, are of pensionable age. A small minority, less than one in ten, are Jewish. Largely because of the upheavals brought about by bombing and evacuation in the last war and by housing clearance and rebuilding that has gone on since, the total population is only half what it was twenty or thirty years ago. Thousands of people have been obliged to emigrate, many of them to housing estates on the eastern fringes of London. This has undoubtedly dispersed many families. Of the old people interviewed a quarter lived alone in the household; in the country as a whole the proportion seems to be one in eight.[1] Taken together, these facts do not suggest that family relationships are likely, in general, to be much richer than in other mainly working-class areas.

The question of change is equally important. The presumption is that more of the present generation of people aged sixty and over have children and other relatives to look after them and are more secure than their children will be when they are old. In Bethnal Green forty-five per cent of the married and widowed people had no, one, or two surviving children, but thirty-one per cent had five or more. We found that those with fewer children saw relatively more of them. Against this we also found that children in smaller families had less chance of gaining relief from the strain of nursing an infirm old person.

In the country as a whole the prospect is rather more complicated and perhaps less gloomy than many people imagine. There are several reasons. Of women married in 1900–9, all of whom are now of pensionable age, eleven per cent had no live-born child.

1. See Chapter 3.

This proportion increased, for people married in later years, to about sixteen per cent or seventeen per cent in the mid-1920s but, according to what evidence there is, has not increased any further. Over the next ten years most of the remaining people who married in the first twenty-five years of this century will reach pensionable age and the proportion of married but childless old people will then remain about the same. But the proportion of unmarried men and women in the population is declining. More people marry than in the past. According to official estimates the proportion of men of pensionable age who are unmarried will decrease from nine per cent to seven per cent and of women from sixteen per cent to twelve per cent between 1954 and 1979.[1] And as there have been such immense improvements in mortality rates at the younger ages over the course of the last half-century, fewer of the people giving birth to one child or two are likely to lose them before they reach their sixties. At present it is estimated that twenty-one per cent of men and twenty-eight per cent of women of pensionable age are unmarried or childless. While these proportions are substantial and require careful verification so that class and area comparisons can be made, there is no prospect of their increasing sharply. The proportion of old people having only small families is likely to continue to increase steadily for about ten years but not thereafter. Of women married in 1900–9 thirty-four per cent had one or two live-born children and of those married in 1925 fifty-one per cent. It appears, however, that family size has not continued to fall for people married since, and, indeed, there may have been a slight increase in the years since the war.

The changes brought about by more marriage, smaller family size, and longer life are producing ramifications throughout the kinship system. More marriage may mean fewer isolated people in old age, but fewer uncommitted aunts who can, whenever they are needed, run to the aid of their kin. Smaller family size may mean not only small sibling groups, more manageable tasks for mother and grandmother, and the concentration of the responsibilities of

---

1. In the same period the proportion of widowers over sixty-five is also expected to decrease slightly from twenty-six to twenty-three per cent and of widows from forty-three to forty-two per cent. Calculated from Table D of Appendix 6, *Report by the Government Actuary on the First Quinquennial Review of the National Insurance Act of 1946*, 1954, pp. 51–2.

parenthood into a shorter span of years, but that aged people will have fewer, and more elderly, children to look after them. The advantage of longer expectation of life, especially at the younger ages, may produce the most significant changes of all in the structure and functioning of the family. A woman born in 1900 expected to live about forty-eight years; in 1951 seventy-one years. Such improvements suggest there are now more families in which there are grandparents, fewer marriages broken early by death, and more children having both parents alive throughout their childhood. One in five of all the old people in Bethnal Green had been widowed more than twenty years and over one in three lost at least one of their parents before the age of fifteen. The longer survival and the greater amount of marriage has given greater prominence to the relationship between man and wife in society, not only because husband and wife live longer together, but because people are less likely to have unattached relatives to whom they owe obligations. The general direction of change in family structure seems to be away from extreme diversities and towards more stability at the centre. As compared with fifty years ago family relationships now seem to be deeper (in generation depth), more symmetrical, and less collaterally extended. The full effects of all these developments on the position of the old need the most thoroughgoing investigation.

Other changes have taken place; of that there is no doubt. The people interviewed in Bethnal Green themselves gave cause for optimism about the present and future. When comparing the present with the past not all the advantage was on the side of the past.[1] Most agreed, for example, that disputes between man and wife were rarer, that men helped more in the homes, that fathers more often took out young children, and that parents were less strict and less cruel; that people lived longer in one home,[2] had steadier jobs, worked many fewer hours, and had a far higher standard of living; that family rituals, such as weddings and funerals, were now more extravagant affairs in which more people were involved, but that a Saturday sing-song, or 'knees up',

1. As shown, for example, in Interview Report 3 in Appendix 2.
2. A School Board visitor's book showed in 1899 that 530 families out of 1,204 in Bethnal Green had moved within the previous twelve months – excluding the 'lowest and most shifting class of all'.

was much rarer and families rather more dispersed. On the whole people seemed now to desire, and to achieve, a greater measure of personal independence and privacy while remaining members of a closely-knit extended family.

The evidence from this very limited inquiry suggests that the extended family is slowly adjusting to new circumstances, not disintegrating. To the old person as much as to the young it seems to be the supreme comfort and support. Its central purpose is as strong as ever. It continues to provide a natural, if conservative, means of self-fulfilment and expression, as the individual moves from the first to the third generation, learning, performing, and teaching the functions of child, parent, and grandparent.

Postscript 1963: Moving towards a General Theory of Family Structure

MORE than half the persons interviewed during the survey described in this book are already dead. Others have left the homes they had (because of a large programme of 'slum' clearance) and are now living on housing estates both inside and outside London. To my knowledge, at least three of the few who were, at the time of the survey, rather isolated from their married children, have now moved outside London to join them. No doubt it would have been possible to keep a careful record of the experiences of all these individuals and such a record would have supplied a valuable commentary on the evidence and the conclusions of this book. Unfortunately, after 1955, I was able to keep in touch with only about thirty of the original sample of 203 – and the number has now shrunk to six. But my continuing acquaintance with these few would cause me to give greater emphasis to certain conclusions reached then.

For example, the woman described on p. 272 remains the most isolated person I have ever met. Her poverty is as real as it was in 1955. She refuses to apply for National Assistance and has now lived for at least eight years on the retirement pension alone. She is not querulous or small-minded about it – but simply, from a firm grip on her pride and self-sufficiency, says no. Similar entreaties to go to clubs and centres or on holiday are also resisted. Her heroic if touching sense of independence has for me symbolized all the complex arguments against systems of welfare and income security based solely on tests of need or means rather than predominantly on universal rights.

There is another sense in which this report might be placed in a new perspective. After publishing a book and getting on with new work an author gets time to ponder whether he was successful in achieving balance and accuracy; time, too, to grow into a slightly different kind of person and so to criticize the decisions he took years previously; time, again, to admit, or reject, the assessments of different readers.

Finally, further studies of old people, in other western countries as well as in Britain, have been published. Certain conclusions are no longer so tentative as they were or, at least, they are no longer so restricted in application. We can speak with rather more authority about the family relationships of old people – and also about their privations. For in terms of the social conventions of the late nineteen-fifties and early nineteen-sixties this report contains both an optimistic and a pessimistic conclusion. It suggests, contrary to much supposition, that the majority of persons of pensionable age lead a fairly secure life within their families: most of them are a source as well as an object of help and companionship. But it also suggests that, at any one time, there is an isolated minority of ten to twenty per cent who have no close relatives, or only one or two, or are separated from the few they have. Of course, the processes of ageing may transfer some people from one category to another. A husband or wife, or an only child, for example, may die. Very few people appear to have been *deserted*, in any wilful sense, by their close relatives. Yet isolation in old age is an immense social problem, affecting upwards of three-quarters of a million individuals in Britain alone. Many live in conditions of discomfort or misery and are particularly vulnerable in illness or infirmity. Society is only slowly awakening to their needs.

It will be noted that I am writing rather more generally than just of the findings in Bethnal Green. That borough is not, as some writers have implied, a sub-cultural island where strange customs have been magically preserved.[1] First, it would be wrong to overlook the facts that prevent it from being any sort of island. It has experienced much more population movement in the past twenty years than most council areas in Britain. Its boundaries, occupational and social as well as industrial, are extremely

1. For example, in referring to the study of kinship in the same borough by Michael Young and Peter Willmott, Eugene Litwak says it focuses on working-class groups with '*passing remnants* of classical extended family relations' (my italics). Litwak's definition of the 'classical' extended family does not correspond, however, with family relationships in the borough. (Litwak, E., 'Occupational Mobility and Extended Family Cohesion', 1960).

difficult to draw. It merges, in so many different ways, with other parts of London and of industrial Britain. To note its vagaries of speech, dress, decoration, and enjoyment is not to question the essential similarity of its family and social structure to that of major sections of the British population.

Second, new studies have been added to those which already in 1957 seemed to buttress the chief positive conclusions about the pattern of family proximity and contact. I list the most important.[1] There have, of course, been others which supply little or no data on family relations.

Surveys of Old People (usually of pensionable age or over sixty-five)

Date of survey	Area	Date of report
1956–7	Stockport (aged 80 and over)	1958
1957	Anglesey	1958
1957	Orkneys	1959
1957	Woodford (younger persons too)	1960
1958	Aberdeen	1963 (in press)
1958–9	Rural area in Shropshire	1963
1958–60	England and Wales (old people in residential Homes)	1962
1959–60	Seven areas: Salisbury, Leicester, Hexham Rural District, Seaton Valley, Glasgow, Wimbledon, and East Ham	1962 (preliminary)
1960	Lewisham	1962 (unpublished)
1960	Swansea (younger persons too)	1961 (preliminary)
1962–3	Britain	1963 (preliminary)

The recent studies show that the great majority of old people with children are not isolated from them. For example, in a rural district of Anglesey, eighty-nine per cent of those having children had at least one living in the same dwelling or parish. In another

1. For full references to these and to other studies referred to in ensuing pages, see 'References to Postscript 1963' on p. 319. For an account of thirty-three minor and major surveys of old people carried out in Great Britain between 1945 and 1958, see Townsend, P. (1959).

rural district of Shropshire the comparable figure was seventy-four per cent, and a further twenty-two per cent had a child within easy distance. In urban and suburban areas the numbers living in the same dwelling or within easy walking or travelling distance fell, but only slightly. In Bethnal Green eighty-five per cent of the old people interviewed had at least one child living in the dwelling or within a mile, compared with seventy-five per cent, as Table 28 shows, in suburban Woodford and seventy-six per cent in the seven areas of Salisbury, Leicester, Hexham Rural District, Seaton Valley, Glasgow, Wimbledon, and East Ham, which were surveyed by Dorothy Cole Wedderburn and John Utting in 1959–60.[1]

TABLE 28

PROXIMITY OF OLD PEOPLE TO THEIR CHILDREN

Children's proximity	Rural districts in:		Bethnal Green (1954–5)	Woodford (suburban, mixed middle and working class) (1957)	Seven areas: (varying class, industrial and population patterns) (1959–60)
	Anglesey (1957)	Shropshire (1958–9)			
	%	%	%	%	%
At least one in dwelling	69	57	52	53	53
None in dwelling but at least one within a mile	20*	17*	33	22	23†
All more distant	11	26	15	25	25
	100	100	100	100	100

* In same parish.

† Within fifteen minutes' walk.

1. I am indebted to Dorothy Cole Wedderburn and also to Peter Willmott and Michael Young for providing a special statistical analysis from their reports.

In all the studies which supply relevant data, old people saw a good deal of relatives living nearby – even when living alone, and even when lacking children (for it should be remembered that roughly a quarter of those of pensionable age are unmarried or otherwise childless). In the Orkneys only fifteen per cent of the 233 old people who were interviewed lived alone, and of these more than half had a relative living next door or were being visited daily by one. Over two-thirds of 600 persons living alone among 2,000 people aged eighty and over who were interviewed in Stockport were visited regularly by relatives, most of them daily or weekly. Finally, in the 'seven areas' inquiry more than half of those living alone had social contacts every day or nearly every day, mostly with relatives. Of the people living alone, eighty per cent of those having children saw at least one of them every week or more often.

Not all the studies which have been quoted contain an elaborate analysis of family contacts and patterns of care, but they tend to confirm all the main features of family structure and life found in Bethnal Green. The Woodford survey is of particular interest, not only because the area is a city suburb but also because roughly half the old people living there could be described as middle-class.

When I had the opportunity of working on the Woodford survey for a short period in 1957 I found not only that relationships between the three generations of a middle-class family could be extremely close but also that lifelong loyalties could be repeatedly reaffirmed in the face of acute personal difficulty.

A widow of ninety-two lived in a semi-detached house with her daughter, aged sixty, her son-in-law, and two teenage granddaughters. It was impossible to interview her because she was stone-deaf, blind, mentally incapacitated, and could not speak. For over four years she had been nursed at home and the family refused to let her go to hospital. She was doubly incontinent and because she had to be attended to frequently during the night her daughter slept with her in a double bed in the front room. The daughter was helped in turn by the granddaughters, who did much of the cleaning, cooking, and shopping.

Fewer of the old people than in Bethnal Green had relatives living in surrounding streets but they (and their families) made more use of cars, and more often had extra rooms in which to accommodate guests for a week-end or holiday. The result was that although they had fewer children and other relatives, they

saw almost as much of those they had as old people in Bethnal
Green. 'The proportions of old people with married children seeing
at least one of them in the previous day was fifty-six per cent in
Woodford, fifty-eight per cent in Bethnal Green. In both places a
further twenty-five per cent had seen a married child at some other
time in the previous week.'[1] Other statistical comparisons produced similar results. A special measure of isolation, when applied
to the information collected about each old person in the sample,
showed that eleven per cent were isolated, compared with ten per
cent in Bethnal Green (see p. 190 above). As the authors say,
despite differences in appearance, occupations, and customs
'perhaps the greatest surprise of the whole report is that [in
patterns of family contact] the two places are so alike'.

A study of a population which also includes a substantial
number of middle-class persons has been carried out in Swansea.
The central subject was kinship, and interviews were held with
young and middle-aged as well as old people. Within the borough
there appears to be comparatively little difference between the
middle and working classes in the numbers living in the wife's
home district and with the wife's parents, for example. An
interim report tells of Swansea being divided up into twenty-six
'urban villages' among which, despite variations of class, size,
density, religion, occupation, and Welsh-speaking, there is none
the less, a 'fundamental broad uniformity in kinship behaviour'. [2]
Altogether eighty per cent of the 325 women in the sample (and
sixty-nine per cent of the 318 men) who had a mother alive had seen
their mothers within the previous week – many of them the
previous day. So although much close investigation of middle-class
family life, particularly in outlying districts of Britain's cities,
remains to be done, the evidence that has so far emerged suggests
only small variations in function and frequency of contact from
working-class family life. My own personal guess is that differences
in total family structure may largely explain what seem to be differ-

1. Willmott, P. and Young, M., *Family and Class in a London Suburb*,
p. 38. It should be noted, however, that nineteen per cent of the old people
approached for interview refused, compared with five per cent in Bethnal
Green.

2. Rosser, C. and Harris, C. A., 'Relationships through Marriage in a
Welsh Urban Area', p. 299.

ent qualitative relationships within middle- and working-class families. The size of the 'extended' and 'immediate' families making up the 'networks' of kin will be smaller and more self-contained for the middle classes.

A survey throughout Britain of persons aged sixty-five and over was carried out in 1962–3, as part of a cross-national survey taking place in three countries, including Denmark and the United States. Few of the results have so far been published. A provisional analysis, however, confirms the broad picture conveyed by different local and area studies. Nearly 4,000 persons aged sixty-five and over were interviewed in all parts of Britain. Of those

TABLE 29

WHEN OLD PEOPLE IN BRITAIN HAD LAST SEEN AT LEAST ONE OF THEIR CHILDREN

(Survey of persons aged 65 and over, 1962)

At least one child seen	Old people with children %
Today or yesterday	69·3
Within previous seven days	17·3
Within previous month	7·4
Within previous year	4·2
More than a year ago	1·8
Total	100

having children, forty-three per cent lived in the same dwelling, twenty-two per cent within ten minutes journey, sixteen per cent within ten to thirty minutes and nineteen per cent further than thirty minutes[1] journey from their nearest child. Table 29 shows that sixty-nine per cent had seen at least one of their children on the day of interview or the previous day and another seventeen

1. These figures refer to the results of the first stage of the survey, which involved the interviewing of a national sample of some 2,500 persons aged sixty-five and over in April–May 1962. A second stage of the survey, involving the interviewing of a national sample of a further 1,500 persons aged sixty-five and over, was carried out in November–December 1962. The survey is a collaborative enterprise carried out by research staff of the London School of Economics, the Cambridge University Department of Applied Economics, and the Government Social Survey.

per cent within the previous seven days. Even when unmarried children were left out of account, more than two-thirds of old people with married children had seen one or more of them the same day or within the previous seven days.

Evidence collected in other western countries goes far to suggest (at least in terms of the rough statistical measures of nearness and frequency of contact so far employed) that old people have similar relationships with their families. Various studies carried out in France, Germany, and Italy show that between two-fifths and a half of old people having children live with one of them; a further fifth generally have one in the near vicinity of their homes. For example, in a survey of old people in a district of Paris, Jean René Tréanton found that forty-eight per cent lived with a child and a further twenty-two per cent had a child living in the same neighbourhood. Even in the United States a recent national study by Ethel Shanas showed that thirty-six per cent of some 1,350 old persons having children and living in all parts of the country in fact lived in the household with a child, another twenty-four per cent within easy walking distance of one, and twenty-five per cent only a 'short ride' away.

Largely because of these facts about proximity it seems that in most western countries about three-quarters or more of old people having children see them every day or at least once a week. In Sweden, for example, the figure is seventy-nine per cent (fifty-nine per cent seeing children every day or nearly every day). In West Germany it is seventy-four per cent and in the United States eighty-three per cent.[1] In a study carried out in and around New York, Chicago, St Louis, and Los Angeles, Marilyn Langford produces evidence about visits by all the children of old people which closely corresponds to that for Bethnal Green.[2] Michael

1. Provisional analysis of the 1962–3 British survey mentioned above shows that eighty-three per cent of those aged sixty-five and over (the same as the United States figure) claimed to see at least one of their children 'every day' or 'at least once a week'.

2. For example, the following are the percentages of *all* children seen;

	daily	weekly	monthly	less often
Four areas in the U.S.	31	37	19	13
Bethnal Green	36	38	17	10

See p. 50 above and also Langford, M., *Community Aspects of Housing for the Aged*, pp. 11–12.

Young and Hildred Geertz even found much in common, so far as family contacts are involved, between three populations of old people living respectively in a residential suburb of San Francisco, in Woodford, and in Bethnal Green.[1]

To all these rather simple statistics we might add an elaborate comparative analysis of family relationships – for those who do not have children as well as for those who do. We could explore the reasons for the slight fall since the war in the proportions of old people living with children (mainly attributable, we might hypothesize, to changes in the family structure of those reaching old age, particularly in so far as they continue to have unmarried children). We could demonstrate from studies in various countries that most old people prefer to live near and in close daily touch with at least one of their married children rather than in the same household.[2] Or we could investigate the complementary findings about the roles often played by grandparents.

A number of studies, including, for example, one by Gordon Streib in the United States, report that more than half elderly grandparents (grandmothers more than grandfathers) are involved, to a lesser or greater extent, in the regular care of their grandchildren. This seems to be true of the middle as well as the working classes, though further intensive research is badly needed. I well remember on successive days talking to two grandmothers. One lived in an attic in East London and had had an eight-year-old grandson to stay with her the previous night. 'I'm taking him to Trafalgar Square and Buckingham Palace today. I do it for his history,' she said. 'He stays with me every week like this. I like learning him about things.' The other, the wife of a baronet, lived in a large house in north-west London. After telling me how she used to read to them every evening while they were small (they lived in the same road), she said, 'My husband and I

1. For example, in Menlo Park (San Francisco), Woodford, and Bethnal Green, the proportions of all daughters of old people seen by them each day were, respectively, forty-two per cent, forty-one per cent, and forty-five per cent. Young, M. and Geertz, H., 'Old Age in London and San Francisco,' p. 131.

2. Professor Rosenmayr and Dr Köckeis report from Vienna: 'Our studies provide ample evidence that in Vienna, as elsewhere, the desire to have a separate household is combined with strong family ties with the aged.' 'Family Relations and Social Contacts of the Aged in Vienna', 1962.

have put aside a large sum in trust for our grandchildren's education. It will cover all their school fees.' Two approaches to education – but one function.

This is not, however, the place for an elaborate examination of all the evidence about family relationships. Indeed, in future years readers of the above passages may wonder why I should have bothered to go to such pains merely to prove that the extended or three-generation family (in the sense defined on p. 126) is very much alive in industrial societies in the latter half of the twentieth century, and has certain crucial functions, not least for the aged. The reason is that at the time of writing its existence is still commonly denied or ignored, even when the 'family' (of parents living with dependent children) is stoutly defended. Until very recently far more was known about kinship in many non-industrial societies overseas than about kinship in Britain. Even now we have not got much further than mapping part of the geography of the family and describing the more positive functions of some of its key figures. Most of us, however, have different relationships simultaneously with a large number of persons to whom we are related, through either descent or marriage. We are conscious not only of obstinate affections but also of tensions, lapses, frustrating obligations, and feelings even of disdain. Instead of being content simply with describing customary behaviour – that most people frequently see some of their relatives of other generations, perform many services for them, and feel warmly towards them – social scientists should be going on to ask: How is it that some parents drift apart from all or some of their married children? Why do they drift apart from some children rather than others? More generally, how does isolation arise? Why do some people remain unmarried and why do others, although they marry, remain childless? The questions spin off endlessly from any deliberation of the permutations of family life.

I feel I now see, in a way I did not when I wrote this book, the crucial and underlying importance to a knowledge of ourselves and our society of the pervading principles of family structure. Many of the findings of this book and others I have referred to above could be fitted into a theory of family structure. Here I can do no more than suggest what it might entail.

*

The primary biological needs or drives to mate, to procreate, and to care for offspring who are slow to mature are satisfied, and therefore also reinforced and turned into basic psychological needs, through the social customs of marriage and bringing up children in the parental household. The initiating social relationship could be said to be that of marriage; a man is now a husband, a woman now a wife. The birth of a child, say a son, adds not one but two relationships to that which already exists: father and son and mother and son. The birth of a second child, supposing it to be a daughter, adds not two but three more relationships: father and daughter, mother and daughter, and brother and sister.[1] Already it is apparent that an individual secures new relationships and roles not just upon his *own* marriage and the birth of his *own* children but also when the events of marriage and childbirth are experienced by the different individuals to whom he is related.

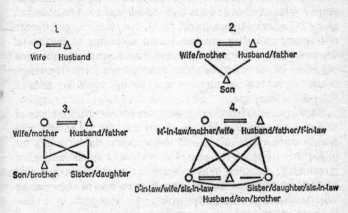

Four stages in the development of a new
complex of family relationships

1. Any increase in the number of *persons* comprising a family group brings about a more rapid increase in the number of *relationships*. If the number of persons is *n*, the number of relationships between them is

$$\frac{n(n-1)}{2}$$

Even in this family, the first child gains a sibling by the birth of a second child to his parents.

To project the simple 'immediate' or 'nuclear' relationships already described, the marriage of the first child, the son, would do far more than start a new 'family' cycle of husband and wife, etc. It would add three new relationships to the complex: father and daughter-in-law, mother and daughter-in-law, sister and sister-in-law (quite apart from any relationships with the kin of the daughter-in-law); and also change three existing relationships to the following: father and married son, mother and married son, married brother and unmarried sister. I use the word 'change' deliberately. Marriage, at least as understood and observed in western society, *necessarily* involves change in the familial relationships of each partner which already exist on either side. Common sense suggests that even when the newly-married pair continue to live in the parental home, the character of the relationships between father and son and mother and son are bound to change (just as we found, on pp. 54–7), that relationships between old people and their children varied according to household composition). The household would have an extra member and old styles of life would be recast in a different form. The repercussions would spread outwards to all the other relatives on both sides of the marriage.

Similarly, childbirth also has wide repercussions in the complex of family relationships. It is not simply the husband and the wife who acquire a new role or relationship upon the birth of their child; their relatives do, also. The husband's father becomes a grandfather, the wife's brother becomes a mother's brother, and so on. As a consequence, the other relationships of *these* people will be affected – with their wives, their husbands, and their brothers and sisters.[1] The expectations of the married couple are, perhaps to a lesser extent, reflected in the expectations of all their near relatives. And the satisfaction of their primary biological and

---

1. The extent of such repercussions has been described elsewhere, particularly in anthropological texts. Firth, for example, notes the difficulty of separating 'one set of kinship ties from that of others in the same system; they are like a set of forces in delicately poised equilibrium; if one is disturbed, others must respond in adjustment also'. Firth, R., *We The Tikopia*, p. 218. See also Homans, G., *The Human Group*, particularly Chapter 10.

psychological needs provides indirect satisfaction of the needs of their near relatives. This is why the ties created by marriage and child-rearing necessarily affect other pre-existing relationships of the adults concerned.

Human beings belong to households and families rather as neutrons and electrons belong to atoms and molecules. The effect of an adult marrying or a child being born is like adding an extra neutron to an existing molecular structure or introducing a new particle into a human cell. Perhaps after an initial period of random or 'exploratory' reaction, the component units will settle down into a new pattern of relationships and behaviour. They divide, and coalesce. The composition or structure of the whole will largely determine (a) the behaviour of the whole, (b) the relation between any two particular units, and (c) the 'character' of any individual unit.

We seem to be trying to develop at least three crucial hypotheses about family structure:

(i) The collective behaviour of any relatively corporate group of kin will vary according to (a) the composition of the group, and (b) the network of kin into which the group is knitted;

(ii) The quality and intensity of the relationship between any two members of an immediate or extended family or a kinship network will vary according to the structure of that family or network;

(iii) The character or personality of an individual will vary according to the structure of the immediate and extended families in which he is reared and to which, as an adult, he belongs.

To take first the 'immediate' family of parents and young children. I am inferring, among other things, that the form and character of the relationship between man and wife, and each parent and each child, as well as their individual personalities, will tend to differ according to the number and sex of their dependent children. Thus, husbands and wives would behave differently towards each other in the families of different structure illustrated in the diagram on p. 248, as would fathers and sons, mothers and sons, and brothers and sisters.

But to pursue these variations solely within the context of the immediate family is not enough. The husbands and fathers are themselves sons and brothers and their relationships with their wives and children cannot be understood except in the context of the structure of the extended family (in our clear but limited sense) and at least the adjoining sectors of the kinship network. This is how so many of the conclusions of this book could be said to fall

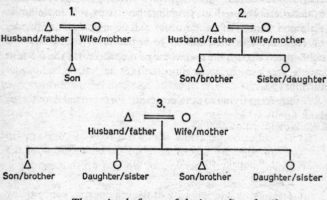

*Three simple forms of the immediate family
of parents and dependent children*

into place. Thus, we found above that husbands helped their wives less often and shared fewer pursuits with them when daughters or other female relatives lived at home or nearby (pp. 66 and 86–8). Unmarried or otherwise childless people had closer relationships with brothers and sisters (and particularly close relationships when both siblings had remained unmarried) than people with children (pp. 120–3).

Again, when interviewing old people and their families in Bethnal Green, I was usually given information which suggested a relationship of reserve, if not hostility, between in-laws. An elderly widow, for example, would speak of a son-in-law like this: 'I've never quite got on with his family. Don't know quite what it is, but his mother's rather superior. Always was. When I go to see my daughter I usually come home before he's back. We don't see a lot of one another – though he's all right. It's best that way.' But occasionally the pattern was broken. Another elderly widow would speak of her son-in-law like this: 'He's marvellous. He's just like a son to me. He gets my shopping on Fridays and we watch the telly together. On Mother's Day he brings me flowers.' At the time one was apt to explain such variations by vague references to common interests or sympathetic temperaments. Later, statistical analysis showed that family structure was an important part of the explanation. People had a significantly closer relationship with children-in-law when they possessed no children of like sex. Indeed, the relationship seemed to be particularly close when the child-in-law's parents were dead or living at a distance. To some extent, daughters-in-law substituted for daughters, and sons-in-law for sons (pp. 100–2). The effects of changes in structure are shown illustratively in the following diagram.

1. More usual relationship

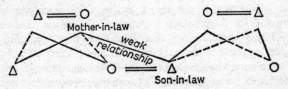

2. Mother-in-law with no son; son-in-law whose mother is dead

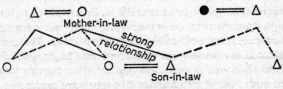

Effects of differences in family structure on relationship between mother-in-law and son-in-law

So far, in developing these ideas about structure, we have limited ourselves to the sex, marital status, and the ascendant, descendant, and collateral kin of individual family members. But the events of marriage, childbirth, and death give the family structure more subtle characteristics, which are important in explaining some features of individual personality and behaviour. Age at marriage and parental age at childbirth vary from individual to individual. Kinship structure may be given a particular cast. One would expect relationships between husbands and wives, parents and children, to differ when individuals marry and have children in their teens rather than in their late thirties or early forties. One would also expect such relationships to differ when the husband is, say, twenty years older than the wife.

Earlier in this book some data suggested that children may postpone marriage or fail to marry at all if they lose one parent, particularly the father, between the ages of about ten and the early twenties (pp. 96–7). This affects one rather than all of the children, and he or she tends to *compensate* the widow or widower for the death of the spouse by keeping house or earning a wage and by being a companion. If such evidence is confirmed and if, as I would expect, the age of marriage is shown to be affected by other structural changes in the kinship network, we would have one major explanation of the recent tendency for more people to marry and for them to marry younger.[1] In the past, far more parents died before their children were out of their teens. Among the elderly sample in Bethnal Green as many as thirty-six per cent had lost a parent by the age of fifteen. This suggests why so many people remained unmarried in Victorian times – or married late.

Earlier marriage, when combined with smaller families completed at an earlier age, has repercussions too. Instead of the mother having five, six, or more children, as in the late nineteenth century, from the time she is twenty, say, until she is forty, she now has two or three children in her early twenties. The average difference in age between the generations may have shrunk from thirty to twenty-three years. Among the consequences will be much more youthful grandparents (at a time when expectations of life have grown) and the first appearance as a common phenomenon in the history of the world's populations of the four-generation family. The practical problems of family relationships will change. For example, instead of it being common for a man

---

1. Of course, this would not supply a full explanation. We should need to take account, for example, of the fact that children now reach puberty a year sooner than the young generation of the war years.

and wife with young children to undertake the care of the last of
their parents to survive into old age, it will be common for a man
and wife whose children have grown up (and are perhaps themselves parents) to argue about the care of *two* or even *three* or all
four of their parents in their eighties.

All this may at least suggest the full ramifications of structural
theory. For the network of kinship is constantly changing,
marriages and births generating new relationships as deaths bring
about the disappearance of old ones, and also adapting itself to
new circumstances. The individual members of the network will
tend to coalesce in different extended families (though, of course,
there may be some overlap). We found that these families usually
spanned three generations and usually comprised six to twenty
individuals in day-to-day contact. Perhaps this functional group
may be smaller in numbers than it used to be (the multiplication of
grandparents and great-grandparents tending to encourage a kind
of vertical splitting of the network, compared with the sole surviving grandparent attracting the pyramid-like structure of a
hundred years ago).

Sociologists (and socialists) are reluctant to examine, still less
abandon, the assumption made by political theorists that the
wider family is antithetical to progress. It is supposed to be a relic
of a stationary society and to contradict the political ideals of
equality, democracy, community, mobility, and prosperity. Talcott Parsons and many others have put forward arguments that it
obstructs occupational mobility and hence occupational and
technical change, and that this explains its decline in industrial
societies.[1] George Homans actually says, 'Our own society has a
single kinship unit, the nuclear family . . .' and later, 'The nuclear
family first left the household and then even the neighbourhood of
other kinsmen.'[2] In the light of evidence given earlier in this
postscript, particularly that from the United States, such statements are now shown to be wrong.

The terms and definitions used by those theorists who have
been interested in the family have remained extraordinarily unclear – and so have the empirical bases for such terms and definitions. Most of the elaborate theoretical analyses that still fill

1. For example, Parsons T., 'The Social Structure of the Family.'
   2. Homans, G., *The Human Group*, pp. 263 and 279.

countless texts and journals are based on very crude, if not slipshod data. The subtlety of the family's response to social change is rarely appreciated.[1]

Western society supplies marriage as a custom to accommodate and regulate the primary biological needs and encourages the married pair to rear their offspring in the home. There is a kind of chain reaction. The biological relationship demands a special intimacy and cohabitation reinforces special psychological needs for love and affection. Your own flesh and blood are necessarily rather special. Your son will call you 'father' and there is no other person in the world whom he can, with like meaning, call that. Similarly, he has an exclusive right to the label 'son' – until perhaps others are born. Even then he will share this right with very few. The biological relationship gives each of you a special preferment to love and affection from the other – even if he has no more right, in the wider democratic meaning of the word, to affection than any other boy in the world, and you no more right than any other man in the world. It is not enough to love mankind and treat all men as equals. Nor, as in the extreme collective settlement, is it possible to treat all children equally in day nurseries, and for the children to live apart from their parents. As Yonina Talmon has shown in some sensitive accounts of the latter, family ties have quickly reasserted themselves, albeit in a modified form. Various forms of the extended family of three generations are

1. Yonina Talmon is one of the few people to have understood this process of response. In one of her studies of collective settlements she describes the way in which children are partly segregated from their parents, live with their peers, and are looked after by nurses, instructors, and teachers. 'Since only very few primary familial roles have been left to the family, it seemed reasonable to expect the family to be of only secondary importance. Paradoxically, this limitation of functions seems to have a beneficial effect on family relations: in so far as the family has ceased to be the prime socializing agency it escapes, to some extent, the inevitable ambivalence felt towards agents of socialization, for parents do not have to perform the two-sided role of ministering to their children's needs, on the one hand, and thwarting their wishes, on the other. Parents do not carry the main responsibility for disciplining their children and can afford to be permissive, all of which limits the areas of potential conflict.' Later, so far as the aged were concerned, 'The curtailment and limitation of obligations seem to reinforce rather than weaken family relationships'. Talmon, Y., 'Ageing in Israel: A Planned Society', pp. 288–9.

perhaps necessary for the satisfaction of basic psychological as well as social needs.

Having established intimate relationships in the home for the first fifteen or twenty years of life it is unlikely that the parties to them would sever them overnight. Western society insists, at some point in adolescence, on replacing the image of a child being cradled in its mother's arms with one of the child being tied to her apron strings. Family relationships do not, indeed *could* not, reflect these images. 'He (or she) should go out in the world and stand on his own feet. He must make his own way now.' The absurdity of the hypothesis of severance is manifest. Even when a father has neither the property nor the means to provide his son with employment he can perhaps assist him, or benefit from him, in many ways. There is a basic need for a man to create someone in his own image – especially a son. He can take pleasure in apprenticeship, training, 'speaking for' his son to his boss, sacrificing himself so that his son can go through medical school and become a doctor like himself. But he also wants to see his son avoid the pitfalls he fell into, and do better for himself. In a real sense the father has a second chance of realizing, through his son, his failed ambitions. It is a compensation for disappointment, and age. If society has deprived the family of occupational allocation, as it were, thereby reducing occupational rivalry between the males of different generations, one obstacle has been removed. The son is no longer a threat – as portrayed so savagely in Zola's *Earth* – to its unity. His advancement and rise in status can to some extent be shared and encouraged by the father. But a price has to be paid. By seeking his son's advancement and sharing his son's resentment of old men blocking promotion and new ideas, he subscribes, if indirectly, to his own premature retirement. While formerly his son was obliged to come to a compromise on a date when the reins would be relinquished, the father now has all too little to say in the decision. This is a problem posed sharply in earlier pages. The old man's voice has been removed from the democratic process.

Already our analysis has pursued paths not anticipated by many theorists. For we have reached the point of arguing that the loss of *authority*, or at least of control over the allocation of work, by the parental generation might in some important respects *strengthen* the relationship between fathers and their sons. If we remember, in addition, that the wives of each generation exist, in a sense to *offset* occupational rivalry between the men and to promote the aspirations of their children, we see that this is another check to divisions which might otherwise occur. This might be one cause, or explanation, of the strength and continuity noted earlier of the relationship between mother's mother, mother, and daughter. Status differences between the generations and the effects of these on family relationships are rarely discussed in terms which discriminate carefully between husbands and wives, and sons and daughters.

Much more could of course be said about the particular relationship between father and son than we have chosen to consider. When the son reaches puberty and during his adolescence the relationship often takes a different form. There may be advantages to the son in being helped over the threshold of manhood by the father, but there are disadvantages and difficulties too. There is a basis for unconscious sexual competition between the two, as well as the son's more general quest for a sexual partner, which takes priority, at least for a time, over established loyalties and obligations. The son is impatient for manhood, marriage, and independence. Resentment over any delay finds an outlet in scenes of dispute and tension. But such tension may be a necessary preparation for the development that is soon to take place in kinship structure. Anthropologists have often shown how the acting out of hostilities in fact prevents them and indeed cements old relationships that have been threatened. During the survey described in this book, I wish I had been more systematically on the look-out for family strains and tensions. They are as much a part of the story of maintaining a structure in equilibrium as close and affectionate contact. Evidence, for example, has been given of friction between man and wife (pp. 89–90), between parent and child (pp. 110–12), between a married person and the spouse's siblings (pp. 115–17), and between parent and child-in-law (pp. 100–2). The strains upon relatives of caring for sick and infirm old people have been documented (pp. 72–4). And the general manner of regulating and limiting conflict through the acceptance by prospective warring parties of certain rules or principles of family conduct has also been discussed (e.g., pp. 129–31). But I would now attach as much importance to the analysis of infrequency of contact between kin, to put it one way, as of frequency of such contact. And I would more consciously check what evidence there was of disharmony – not only for what it tells us about particular relationships and personalities but also for what it tells us about the maintenance of structural equilibrium within certain parts of the kinship network.

It is none the less evident that any relationship between two members of the family, such as the one between father and son that we have been considering, goes through certain phases over the cycle of life. After a period of coolness, uncertainty, or hostility, the son will get a job, marry, and start a family. He will suddenly find himself behaving, as a husband and a father, in just the way for which he criticized his own father. As a result he may become more tolerant of his father, and more reconciled to his idiosyncrasies. He will recognize more surely the value of having grandparents on call. Many sons, I would suggest, are likely at this stage of their lives to go through a kind of reconciliation in their relationships with their fathers. In a sense they can share the burden of being a father with someone who has been their 'father', just as many fathers can continue to fulfil, through their sons, the need to procreate and teach the younger generation, and maintain touch with it. As evidence of the need of older people for grandchildren I would cite evidence from this book and elsewhere of the tendency of unmarried or childless persons in middle or old age to look to the children of collaterals in substitution.

My argument is incomplete. However, it suggests not only the basic *continuity* of the primary relationships between husband and wife and parent and child but their complex and automatic response to the process of ageing and also to each birth, marriage, and death which occurs in the rest of the structure of which they are inescapably a part.

APPENDIX 1

A Further Note on Method

A GENERAL description of the methods followed in the main inquiry will be found in Chapter 1 of this book. Sometimes in the text additional remarks explain the manner of arriving at particular findings, for example about earnings on p. 82 and about social isolation on pp. 188–91. This note refers specially to accuracy, representativeness of the sample, and statistical validity.

Accuracy

The principle adopted in the Bethnal Green research was one of establishing each individual's chief relationships and activities to provide a framework or context within which it was possible to introduce appropriate questions and evaluate answers. The consistency of much information was convincing. Answers to widely spaced questions often 'hung together'. This was perhaps the most valuable test of their accuracy.

The old people were visited without previous warning and most were interviewed on the spot, although appointments had to be made with a few who were busy or ill. It was therefore possible to see many of them going about their daily affairs in their habitual surroundings, preparing meals, looking after grandchildren, sewing a dress, and being visited by relatives and friends. As the interviews were spread over the twelve months of the year and took place morning, afternoon, and evening, and sometimes on Saturday or Sunday, many statements of fact could be substantiated by direct observation. Over twenty per cent of the interviews took place in the evening or at the week-end and at forty per cent of them relatives other than a husband or wife were present or were seen briefly or for long spells before, during, or after the interview. Some of these were living in the same household or dwelling but many were just visiting the old people. At only seven per cent of the interviews were friends or neighbours seen, however briefly.

The interview schedule, with its mixture of general and specific questions, allowed the flexibility necessary to adapt to the person being interviewed. Careful attention could be paid to spontaneous remarks. It proved unexpectedly easy to move from the formal role of interviewer to a relationship of friendliness in which, for example, family photos were exchanged. An introduction from the family doctor, which could be produced if necessary, also helped to reduce suspicion of the motives of the research. A letter of thanks which restated the objects of the research was sent to each person.

Another important object was to explore some questions very thoroughly, particularly those regarding the social relationships taken most for granted. Questions had to be specific and meaningful. Systematic exploration of close relatives and friends one by one proved to be the best prelude to the more involved questions about daily life and social problems. This has an important bearing on research in this field. Unless data about the whereabouts of and contacts with relatives are gained, in many inquiries a misleading picture about personal activities and needs is likely to be built up, because so many people take family activities as given. This particularly applies to research concerned with the effect of social services on the family.

The importance of asking meaningful questions can be illustrated by the example of illness. People were first asked whether they had been ill in bed at home for any reason in the last two years and if so, who had looked after them, and who would look after them during any future illness. This soon proved to be inadequate as a form of questioning. A number of people said they would 'manage on my own'. They often took the help of relatives for granted and thought the question of help referred only to a neighbour or friend who would fetch the doctor or their children. Those who had not experienced illness for many years sometimes found the question difficult and liked to think they would not be dependent on others in the sense that relatives or others might have to give up work or prepare their meals. Supplementary questions were therefore asked which limited the meaning of 'help in illness' largely to the provision of meals and drinks, making the bed, and assistance with personal toilet when the old person was confined to bed. And when the source of help was unclear specific questions were put about neighbours and relatives living nearby.

Throughout the research one of the most difficult problems was that of taking proper account of people's diversity and of the apparent disorganization in their lives. There was a great temptation at each stage to make life appear more logical, orderly, and predictable than it was. The work may have suffered because of this unwitting distortion. People vary and their lives do not always pursue a steady course; contradictory opinions are held at one and the same time and different meanings are put upon the same words, particularly those with moral overtones, at different times. The result is that there may be less system in social organization than we suppose, or, at the least, a trickier balance of complex social influences.

Representativeness of the Sample

Getting names and addresses from doctors in Bethnal Green was chosen as the means of securing a random sample of people of pensionable age in the borough. There was no chance of gaining access to the Ministry of Pensions list of retirement pensioners, and a list compiled by the Borough Council at the time of the Coronation covered only two-thirds of those of pensionable age and was, in any case, partly out of date. The names of one in three of the general practitioners were picked out at random. The research was finally based on records consulted at seven practices, which were fairly well distributed over the borough. So far as is known about ninety-eight per cent of the population of London are covered by doctors' records, and it is assumed that the sample was drawn from some such percentage of the old people in the borough.

Chapter 1 describes the result of visits paid to the address of people who finally qualified for inclusion in the sample. As most of the interviews were carried out by one person some months elapsed before all the addresses could be visited. This delay may have resulted in the sample becoming partly out of date and unrepresentative. Fifty-eight of the 261 could not be interviewed, thirty-eight because they had died, had moved out of the borough, or could not be traced, ten because they were in hospital or residential Home or were ill at home, and ten because they refused an interview. These ten people who refused formed less than five per cent of the sample.

The representativeness of the sample can be checked in a few, but only elementary, ways. Table 30 shows the distribution of the

TABLE 30

DISTRIBUTION OF OLD PEOPLE IN DIFFERENT ELECTORAL WARDS

Wards	Total number of people on Electoral Register	Number of old people in sample inquiry	Old people as % of number on Electoral Register
North	7,550	30	0·40
East	8,225	35	0·43
Central	8,591	65	0·76
South	8,805	47	0·54
West	7,314	26	0·36

sample over the five wards of the borough, and Table 31 compares information given about their household composition by the women in the present inquiry with similar information that was obtained from a special analysis of the 1951 Census. The two groups may not be exactly comparable, because of differences in applying the definition of 'household' and in the sub-categories. Six per cent of the sample were aided by the domestic help service; separate analysis showed that this was exactly comparable with the figure relating to the whole population of pensionable age. Similarly, twelve per cent of the sample belonged to an old people's club; information from the Old People's Welfare Committee about total membership at the time of the interviews suggested the proportion should have been eleven per cent. So far as the various figures go, it seems the sample gives a fair representation of the elderly population in the whole borough.

Statistical Validity

Statistical tests have a limited but important role to play in research of this kind. They help to discipline the analysis, especially in forcing the research worker to make explicit definitions and take account of the quantitative element in his findings. Their applica-

TABLE 31

COMPOSITION OF HOUSEHOLDS OF WOMEN OF SIXTY
AND OVER

Others in household	1951 Census 20% sample	B.G. sample inquiry
	%	%
No one	32	28
Husband only	21	25
Unmarried child(ren) (and husband)	24	23
Married child(ren) (and others)	10	14
Others	14	10
Total	100	100
Number	1,067	139

tion cannot be pushed too far. Some of the most interesting generalizations involve a constellation of factors which cannot be tested easily, if at all. Much of the research material, even the quantitative material, cannot easily be put in a form testable by standard methods. Even the material that remains, however, could well necessitate several hundred tests if the research worker was determined to validate his findings as strictly as possible and was able to use time and money extravagantly for such a purpose. Moreover, as so many statisticians acknowledge, general comparisons between social groups can often produce significant differences which begin to look very misleading once the constituent parts are examined, or once the definition of categories is altered even slightly. For such reasons statistical tests need to be used with caution and discrimination.

Certain experiments were tried, especially in comparing two groups which could not be regarded as independent. For example, in comparing eldest and youngest children in their frequency of contact with the old people any differences could be obscured by the structure of the family and the sex and marital status of the old people.

One particular difficulty arose in attempting to use average frequencies of contact for expressing certain differences between relatives. At first it was hoped to summarize information in such terms as 'the average son sees his mother x times a week and the average daughter her mother y times a week'. This would have simplified the job of conveying differences between sons and daughters, brothers and sisters, sons-in-law and daughters-in-law, and so on. It could not be done. The statement, say, that the average son is seen three times a week is not particularly helpful if eighty per cent of all sons are seen either daily *or* once a week or less. Following advice, most tables about contacts between old people and their relatives were expressed in frequency distributions, i.e., percentage seen daily, weekly, etc. Table 13 provides an exception. For each old person his contact with his children was averaged. Thus, a person seeing two children seven and three times a week respectively was counted as seeing his average child five times a week. By this method a more normal statistical distribution was obtained and the differences between small and large families could be tested under reasonable conditions. The χ^2 test, the t test, or the analysis of variance test were used for purposes of statistical analysis.

Three Interview Reports

THESE reports of interviews with old people are given in full. Permission was obtained from the people concerned, provided fictitious names and addresses were used. A few other details, such as occupations and ages, have also been changed to prevent identification. The reports follow the interview schedule used and indicate its scope. This selection is intended to illustrate the differences in the circumstances of the old people interviewed.

INTERVIEW REPORT 1

(i) 2 February 1955. No. 157. 7.30 p.m. 2 hours 15 minutes. Informant alone for first half-hour, then wife too. Second call. Seen subsequently on two further occasions.

1–5. Mr Noggs, 25 Angel Street. Aged sixty-eight. Married. Born, Finsbury.

General

Mr Noggs is a youthful-looking man. He is plump with a slightly moon-shaped face and has thin black hair. His wife is thin and frail and careworn. She talked in a resigned but quiet tone. Although the husband seemed to be at ease when we were on our own and swore frequently, he behaved quite differently when his wife was in the room, saying little and that with less relish.

6. Household

   i Emily – sixty-five – married – wife.
      John – twenty-three – single – son.
      Henry – thirty – single – wife's nephew.

  ii Informant (head).

 iii Seventeen years (in house). Before that they lived for eighteen years in the same street. I asked this question before the wife came into the room and he gave only a vague estimate. She knew the number of years precisely.

   iv 'We came here because at number 28 we only had half a house. The children were growing up and we needed more room. Yes, we put in for it to the landlord.'

   v Besides the son living in the home the informant has two daughters, who married in 1945 and 1946, then leaving home. In 1946 Henry, the nephew, came to live with them, because his mother (Mrs Noggs's sister) had died.

   vi 'We're happy here. God forbid [moving out]. I wouldn't like to go in flats. I've got that comfort out in the yard and that's all I want. This is just comfortable. I don't want no ballsing about with rows and noise in flats.'

   vii 'I don't think it's a good idea' [living with married children]. The wife, however, thought it a good idea to live near.

7. Type of Dwelling

   i Terraced cottage on two floors.

   ii Five rooms including kitchen, and a big yard.

   iii No bath. W.C. in the yard.

   iv The home is very much like many other terraced cottages built 100 years ago. The floors slope and pieces of wood have had to be fitted on top of the doors. The front living-room is sparsely furnished, indicating a poor standard of life in former years. There is just one small mat on the lino-covered floor, a table, a couple of chairs with wooden arms, a sideboard, and one or two fitted cupboards. On top of the two fitted cupboards in recesses on either side of the fireplace are photos of the weddings of the two daughters.

8a. Occupation

Mr Noggs has worked all his life for various firms as a builder's labourer. 'If I'm able to carry on I'll carry on. If I can carry on till I'm seventy – if my health holds out. What's the good of me retiring? The pension's no use to me. What can I do with that? The Government don't give you enough. No, my wife doesn't want me to retire. Yes, I think I'll want a rest when I'm seventy. There's some of them living on this bleeding assistance. Casuals. They're a lot of lazy bastards.' His wife was a laundry hand for many years but she gave it up at the age of fifty, because she had TB and had a long spell in hospital. Their son is a punch-card operator.

The nephew is a carpenter, and both earn good money. Mr Noggs said he had no hope of an occupational pension but his employers did not retire men when they reached any set age because 'labour's short and if you can carry on they'll keep you'. He had changed his firm, but not his job, since reaching the age of sixty.

9. *Source of Income*

   i His wife has a retirement pension of £2. (She continued paying insurance contributions after retiring at fifty until she was sixty.)

  ii No national assistance.

 iii No other income.

 iv No savings.

  v Total income (earnings) £7.

 vi As with many other older couples, it was obvious the wife did not know what the husband earned and he did not know what the son and the nephew in the house gave her. He did not know whether she had any money from the two married daughters. I was able to ask Mr Noggs what he earned and what he gave his wife when he was alone, but I did not see his wife alone. There was an awkward silence when I asked how much board money she received from her son and nephew. She looked at her husband and then she said, 'My nephew gives me more than the other because he's earning better money'. In such cases it seems quite wrong to press for details. (On a subsequent call she said her son gave her £2 and her nephew £2 10s.)

 vii Wife used the tobacco vouchers she was entitled to.

11. *Selected items of expenditure*

Rent 19s. 3d. Coal 15s. in winter but averaged between 7s. 6d. and 10s. No sick club, clothing, or Christmas club. Life insurances 2s. 7d. There was a cat in the home.

12. *Health*

   i Active

  ii (*a*) Very little limitation of movement. But he did say, 'It knocks me. My breath. I've been working on rooftops. I have to have a few halts on the way up. It takes the go out of you but you've got to expect it when you get older.'

  (*b*) No pain in feet.
  (*c*) No recent falls.
 iii Normal physique.
 iv 'I got a bit of a cold but that's all. I've jolly good health.'
  v Alert.
 vi (*a*) Five years since last visit to doctor. 'I don't want to see him.'
  (*b*) No treatments by doctor in last year.
  (*c*) The only time in his life he was in hospital was for small-pox twenty-five years ago.
  (*d*) No experience of domiciliary nursing.
 vii His wife has been in very bad health since the war. She is thin and looks older than her husband, who has no grey hair on his head and looks like a man in his forties or fifties. Talking about her health, his wife said, 'I've had operations. I've had T B trouble ever since before the war. I had a lung removed. I haven't worked since. I have to go out now and again to the hospital but they tell me they can't do much for me. No, I don't sleep well. We sleep apart. The doctor said we had to. You see one's up and one's down, but we never quarrel.'

13. No Welfare Services or Clubs

 'We're not interested [in an old people's club]. I don't want to sponge. I'm not interested.' His wife tried to modify his attitude by saying, 'Some people are quite happy and enjoy going out to those things. If one or other of us were left alone, you might be glad of company. Some of these people are quite happy.'

14. Household and Personal Services

  i Her youngest daughter living in the next street comes to do her shopping every day. As for cleaning, 'My girl helps in between.' Mrs Noggs does all the cooking and sends most of her washing out (3s. per week).
 ii Son and sometimes nephew do odd jobs, such as getting coal up, washing up, cleaning windows. Mr Noggs does nothing in the home, apart from occasionally chopping wood or tidying the yard.
 iii Son deals with any official letters and forms.
 iv Wife pays rent, insurances, etc. Mr Noggs said, 'There's

some dilatory people who don't pay up regular. We always keep out of debt.'

v As earlier with income, it was difficult, when both were present, to get at the exact amount for housekeeping, but Mrs Noggs said, rather reluctantly, 'I get about £8 altogether but my nephew gives me more than my son.' However, this turned out to be an underestimate. On a subsequent call she said she had £9 10s. altogether, £5 from her husband, and £4 10s. from her son and nephew. This did not include her own £2 pension.

vii Her youngest daughter usually collects her pension. 'In good weather I sometimes go because it's only at the top of the turning.'

ix No illness in last two years. If Mr Noggs were ill, his wife would look after him, but he couldn't remember the last time he'd been in bed. So far as she was concerned, 'My husband would go to work. My sister opposite would pop in and my daughter would come in. My son would go round for her.' She had been in bed for two days the previous winter and her youngest daughter had prepared meals and looked after her.

17. Friends and Neighbours

'Yes, we've got good neighbours. We don't gossip. I don't interfere. I mind my own business.' He has no friends among them. His wife said, 'We've lived down here thirty-five years and we've never had no quarrels. No, we don't pop in. If you really wanted something they'd help you. Nearly all have got families and they help one another.' She said they have no friends living locally of whom they see a lot. Both denied they are visited regularly (by a friend or neighbour), though the husband meets casual friends at a local pub.

18. Holidays, Outings, Pastimes, Festivals, etc.

i 'We've never had a big holiday. We've never been able to afford it. I had a week off last year. We went out rides, just a little bus-ride.'

ii They do not visit relatives for week-ends because they have so many living near.

iii 'They all come round Christmas morning – our children and their husbands and our nephews and nieces. In the afternoon we go round to the girls. They [the boys] can please themselves.'

iv The husband 'likes a bit of gardening'. He has not been to the pictures for 'years', and his wife said, 'I've only ever seen one talkie. We like listening to the plays on the wireless. Sometimes I have a jaw across the road [her sister's].' She said later, 'I never go out of an evening. I listen to the plays and so does my husband. He never goes out. Sometimes he stays late and has a drink in the pub and is not back maybe till seven but when he comes in on a Saturday at two he stays in. He doesn't go out again.' And her husband said, 'I expect her to be here when I come.' And she added, 'Yes, I mustn't be out. He likes to know where I am.'

v The wife regularly corresponded with those members of her family who lived some distance away, for example, the daughters of an elder sister who died some years ago, who lived in other parts of London and one who lived at Margate.

viii C. of E. but not churchgoers. 'We know how to behave ourselves. We don't want no mastering or doctoring. It's how you was brought up when you were young.'

19. Family Life

As in so many cases there is a distinct division in the roles of husband and wife in the household. He has his work and she has her family. When I asked whether man and wife got closer together when they were older he repeated what had already been said. 'We don't notice it. I always expect her to be home when I'm back. We're all right. We make no squabbles or fighting.' When I was asking about the wife's family, the husband seemed rather impatient and said once or twice in reference to family activities, 'It don't interest me.' These references were not so much to his children but to his wife's sisters and their children.

They have three children, the son being at home, the youngest daughter living in the next street with her two children, who were seen every day, and the eldest daughter living at Clapton. She calls on her mother twice a week, about once a week with her husband

and children. Explaining how the eldest daughter came to be living
at Clapton, Mrs Noggs said, 'She couldn't get a place round here.
My Rosie [her youngest daughter] got her place because I spoke
for her.'

Mrs Noggs said, 'My mother had eighteen children. Two were
born dead and there was sixteen girls and two boys, but she reared
only eight.' Three sisters are still alive. One lives opposite with a
single daughter and she has a married daughter in the same street.
These are all seen every day by the wife but not by Mr Noggs.
There is a single sister living at Epping. Another sister has moved
to Bow, a mile away, and is now seen only once a month. Her eldest
sister seems to have had an important influence on the family.
Although she died some years ago Mrs Noggs maintains frequent
contact with her children. One of them is living with her, and two
daughters live about five minutes' walk away and see her every
day. These two, one of them single, live together and the married
one has a little girl who comes every day from school to have tea
with Mrs Noggs.

Referring to her mother, who died in 1930 at the age of eighty-
three, she said she lived in the present street all her life. 'We looked
after her every day. I took her a hot dinner. We always looked
after one another.' She still has some contact with two or three
cousins who live a mile away.

The husband's mother had eight children but 'all except two of
us died as babies. She bred too quick. She didn't have the strength
to keep bearing and she died when she was thirty. We all drifted
apart and my father married again. Me and my sister were the only
two alive when she died. We went to my father's mother and father.
When the old man got married again we had to battle for ourselves.' His sister died at the age of fourteen, and so he has no
relatives left alive on his side.

Asked what was the happiest time in his life, he said, 'We made
our own pleasure. We always made our own happiness.'

20. Changes in Family Life

His wife said, 'We're a thousand times better off. I remember
when my mother and the rest of us earned 1s. 3¾d. for seven gross of
matchboxes, and then my mother did a day's washing. I don't have
to think about where the next meal's coming from like I did then.

Even when you did get wages again you had to pay back a few shillings what you'd borrowed when you were short.' The husband seemed to think this was an implied criticism of himself and said, 'We never had the unions in them days. I know when I went out day after day and didn't earn a penny because of the weather.'

There was an interesting difference between husband and wife about their ideas of the richness of family and other contacts. The husband said, 'People today aren't so friendly. They can't afford to come and talk to you. They can't afford to mix up and have a good chat. Some people who've got on better than you can't be bothered with you. You used to get people saying good night and all that sort of thing when you passed them in the street. It's not the same now.' These remarks applied as much to families as to neighbours and it was quite obvious that his wife didn't agree with him, though she tried to conceal it to some extent. She said, 'We all cling together – *our* family. We always have. Take my sister across the road. Her son lives a long way away and he never misses a week, and he's brought her 2s. 6d. since he's been married. And her daughter's always going in to her. The family next door has got no parents – there's four sisters. There's two single ones at home but you always see that lot together.'

They agreed their parents had been 'very, very strict'. Both acknowledged the influence of their mothers but as Mr Noggs's mother had died young he said, 'My grandfather's family was always helping each other.' His wife's attitude to her mother was typified by her remarks about christening. 'You always had a tea after the christening. It lays to you when they're christened. Usually it's after about three months. It used to be three weeks. That's changed. And you used never to see a baby being taken out till it was christened. My mother always used to say, unless a woman was churched the baby shouldn't go out. Unless the woman was churched she hadn't been received into the eyes of the Almighty.'

When Mr Noggs's mother died he was taken over by his grandparents for a time but when I asked a general question about the early death of parents, he said, 'Children would have to go into a school or their uncles and aunts would have the kiddies. But they were mostly shot about [he meant in first one home and then another]. One aunt might only be able to have one. They used to

help each other in that respect.' (This with a sly look at his wife.)
Talking about young people and their children, his wife said, 'Some
of the girls today get too much money. If they go up the road with
two children, the children will have a cake each and then they'll
want more, and they'll get more. We used to be satisfied with a pen-
north of chips. No, I don't think wives should go to work. Wives
shouldn't go to work if the husband's earning a living wage. I
think a lot of them do it to dress up.'

About death and funerals, the wife said, 'People respect their
dead better today. They used to stop at a halfway house at the
burial. The best part of them would have more than they ought
to have done. In dozens of cases there'd be a fight on the way back.
Yes, they'd disagree about the things in the mother's home.
There was always some of them who would have a few over the
eight. And if there was anything in the family [disagreements] it
all came out, they had their battle out. Perhaps it would be some
brothers and sisters because one took more insurance money than
the other.' Asked what this meant, she said, 'Well, one might be
paying in one penny for the mother and she'd get £8 for that penny,
but another might be paying in tuppence and she'd get £16. One
might say to the other, you're only waiting for Mum to die to get
that money.' And just after that she added, 'The eldest boy could
claim the lot if the last parent died. Yes, I think that happens now.
The eldest son could claim the lot. As a rule though it's shared
equal. I do know that. A woman's mother living up the street died
only last week. The money was shared out and even a sister in
America can claim her share. I know that for a fact. Yes, it's
usually if there's one of the children at home who takes on the
home. But you have to ask the landlord for the tenancy.

'Oh, they all have a big show with weddings now. *We* went back
to work when *we* were married. One of my daughters had it kept up
at her husband's mother's place, because it was a bigger place than
here, and my Rosie had a big hall. Oh yes, all the family would be
there, even cousins. There weren't many white weddings in those
days. When my mother got married she was in a mauve bonnet and
a Paisley shawl, and when I got married I just had my best frock,
and he managed a suit. It was only those with money who went on
for three days. That wasn't our station of life. That was the bigger
pots. Each of my sisters had grey weddings.'

21. Loneliness

'No. We've always got something to occupy our minds.'

(A kinship diagram like that on p. 48 was made out in this and other interviews.)

INTERVIEW REPORT 2

(i) 4 August 1955. No. 115. 1 hour 25 minutes. First call. Informant only. Seen on six or seven subsequent occasions.

1–5. Miss Merrivale. 170 Pinchbeck House. Aged sixty-nine. Single. Born, Bow.

General

Miss Merrivale is a pale, very thin woman with a rather pleasant shy smile and wispy grey hair. The thinness of her arms seemed to indicate malnutrition. She was diffident about the interview and perfectly willing to talk, although extremely shy. I raised the question of why she had not got married and she suggested that it was partly because she and her mother had been so close and her mother widowed, but also because 'I didn't meet anyone that appealed to me'. To reach her room one has to climb several flights of an old tenement block between two or three other blocks. At the end of a narrow dark passage is her room. There seemed to be little question that she is voluntarily living in poverty.

6. Household

   i Lives alone.

  ii Informant (head).

 iii Has lived at same residence thirty years.

 iv 'My mother and I couldn't get anywhere else.'

  v Has lived alone since her mother died fifteen years ago in 1940.

 vi 'I would like a change, but I don't think I stand a chance.' She suggested she'd like a ground-floor flat, possibly in a house where there was a yard or garden. When I suggested she might put her name on a housing list although it might take some years to come through, she commented, 'I don't think it's worth it. I'd be in the other country before my name came up.'

7. *Type of Dwelling*

i Private tenement flat, third floor.

ii One room.

iii She shares the lavatory with neighbours in their one-room flatlets, shares water supply, and has only one gas ring. There is a washroom on the same floor which she does not use, preferring to go to the local baths.

iv In the room is one small iron bedstead, a single slender wooden chair, a small table, two or three large cardboard boxes in which are some of her belongings, no mats on the lino floor, and the one gas ring above the tiny iron grate. There is one large fitted cupboard in which I could see a few oddments of margarine, sugar, jam, tea, and so on but very little else beyond a few pots and pans. On the small table was half a cup of tea and one roll which was half eaten. All the signs pointed to an extremely bare subsistence, if not poverty.

8b. *Retirement*

She worked as a dress machinist most of her life but retired at the age of sixty because 'I wasn't very well at that time so I left. Anyway I don't think they liked their women staying on over the age of sixty. I was glad at the time. No, I'm not sorry I gave up work then.' She seemed to minimize any changes that retirement had brought and merely referred to the reduced income. She had been earning between five and six pounds then, which was at the end of the war.

9. *Source of Income*

i Retirement pension of 40s.

ii No national assistance.

iii No other income.

iv A small amount of savings, certainly no more than £50.

v No earnings.

vi None.

vii She did not use tobacco vouchers.

10. *Money Problems, Applications*

She said that she knew about national assistance but did not

T–K

want to apply for it. 'I'll have to apply when I need it, but while I've got a little savings I'll draw on that. There's nobody I've got to leave it to, so I'd rather use that than cost the country any more.' She knew perfectly well that she would be able to get some assistance if needed.

11. Selected Items of Expenditure

Rent 6s. 8d. Coal only about 3s. 6d. to 4s., because she said she made do with 'half a hundred in the winter, because I can't stand a lot of firing'. No subscription clubs. No life insurance. No radio. When I was questioning her about the amount of money she needed to spend in any one week, I first suggested that perhaps she might spend around £3 a week but she insisted, 'No, not as much as that. I only go over my money by a few shillings.' It thus appears that she must live on something like £2 5s. a week, drawing about 5s. weekly from her savings.

12. Health

  i Fairly active.
 ii (*a*) Very little limitation of movement.
    (*b*) No pain in feet.
    (*c*) Some giddiness but no falls.
iii Very thin and, I thought, undernourished.
 iv 'Fairly well but a bit chesty.'
  v Alert.
 vi (*a*) Her last medical consultation was six weeks previously
        to have an ear syringed.
    (*b*) One medical consultation last year.
    (*c*) She had never been an in-patient in hospital.
    (*d*) No visits from the district nurse.
vii She sleeps 'too well' (that is, from 8 in the evening till 7 in
        the morning).

13. No Welfare Services or Clubs

'No. I could go to one of these old people's clubs. Some of the people in these buildings go but you only see all the people who live here. I have a read.' Questioned further about this it appeared that such a club did not appeal to her. She was shy and feared membership of a club would lead to associations interfering with her privacy.

14. Household and Personal Services

i–vii It was quite clear after a whole series of questions that she does all her own household jobs and odd jobs of various kinds and collects her own pension.

  ix She has not been ill in any serious respect for a good many years but if she were ill she would 'send down to the Superintendent of these flats. If I was ill I suppose I'd have to go into hospital. I don't think of those things. If I'm not feeling well I look after myself. I'd rather manage that way. I'm independent.' It appeared that she did not even think that she would trouble the neighbours to send for a doctor and said that if she could she'd go and tell the Superintendent herself. On a subsequent call she had had a cold but sought the help of no one. She made one journey to the shops and then retired to bed for two days.

15. She occasionally fetched an errand for a widowed woman of great age in a nearby flat. Apart from this, she performed no services for others. She looked after her mother in the last years of her life.

17. Friends and Neighbours

I was able to put a great number of questions about neighbours and more or less established all the contacts with all the people living nearby. Apparently her particular block has many single-room flats and most of the people living there are fairly isolated. In the room on her left is a middle-aged woman whom she rarely sees and on her right a man. They never went into each other's rooms, only exchanged a greeting in the passage or on the stairs. 'The one that side is at work most of the day and so is the other. I seldom see them. The only one I see is an old lady on the landing. I fetch things for her sometimes. Not every day, just now and again in the week. I'm not a one to get thick. Her children come to visit her. No, she's not a friend, just a neighbour.' It appears she meant that although she would drop in on this old lady, she did not stay very long and did not consider her a friend. She called two or three times a week, collected an errand, but did not linger in the woman's home more than a few minutes. Persistent questions about friends failed to reveal a single one. She replied to a whole series of questions about her evening activities, a visit to the cinema and so on. One very good indication of this was that she said that she had no one to sign her pension book each year, but had to go over to the Citizen's Advice Bureau to get the signature of someone there.

18. Holidays, Outings, Pastimes, Festivals, etc.

i When I asked if she'd had a holiday this year or was going on one she said, 'I've been to Southend twice. No, only outings for the day. No, I didn't go with anybody.' She caught the train, sat on the promenade, had tea, and came home, by herself.

ii She never stays with any friends, and has no relatives.

iii 'At Christmas I had an invitation in to a neighbour.' But she did not go because the woman had children (the woman living on the landing referred to earlier). At Easter, birthdays, and other occasions her days are spent mostly as any other.

iv She said that she goes by herself to the cinema once or twice a week but apart from occasional walks in the park there are no other outside activities. I kept questioning her about this and found that she had no radio to listen to but plays the mandolin, because she had been a member of a band in her early life. With great pride she showed me the mandolin case and pulled out a whole pile of tattered music, among which I saw 'Meditation' by Gounod which she called 'Ave Maria'. There were one or two pieces from *Tannhäuser* and *William Tell*. 'I make my own amusement when I want to.'

vii As her mother had died some fifteen years ago and was virtually her last relative, I questioned her about the arrangements at the time of death and afterwards at the funeral. 'I managed all on my own. There was nobody but me at the funeral.'

viii C. of E. but not a churchgoer.

19. Family Life

Her case was the most isolated yet encountered. She was the only child of her mother and the mother did not die until the age of eighty-eight in 1940. Her father had died when she was only eleven and she and her mother 'were just like pals. We went everywhere together. We worked at the same place until the last few years of her life when she stayed at home. That was my worst trouble [mother's death.]' When I questioned her about her mother's siblings she said that her mother had had three brothers and two sisters and that they'd all died much earlier than her mother. It appeared that the last one died before 1930. Both she and her mother had lost touch with the children of these brothers and sisters and the informant mentioned that her mother often used to speak of what would happen to her daughter when she in fact died. 'I know I have cousins but I don't know where they are. No, I don't know the address of any relative.' The same appeared to be the case for her father's relatives. 'I've never had any relatives in Bethnal Green and I've never seen any of them for more than twenty years. No, I'm not sorry I haven't any relatives in Bethnal Green.'

She said that her biggest problem has been 'getting a living'. When I asked what was the happiest time in her life she said, 'I've made myself happy at all times'.

20. Changes in Family Life

I didn't persist with these questions because it was obviously difficult to talk about the changes in family life with a person who had no family. She did, however, say that children didn't seem to have the same idea of duty to their parents these days and she particularly complained about young children in flats. 'They're awful now. I don't think they're brought up properly.' She said that there'd been a lot of changes since the old days but that people were not so friendly and families, so far as she could see, didn't seem to cling together so much.

21. Loneliness

She was most emphatic in saying that she was not lonely. 'I make my life. If I feel miserable I go out for a walk in the park.' She indicated in answer to other questions that she'd been used to a rather lonely life and therefore found it easier to amuse herself.

Additional Note

It was difficult to believe, after the first call, that Miss Merrivale
was as isolated from society as appeared to be the case. She was
visited on six or seven subsequent occasions. On all points the first
interview was confirmed. Invariably she was at home, invariably
alone. On Christmas Eve, 1955, she was found to have received no
Christmas card and indeed was expecting to spend Christmas day
alone. The only evidence of Christmas was a large sheet of Wool-
worth's Christmas wrapping paper which she had put in an old
picture frame. On a later call I found that the only neighbour with
whom she had any contact had now moved out of London. Miss
Merrivale missed her but persistent questioning failed to reveal any
other person whom she now visited, even briefly.

INTERVIEW REPORT 3

(i) Main interview, December 1954. 3 hours 15 minutes. No. 49.
First hour with husband, nearly another hour with Mr and Mrs T.,
married daughter, and two granddaughters, and final hour or so
with the old couple alone. I saw this couple on six further occasions
in the course of the following year and a half and additional
information obtained during these calls is appended to the following report.

1–5. Mrs Tilbury. 13 Braintree Street. Aged sixty-eight. Married.
Born, Bethnal Green.

General

Mrs Tilbury is a plump, motherly-looking woman with her grey-
black hair swept either side of her head to the back in a knot like a
gipsy, with dark eyes surrounded by wrinkles, and she wore a pair
of drop garnet earrings. When she laughed, her face creased in
smiles. Her husband is a youthful-looking man with greying hair, a
deeply lined, leathery face, and a rather military bearing.

6. *Living Arrangements*

   i   Arthur – sixty-eight – married – husband.
   ii Husband (head).
   iii Has lived there thirty-nine years, except for a period of
      eleven years during and after the war when Mrs Tilbury,

together with her two daughters and their families, was living in a bungalow on the coast. At that time the husband lived in the present house and went to see his wife and family at week-ends. 'During the war when there was all the bombing we rented a bungalow. He [husband] used to come down week-ends. I had all the family with me. A niece and her child too.' There were then four married women living with their children together, because of the absence in the Forces of the husbands.

iv   Mrs Tilbury's parents lived in the house previously, and she and her husband and family lived with them for twenty-five years, until their death after the war.

 v   The last change in the household composition was after the end of the war when her father and mother both died and their youngest daughter, Phyllis, got married.

vi   The old couple do not want to move but in the next few weeks will have to do so because of the scheduled demolition of the house. On my first call, the informant said, 'No, I don't want to move. I want to be carried out of here. My daughter lives in Wimbolt Street. We want to go there. We've heard of a couple of Jewesses with a downstairs flat and we are trying to arrange a change with them [through the L.C.C.].' On the last call at that house Mrs Tilbury came in to tell her husband that she had just been to the housing office. 'We're to have it. They're to exchange. We were hoping it would be all right. Oh, my legs. I just can't get about. It's taken me all my time to get there – and the waiting. They told me we were to have that place, but they said something about the builders wanting to do it up, and when I went upstairs to the builders, they thought we were in for an ordinary exchange. They said we had to take our chance just like the rest of them. But then I explained and said that we were having to get out because of the schedule for the slums. They said they'd have to do it up but they couldn't tell me when it would be done. I told them we didn't want the hallway and kitchen done because that has just been done recently and it was nice plastic paint, but they've got it all down though,' she assured her husband. Later she said to her husband, 'You'll feel it when you're there. No yard. It's all confined there. I

thought I was going to get claustro-something, but I expect
I'll get used to it. I shall make myself comfortable there.'
They explained to me that originally they had been offered
a place in Hackney but they made very strenuous efforts to
get near their youngest daughter, and finally found that they
could obtain a flat from two single women who wanted to
move out of Bethnal Green. Because they were entitled to a
place in Hackney they have arranged for these two women to
go into that place. Mrs Tilbury said she had to go up to the
housing office several times, 'to tell them'. When I first called
she was terrified she would be moved a long way from her
daughter, but at the final call when they knew that the flat in
Wimbolt Street was assured, they were both resigned to the
move. The husband said, 'It'll make a difference though,
without a yard. I used to breed wire-haired terriers and
chickens and rabbits. You know old Dr Franks who was in
the Bethnal Green Road before Dr Wames? I used to keep
him supplied with eggs.' Explaining why he wanted to move
into the flat in Wimbolt Street, he said, 'Why I want to go
there is if we went somewhere else, me and the missus would
be lonely. She can go over to Phyllis's and watch the television when I'm asleep [he works at night]'.

vii Neither of them has any great objection to living with one of
their married daughters if it became necessary. But they
recognize that they want to preserve some independence.
What they wish most of all is to be near one another. Mrs T.
said, 'I wouldn't mind going out into the country. If her
mother went,' she said, pointing at her granddaughter, 'if
she went to the country I'd go with her.'

7. *Type of Dwelling*

i Terraced cottage. Refaced at the end of the war.
ii Four rooms and a kitchen and yard.
iii No bath.
iv A narrow passage led to a pleasant, square kitchen with an
old iron grate and fireplace, a large window looking out on
to the garden, an old dresser with Victorian china on it, two
armchairs, a table, and a few wooden chairs. On the walls
were hanging photographs of a nephew and two of the

husband's brothers. In the front living-room, where furniture and bedding had already been stacked in preparation for the move, there was a piano with two pot Alsatian dogs on top and numerous photographs of the family. I was shown a box of photographs of most of the close relatives, including children, grandchildren, in-laws, nieces and nephews, grand-nieces and grand-nephews, cousins and cousins once removed, parents, and even grandparents.

8a. Occupation

Mrs Tilbury has been a machinist for many years and her parents and grandparents and great-grandparents used to be silk weavers. Her health has been bad this year and she has been unable to do very much outwork. Her boss had 'been round four times this month, it getting near Christmas, asking me to do some work for him. I tell him I can't do it, the doctor won't let me. I can't even do the dresses for my grandchildren.'

The husband is a night guard at a factory. He works sixty-five hours a week, usually starting at 6.30 p.m. and finishing at 7.30 a.m. He has been in this job for nine years. Asked if he wanted to retire he said, 'I don't want to stop. I want to go on for as long as I can. Confidentially, they think I'm three years younger. They usually lay them off when they're sixty-five. I want to stick there as long as I can. How would I do if I gave up? We'd be living on nothing [he recounted the cost of coal, gas, lighting, and rent and food in comparison with 54s. he'd get on retirement]. I don't want to exist, I want to live.' He recounted with pride a remark that had been passed on to him that his boss had made. 'He said to this bloke, if you want to know anything, you ask Tilbury, he knows everything.' On the first call when I saw the wife alone, she said, 'He's saved them from fire three times. He used to be a meat pitcher. We've been used to good money. He's been on sickness benefit for nine or ten weeks now [by the time I called the final time it had proved to be eleven or twelve weeks]. He went to work with a broken bone in his back. I ask you. There's not many men could do that. He's been through it these last years. He's got so much courage though.' The husband said later on, 'It would be murder if I retired. We've always liked having a good table. A chicken and plenty of meat like. When I worked up the market [until six years previously] we never bought meat from the butcher, I used to get it there. We're used to a chicken and it's much less than meat I can tell you, now. We couldn't do all that if I retired. We wouldn't have anything.' He had worked for most of his life as a porter. 'That was all night work too.'

10. Earnings normally £8 a week. Some savings but not amounting to more than £100. No pension or other source of income. No regular payments from children.

11. Selected Items of Expenditure

Rent 16s. 7d. Coal 7s. No clothing or Christmas club. Gas 6s. Light 2s. 6d. Insurances 2s.

12. Health

    i Fairly active.

    ii (a) She can't climb stairs because of heart trouble. She finds it difficult getting about and says she doesn't like going on her own on to buses and travelling about.

       (b) She had pain in her feet.

       (c) She had a fall the week before the first interview, when she slipped in her yard, cut her knee and bruised her arms and shoulders.

   iii Plump.

    v Alert.

   vi (a) Last visited doctor one month ago. 'He tried to persuade me to go to hospital on account of my heart trouble. But we don't want to leave here. So long as we can manage.'

      (b) She had seen her doctor three or four times in last year.

      (c) Never been in hospital.

      (d) Never had district nurse.

  vii Her husband has had several illnesses in recent years. He said that he had three lots of stitches in his stomach. His most recent trouble occurred in August of this year. He was twelve weeks off work. For six weeks he was in Bethnal Green Hospital. 'I was having all my teeth taken out and after they'd taken one lot out I went to the dentist again and there was a doctor and nurse there and they said I had to have gas and I don't know what happened when I had gas. I suppose I may have struggled. But when I came out I could hardly stand up. I couldn't sleep that night for the pain and the temporary doctor said I had acute lumbago. The next day I saw my own doctor and he said I had acute fibrositis. So I said which is it? And went back to work, but it seemed to get worse, and they told me to go along to the outpatients at Bethnal Green Hospital. The doctor there said I couldn't come out. He said he didn't know how I managed to stand on my feet at all. They said I'd broken a bone in my spine. I'd got to wear a belt, like a woman's corset, to support my back. They didn't tell me but I know what they thought. They thought I had some cancer in my spine but it turned out it was the bone. But I can't say enough of my treatment in hospital. If I'd been paying £20 a week I wouldn't have got better treatment. There's a class of people that go in and are always complaining. Can't they have a doctor and nurse to themselves? My doctor said to the man in the next bed, "You be like this one, it's will-power that's getting him right."' His wife said, 'I haven't told him this but I heard all about him from others there. He was always laughing and cracking a joke.' And her husband said, 'Well, it's no use lying there with a face like that.' And he pulled a very long and hideous face. He had been in Bethnal Green Hospital two or three times since the war. 'I'd had a perforated duodenal ulcer, that's what all these stitches over the stomach are. They told me it was a very serious operation before I went in, but I said, "Doctor, I don't mind what it is as long as you get me out of this pain."' He also showed me some very bad scars on his wrist which he got in the first war, when a bullet went through his wrist.

His wife, referring to her poor health, said, 'What worries me is I can't get about like I used to. I'm always thinking about that. I only wish I could do more. I get so nervous too. They took me to one of those shows on ice [her youngest daughter and family took her to see this some time back]. I couldn't enjoy the show because I was thinking about them moving stairs. My son-in-law and my daughter had to carry me over them.' She also gave an instance of the help that her daughter gives her. Recently her daughter went to the doctor for a prescription. 'My girl went over with some medicine for me. When she said she'd come about Mum and not Dad, the doctor said, "It's your Dad who's really in trouble. It's your Dad we want to get better."'

13. No welfare services or clubs. They are too concerned with their own family to want to join any club, but Mrs Tilbury said that she 'can't get about to these things'.

14. Household and Personal Services

   i Mrs Tilbury still does a good deal of her own shopping, cooking, cleaning, and washing. 'My daughter does some. She's a bit rough and ready, like me. She wanted to stop off work. She said she wanted to turn her job up so that she could look after me. But I didn't want to stand in her light.' The daughter works as a waitress in the City from 10 till 3.30 p.m. 'She comes over here before she goes and cooks me a bit of dinner. My two granddaughters come from school and have it with me.'

  ii Daughter and husband help with odd jobs such as windows, fires, repairs.

 iii Husband deals with official forms and the like but the informant seems to do a good deal of the negotiating because her husband has to sleep in the day.

  v The husband gives his wife £5 for housekeeping (which also covers the rent), but he also pays for the coal.

 ix If the informant is ill, her youngest daughter living a couple of minutes' walk away would look after her. 'When she comes in here she says, "I'm going to scrub up", and nothing you can do will stop her.' She has a very good neighbour living opposite who will run any errands or do anything to help, and her grandchildren are always fetching her errands.

15. Services performed for others

A couple of years ago the informant went to look after her eldest daughter who was ill with TB. 'I stayed with my daughter six weeks. I really did knock myself up. But Grace was helping me [Grace is the sixteen-year-old granddaughter] and she said why didn't I come back home for a day or two because she thought she could manage. Well, it went on and went on and my daughter was in a sanatorium for a year and ten months. I wanted her children to come over here. But Grace managed it all. She said she wouldn't come because she said, "Daddy won't look after himself." She's a proper little mother she is. She did everything right. I wish you could see her.'

Mrs Tilbury frequently looks after her youngest daughter's two children, at lunch time when her daughter is at work, and she fetches the youngest one from school and sometimes the eldest, around four o'clock. Indeed, on one visit, she came in with the youngest granddaughter and the older one followed later. Once a week when her daughter goes out with her son-in-law to the cinema she has the two granddaughters to stay with her. She said, 'I like to make things for my grandchildren. Everything they've got on is what I made [and indeed the two granddaughters were beautifully dressed]. I was hoping to do it for them this Christmas but I just haven't been able to.'

The ties with the granddaughters are extremely close. 'They save up their money and every time they go away they bring us back something. They never miss us with a Christmas box. They brought round what they've got for their Mum and Dad, an umbrella and a pair of braces. They said that now they were going to try and get ours.' And the husband said, 'I give 'em sixpence each every week. And I give 'em ten bob each at Christmas. Then they can buy what they want.'

Mrs Tilbury looked after her aged parents. They did not die until after the war, at the ages of eighty-seven and eighty-five respectively.

Referring to the frequency with which the three generations have tea together, the informant said, 'We often eat together. They all come here. We've had them here every Christmas. My husband gets a turkey and we have a real good party. I don't know what we'll do this Christmas though [because of the move]. I suppose we'll go round to my daughter's.'

17. *Friends and Neighbours*

Mrs Tilbury pointed out that her immediate neighbours had already been moved out, and she said that she didn't have very close relations with many of them. 'Only one pops in for chat. A woman living opposite.' The husband, when he was alone with me, elaborated about friends and neighbours: 'We've any amount of friends. The woman across the road comes over nearly every day and has a chat. My wife, she only has to go up the top of the street for an errand, and it may be two hours before she's back. They all stop her and have a gossip. You can't go round the corner without bumping into someone you know. And [referring to relatives] they all knock at the door, they all stop here. They come in and sit down and then they go.' He warned me not to take too much notice of those who said that children neglected their parents. 'There's one old girl living alone near here, she must be eighty-nine. Her son and daughter have been begging of her to go with them. But she won't. She just won't. There's a lot like that.'

18. Holidays, Outings, Hobbies, Festivals, etc.

  i No holiday this year, but it is the first for many years. 'We've got a friend at Southend who used to live next door. We used to go there for a fortnight every year' (i.e., husband, wife, daughter, son-in-law, and granddaughter).

  ii Mrs Tilbury used to go and stay with her eldest daughter quite frequently, but has been unable to do so lately because of her health.

 iii Generally at Christmas they all have a big party with children, sons-in-law, and granddaughters. Until recently this also included Mrs Tilbury's parents. Some of the brothers and sisters and nephews and nieces also come. 'We always cling together. This will be the only year we've not had them here.'

  iv Mrs Tilbury used to go quite a lot with her daughter to the cinema, but she hasn't gone now because of her health for over four months. Her husband has not been to a cinema for years. 'We listen to the radio a lot. Children learn a lot from them. We listen to the programmes for schools. I can tell you, you learn a lot.' As said earlier Mrs Tilbury looks after the two grandchildren when the daughter and her husband go to the pictures.

 viii C. of E. They said they weren't churchgoers. 'I reckon you can be just as good if you don't go to church. I'm not against religion, but I've seen something.' (He implied that what he had seen of churches and ministers of religion had not appealed to him.)

19. Family Life

This couple provide a classic example of the old living within a three-generation family setting. Mrs Tilbury showed me two photographs of her youngest daughter's two daughters, in stage garb with top hats and carrying canes. 'They're both stagey. They've been doing step dancing all over the place for charity. They've been up the Chase Settlement step dancing and all that sort of thing. They earned over £200 for the Cancer Campaign. We're very proud of them. I remember in Ramsgate [when the whole family was down there three or four years ago] the youngest one, Jane, was a proper little lady, holding music for a professor. Right in front of a very big audience. I love my grandchildren. They never pass the door. They're perhaps going for a box of Aspros for their Mum and they stop at the door and knock and when I open it I say, "What have you come for?" And they say they just want to come in and see me. They call me Nan.' When the daughter and two granddaughters were there during the last interview at the house they each gave the grandmother and grandfather a very affectionate hug and for some time during the interview the six-year-old granddaughter sat on her Grannie's knee. Mrs Tilbury said her youngest granddaughter, Jane, aged six, had been asked at school to write down three big wishes. 'The first wish was for her sister to keep on with her school, the second was she wanted her Mum to live for ever, and the third was for her Nan, that's me, to get her legs better.' The youngest daughter, Phyllis, who lives just round the corner, is seen at least two or three times every day, and as said earlier, she comes in and gives her mother a great deal of help with the cleaning, cooking a meal, and so on. The eldest daughter comes down with her family every Sunday now. Referring to Grace, the eldest granddaughter aged sixteen, who was a 'little mother' when her mother was in the TB sanatorium for nearly two years and looked after her father and sister, she said, 'Grace was going to stay on at school. The teacher said to us, "Don't let her go in a factory. She's not that sort of girl. Let her go in an office." But she had to stay at home to look after her Dad and sister. Now that her mother's home again I expect they'll try and find her a job.' It should be noted that Mrs Tilbury originally had seven children; two were still-born, two died of whooping cough in their second years, and a third died of convulsions after two or three months.

'My mother and father lived with us for twenty-five years. They were in their late eighties when they died at the end of the war. They was weavers like my grandfather and my grandfather's father. I've still got an old aunt living in Wanstead. Aunt Jane. She's eighty-seven. I used to go down to her and do her curtains and clean out her place. I liked to know she was all right. But I can't do it now. A couple of months ago I went down with my granddaughter [Jane]. Henry [the aunt's husband] shook and cried. It frightened my granddaughter. He said he thought they were all alone in the world. He thought we didn't want them, me not going. It did me no good.' As indicated on the kinship diagram, Mrs Tilbury still has close relations with a sister, a brother-in-law, a cousin, a cousin once removed, and several nephews and nieces and grandnephews.

Referring to the fact that her youngest daughter married at the age of eighteen, the informant said, 'She was only a kid, but what with all them Americans about in the war, we thought it was the best thing. She'd only been going with him a month. Out round our bungalow, I came across all sorts of hearts with daggers, and I knew it was getting serious. He came and said he wanted to get married to her, so I said, "Oh well, I don't know what we're going to think about this, but you'd better go and ask her father." He was in the garden, so he went out there. But it being the war we thought it was all right. My eldest daughter didn't get married till she was twenty-five. It was round the time when Dad was ill. She nearly didn't marry him at all. One day she said to me she was thinking of giving him up. She said it was hardly fair for her to get married when Dad was ill. I told her not to be silly. I didn't want to stand in her light and nor did Dad.'

20. Changes in Family Life

About former times, Mr Tilbury said, 'It was a hard time when I was young, we're happier now. We're more comfortable. We're happier together and more united. You've only got to look at these children. They're dressed up spick and span when they go to school.

When *they* used to go to school there was hardly any of them with shoes on; you give me these people who say, "What about the good old days?" They were the bad old days. I don't want to see those days again. That's the truth. You never see children with a ha'porth of chips outside the pub these days. Families are more united than they were. You've only got to look at the babies in their prams. They're a picture. They used to put them in the bottom of an old chest of drawers. Or in the bottom of an old banana box. Things are a lot different now. And you don't see the rowing and fights like you used to.' And his wife interrupted, saying, 'When we lived in Haverfield Road when we were first married, a woman stuck a head out of the window and looked down at me, I was outside my house, and she said, "The Queen's dead. Can't you see I'm in mourning?" she said, pointing at her eye. It was all swollen and black. Every Saturday night you used to see a bundle with somebody or other.' She looked at her husband and added, 'Me and him used to have a bundle. But we've got used to ourselves now.' The husband said that 'Husbands and wives get along better now. Her husband,' he said, looking at his daughter, 'wouldn't think twice of doing the washing.' And Myra, the eleven-year-old granddaughter, said, 'Daddy does Mummy's hoovering sometimes too.' Her grandmother reproved her, saying, 'You shouldn't tell tales out of school'.

'We've been happy all our life. The only bad patches were when we lost our children. I lost a boy, he was only two months, with convulsions.' She looked at her husband and said, 'Losing our children and your illnesses were the worst times'. Apparently when she was machining earlier in her life, they used to have a shop window in the front of the house. 'I used to have the place as a shop window. I used to put all the dresses and pinafores in there and we always used to have people coming in and out.' The husband referred to the advertising stunts that used to go on when a new shop opened in the district. 'The brakes used to go round with a band in them, they were all playing from there. They'd throw out hand-bills to the people. It'd be for some shop that's opening as a butcher's. Or another that was opening as a grocer's. You don't see any of that these days.' And later he said, 'The shops used to stay open sometimes till midnight. And you used to see the people going into the shops when the pubs closed. Christmas night they'd

be open till one and two in the morning.' Again he said, 'But I
don't want them days back again. They say the good old days.
They was the bad old days. I don't want to see them days again.'
Mrs Tilbury, talking about the weaving that had been done by her
father, grandfather, and great-grandfather, said, 'We kids used
to make a bed up under the loom. And the men used to work upstairs. But when the missus went in they'd take off their aprons and
throw them over their work. They wouldn't tolerate the missus
looking at them working. They threw the apron over it.' Talking
about her family she said, 'I was the roughest one in the family,
of all my sisters. All my sisters was respectable. They was people
you could take anywhere. They didn't have a lot but they always
kept themselves nice. My eldest daughter's like that but my
youngest's like me. She's rough and ready.' She referred again to
the spotless way in which her granddaughters were turned out.
'The kiddies today all look better. They're all dressed nice. *We*
never had underclothes or shoes. We was lucky if we had a $2\frac{3}{4}$d.
pair of socks. The boots only cost 2s. but we didn't always have
them.' And the husband said, 'It wasn't till I was nearly thirty
that I was even able to have a suit, and that only cost five and
twenty bob with two pairs of trousers. And an overcoat only cost
£1.' Twice Mrs Tilbury referred to 'my Dad's photo, taken
when he was weaving, when the Prince of Wales visited the
borough'.

Mr Tilbury told several stories about the days when he returned
from the Western Front in the First World War. He told of going
about in blues in Manchester when shopkeepers used to give him a
basket of fruit or a couple of haddocks for nothing. 'When we got
to the station, there was a whole train load of us and we was all
lousy I can tell you. I was caked in blood. And the other side of the
barriers the nurses were there with trays giving you this and that.
You didn't know what to take first. They'd be throwing you bags
of fruit and biscuits and sweets and everything. There is some good
people in the world. We had none of this military nonsense. If
you was a sergeant or a corporal or a private you was all mixed up.'
Mrs Tilbury said, 'You didn't need to go in the Army. He was in
the meat trade and Sonny [her husband said, 'Everybody called me
Sonny because they called my father Sonny and that name stuck']
could have stayed at home. But Mr Clever went.' And Mr Tilbury

said, 'Well, I wouldn't like to have said after the war that I wasn't in it.'

21. Loneliness

'No, we've always got plenty of people seeing us. We've always got our family. We've always been clinging together. I think families are more together than they used to be. Mind you, I don't say that's everyone. I don't class them what goes to pubs. We cling together.'

Interview after Move into Council Flat in December

When I called the day before Christmas Eve, Mrs Tilbury and her daughter Phyllis were supervising a coalman carrying bags of coal into the downstairs flat into which Mr and Mrs Tilbury had moved a few days previously. 'Mum's been burning bits of wood, any old thing – it's been dreadful,' Phyllis told me. The new flat lacked all the character of the former cottage, but its amenities were undoubtedly better. An all-night inset fire was in the living-room, there was a bathroom, a good kitchen sink, and spacious cupboards. The walls had been newly covered with flowered wallpaper and a new piece of 'oil-cloth' was on the living-room floor. Mrs Tilbury said, referring to her husband, 'I don't know where Dad found the money, but he found it. . . . I bought this sideboard off the people who were here before – it's very nice. It's one of these antiques. I thought I wasn't going to like the place before, I thought I was going to feel shut in, but I shall get used to it. I shall settle down.' She was worried about the fire, 'I'm not used to it', and although there was a hearth and a fender had bought a fire-guard. Mrs Tilbury showed me two taffeta dresses she was making for her two granddaughters. 'I must get on with them tonight. I must finish them for Christmas.' Phyllis told me she had bought a signet ring and a handbag for her eleven-year-old daughter, 'I've put some lipstick inside but I shall tell her not to use it yet.' She laughed and seemed to view with pleasure her daughter's approach to womanhood.

Further Interview with Mr and Mrs Tilbury on 13 June 1955, 3.30 p.m. $1\frac{1}{2}$ hours

Bethnal Green

Asked why they did not wish to move out of Bethnal Green, and

why they liked the borough, Mr Tilbury said, 'You know everybody. It wouldn't be the same atmosphere anywhere else. There's
no snobbish with the people. Everyone in Bethnal Green seems to
have money. Yes, an insurance man was telling me that in Bethnal
Green he never has to go twice for the money. You never see them
on the floor these days. There's never the borrowing like there was.'
His wife commented, 'You'd never go long if you were on the floor,
though the people are rough. I remember, Sonny,' she said, looking
at her husband, 'when the fellow down the turning came up to you
and said he'd heard you'd been away for a few weeks.' 'Yes,' said
the husband, 'he put his hand in his pocket and gave me a pound.
"Ta-ta," he said, "I'll see you soon."' 'Rough as they are,' said
Mrs Tilbury, 'they're as good as gold. I've seen some of them that
he's brought home to my place. I've said get them out of my place
as quick as you can, they looked that rough. But they're as good
as gold.'

When I asked why it was that her son-in-law seemed to want to
move out of Bethnal Green, Mrs Tilbury explained, 'Sons-in-law
don't go mad on the mothers and fathers-in-law. He's got a nice job
in Ford's in Dagenham but my daughter doesn't want to leave
Bethnal Green. I think it might make a difference in their lives.'
The couple then thought it necessary to emphasize the quality of
their daughter's husband and said that he only 'drinks once a
month' (that is, only once a month with Mr Tilbury). Talking
generally about problems of setting up home upon marriage, Mrs
Tilbury said, 'He'd like to go in for buying a house. A lot of young
'uns live with parents these days. Phyllis [her daughter] set up
home here after the war. The capers we had to get the place. She
put her cot and Myra's bed and all her stuff in one room in our
place and even then they didn't think we were overcrowded.
Course, she wasn't really living there.' She made one quite
interesting remark about her son-in-law and his wish to move
further out. 'I really think he wanted to go to East Ham where all
his relatives are. I think he wanted to be near all his old aunts so
that he could go and see them.'

Neighbours

The couple moved into this new flat some six months ago and the
husband said, 'I still don't know the neighbours'. And his wife said

that they were very good. 'They say good morning or good evening. I miss a lot of the old neighbours but I knew some of them round here from my girl living here. There's an old girl aged eighty just here who's all shrivelled up with cancer. She cries sometimes and when I hear that woman cry I want to go and knock. She lives with her daughter. But I don't know whether I should.' Later, on 'good' neighbours, she said, 'I don't like nosy people. There's one woman upstairs who keeps talking about sweeping the dust down. I say they're upstairs and I'm down. You should keep yourself to yourself. Yes, they'd only come in when there was trouble.' In a jocular remark about chatting to people in the street and the number of friends they could talk to, Mrs Tilbury said, 'My girl says she won't come up the road – there's too much jawing and it would be a couple of hours before she would be back.' And when her husband interjected that he wouldn't come up the road with her, she remarked, 'Yes, he's frightened it would cost him too much.'

Families in Occupations

A few comments were made on the tradition of handing jobs down from father to son, in the docks particularly. Mr Tilbury said that when he first worked in the meat market it was very common to get a job for a son or a nephew or someone like that and Mrs Tilbury remarked that when the foremen in the docks were choosing men for the day's work it was usually the relatives and those in the gang who were selected.

Housekeeping

Mrs Tilbury, 'I remember when I first got married I got a pound a week wages. He used to have more than I did for beer money [her husband protested at this]. Yes, he did, and I'm not afraid at saying this. I paid 6s. 6d. rent out of that and put away 2s. 6d. every week in a yearly club and drew it out Christmas. That shows you how far the money went in those days.' Mr Tilbury was rather scornful of money clubs. He said that 'If you draw a loan out of those clubs you're paying interest on your own money.' Mrs Tilbury said, 'Even with £5 or £6 a week these days you are singing "do not forget me" on Tuesday.'

Grandmothers and Grandchildren

Mrs Tilbury, 'I look after them all their holidays. I go up and sit
with them. I worry my life about those kids. They're so venture-
some. But that's what I'd like to see. [She returned to a comment
she had made at a previous interview.] I'd like to see them giving up
their dancing now that Myra's got to a Grammar School.' Saying
that nearly all the households in the blocks of flats possessed television sets, she remarked that her granddaughter 'said to her
father, "You ought to be ashamed, Dad, not having a tellie." Yes
she did.'

Housework

There seemed to be a slight element of conflict in her views about
her daughter being 'houseproud'. She had said before how spotless her daughter's home always was and how a person could call
at any time of day and find it in perfect order. 'The best part of
young 'uns these days want a good time all the time, but my
daughter on a Saturday night will start doing her washing. I
think sometimes it's too much. I've said to her, you'll drive him
out.' Both Mr and Mrs Tilbury agreed that 'Young husbands
definitely do more in the homes these days. My son-in-law cleans
the windows and does the paintwork. A lot of men do that.'

Funerals

Mr Tilbury supplied most of the following information. 'Some
of the relatives wouldn't follow. They'd go down to the grounds by
bus. The father would organize it if the mother died but if both the
parents were dead it would be the eldest son or daughter. They'd
get round the others and work it all out. When they followed the
eldest son would go first, supposing he was twenty, and then the
next one, supposing he was eighteen, and then one sixteen, and so
on by age like that. So the next followed on. The children might be
in the first coach and the brothers and sisters in the second. No,
the nephews and nieces wouldn't go. Yes, relations were always
asked to follow. That would sometimes cause an argument. He
didn't ask me to follow. She didn't ask me. Sometimes they'd come
straight out of the cemetery and go for a drink and then they'd get
on the booze and finish up singing or fighting. There'd be argu-

ments over the insurance money. It used to be the eldest who took
the possessions, but now it's all changed and it's shared. When
my mother died the insurance people paid for the funeral and then
we all had to go up to Mare Street to get £2 18s. It was all agreed
that £2 18s. would go to my widowed sister. What money we had,
like £5, we put together and bought a stone for them – it cost £22.
Yes, you do that out of respect.' Mrs Tilbury interjected, 'What
makes me wild is that they never keep it up [looking after the
grave]. Mr Tilbury continued, 'Sometimes they'd have a handker-
chief round the head in the old days. That would be to keep the
jaw from slipping. And then there was money over the eyes. Yes,
they'd be washed first till the undertakers come. All the relatives
would come and maybe they wouldn't be buried for five or six
days, but if they turned the undertakers would come and screw them
down. They don't go into black like they used to for the dead. The
widows used to wear their weeds. I think it's a good thing you don't
see that these days. If it was a young widow everyone would say
something fresh to them. The war widows used to have rosettes in
their hats – black with white in the centre. There'd be three or four
months' full mourning and the young children would wear white
frocks with a black sash or bow for a couple of months. But you
don't see any of that now.' Asked whether neighbours had a collection for a wreath, Mrs Tilbury said that that still happened. 'It is
usually a woman who collects. Any woman with a good front who
could get it out of people.' And asked about widows marrying
soon after the death of a husband, Mr Tilbury said, 'Some of
them had them in line before the old man was cold.' Mrs Tilbury
observed that years ago a widow had nothing to fall back upon,
such as a pension, and so was obliged either to go out to work or to
find a husband quickly. 'Years ago a widow got nothing when her
husband died, so if someone had a bit of money they were in.'

Examples of Diaries Kept by Old People

THE following four diaries (two of them shortened) were selected from twelve that give some illustration of the patterns of daily life of old people in Bethnal Green. With a few minor alterations to conceal identity and correct spelling and punctuation they are printed as written. Among a few simple instructions people were asked to note the time of day when getting up, having breakfast, calling on relatives and friends, etc., and to note in particular whom they met and what they did together. Altogether twenty people, selected to represent as fair a cross-section as possible of those interviewed, were approached. A few refused because they were unable to write and a few because they did not want to do it. Twelve kept a diary for a whole week.

WEEK'S DIARY NO. 1

21–27 March 1955

Mrs Tucker, 16 Bantam Street, aged sixty, living with infirm husband in terraced cottage

Monday

7.45 a.m. I got up, went down, and put my kettle on the gas – halfway – then I raked my fire out and laid it, swept my ashes up, and then cleaned my hearth. Then I set light to my fire, then sat down for a while, then I made tea and me and Dad had a cup.

9.20 a.m. I went out for the *Daily Mirror* and fags for Dad. About eight people said 'Good morning' with a nice smile, then I replied back. Then I went home and prepared oats and bread, butter and tea and me and Dad sat for breakfast. When we finished I cleared away and swept and mopped my kitchen out.

11.15 a.m. I started to get dinner on, then Mrs Rice, a neighbour, asked me to get her coals in, and she will take my bag-wash, also get my dog's meat. We had a nice chat about Mother's Day. I showed her my flowers and card which Alice sent. It was very touching, a box of chocs from John, stockings and card from Rose, card and 5s. from Bill, as I know they all think dearly of me.

1.0 p.m. My daughter Alice came with baby. We had dinner together.

2.0 p.m. My daughter Rose and husband came. I made them a cup of tea and cake.

3.15 p.m. Dad and I sat to listen to radio.

5.0 p.m. We both had tea, bread and cheese Dad, bread and jam myself. When finished I cleared away again.

7.0 p.m. My son John and his wife called to see if we were all right before they went home from work.

8.0 p.m. I did a little mending.

10.0 p.m. We went to bed.

Tuesday

8.0 a.m. I put kettle on. While waiting for it to boil I lit my fire, swept up, cleaned my hearth, then made my tea and sat for a while.

9.0 a.m. I went for the *Mirror*. I had a chat with Mrs Hoover. She told me about her husband being queer, I felt very sorry for her, although I have my own bad. Then I got my potatoes and went home, had breakfast, plate of oats for Dad and me.

10.10 a.m. I cleared my kitchen up and went out for stewing meat around the corner at Stan's, only 1s. 6d. Came back and put it on.

11.30 a.m. I went around to see my little granddaughter Carol in Tudworth St. A lady asked me how I was. She told me when her boy was three he used to miss the food off the table such as spam or pies, she spoke to him about it, he was feeding his pussy, he said. She gave him a bit to *give* his pussy and, as he called it, a rat came out of a hole and we had a good laugh. Then I came home with my granddaughter. I am happy when she is here and so is Dad.

1.0 p.m. We had dinner, then I read the paper.

4.30 p.m. My daughter came. We had tea together, then she took baby home.

5.30 p.m. Listened to wireless.

7.0 p.m. My son and wife called in. Stayed till 8, then went home.

9.0 p.m. We went to bed.

Wednesday

7.45 a.m. We were up as I had to go to Doctor's with Dad. We just
had a cup of tea and off we went at 9. Then we came home to
Quaker Oats and bread and butter – that was 10 o'clock. I lit my
fire, then cleared my kitchen up.

11.0 a.m. I went to the chemist first, then got my potatoes and a
little piece of meat. I made a lot of it. I put it through the mincer
with other little things and made a nice pie.

1.0 p.m. We had dinner and cup of tea and my daughter stayed
with baby Carol. Nobody came after 6 o'clock, except my son
John came with his wife to say good night before they went
home from work.

9.0 p.m. We went to bed: I didn't feel so well with my back.

Thursday

7.0 a.m. I got up a bit early as it was early closing and I can't rush
about and I can't always expect the children to be right on spot
every time, so while God above gives me a little health and
strength I must use it.

10.0 a.m. I went for my shopping which didn't last long as I don't
get my money till Friday and Saturday, so we make the best of it.

12.30 p.m. We had dinner, then had a rest. My daughter came with
baby then.

2.30 p.m. I fed my dog and cats, then a neighbour asked me to have
her key and see her coals in, as she was visiting a sick friend.

5.0 p.m. My grandson came to see me. He loves to have tea with
me. He went home at 8 o'clock.

9.30 p.m. We went to bed.

Friday

7.30 a.m. I got up, lit my fire, had a cup of tea and then washed my
woollens out, and then I started to do my bedroom, that lasted
up till 11.15, then I got ready and went to the post office with
Dad. I got a few errands on the way and some fish and chips for
dinner, then I fed my birds, cat, dog, had a rest, then went out.
(Two married daughters and three grandchildren came and had
a midday meal.)

3.30 p.m. We went and sat in the park, had a little stroll, then home to tea.

5.0 p.m. We had egg, bread and butter for tea.

6.30 p.m. John and wife came as they always do, then I washed up and cleared up my kitchen. Listened to wireless all night, in between I did a bit of ironing.

10.30 p.m. We went to bed.

Saturday

7.0 a.m. I got up, fed my birds, gave the dog a cup of tea, then had a cup myself, I then got water for cleaning. My back and legs don't keep good, so I have to mop out with Dettol.

9.30 a.m. I went with Dad to the post office and got a few things on the way.

11.30 a.m. I went out to get meat for Sunday and potatoes. On my way back I met my brother, I hadn't seen him for two years. I went and had a drink with him, he was ever so pleased to see me. I hurried back because I left my three grandchildren indoors. I have them on Saturday while my daughter Rose is on the stall with her husband in Bethnal Green Road, but I am pleased to have them. I sent them to the pie shop. I made them hot cups of tea when they came back.

4.30 p.m. We all went for a stroll to Woolworths [in Hackney] and looked at stalls and shops.

6.30 p.m. Their mother took them home.

9.30 p.m. Dad and I had a walk. Had one drink, then home for the wireless, then to bed.

Sunday

9.0 a.m. Up and had breakfast, egg, bread and butter, fed my birds, dog, cats, then I ground all the hard bread I collected from my daughters through the mincer for the little birds outside. I bagged it up and that lasted all the week putting a bit out every morning.

10.30 a.m. I got my dinner all on, then cleared up.

1.30 p.m. Dinner and then a rest.

6.0 p.m. Tea. My son [George – eldest] came with his wife and baby. Brought a box of chocolates. They stayed till 10 o'clock. (Also Alice, Rose, and John.)

10.30 p.m. Went to bed, as we missed the papers very much.

WEEK'S DIARY NO. 2
21–27 March 1955

Mr William James, aged seventy-three, widower, lives alone in
two-room flat on first floor in Gretland Street. Formerly a market
porter

Monday

7.45 a.m. Got up, made a cup of tea.

8.0 a.m. Started to clear the place up. Cleared the fireplace out. I
  had the sweep coming between 9.30 and 10 and they are very
  strict on time. And at 9 had some bread and marmalade for
  quickness and he came at 9.45. He stayed about 20 minutes –
  another 5s. gone. Well, I had to sweep up and clear the place up
  and got out at 11.15.

11.15 a.m. Went to the paper shop, got my *News Chronicle* and my
  ration of twenty Woodbines and went to my daughter's place
  in Thirsk Street at 11.45. Sat down for a while and had a smoke.

12.15 p.m. Washed her breakfast things up, swept the kitchen up
  and then had another sit down talking to Mr Bird (budgie).
  Then found some cold meat, so I boiled some potatoes and had
  some dinner with a nice cup of tea.

1.30 p.m. Sat down and read the paper and listened to the wireless
  and of course dozed off till 3.0 p.m. Got up, washed up and got
  ready for the girl to come home at 4.20, made a cup of tea, then
  the grandchildren came home at 4.40 and you know what they
  are for talking and at 5.30 I went home, buying the paper as I go
  along. Got home 5.50.

5.50 p.m. First thing light the fire, then lay the table, make the tea,
  boil an egg and finish up with marmalade. Then sat down and
  read the paper. Then got up, washed up, had a wash, sat down
  till 9. Then went to the club and had a chat and a game of cards
  till 11, then home and so to bed 11.30.

Tuesday

8.0 a.m. Got up, made a cup of tea. After that cleared the stove out,
  chopped some wood and laid the fire for tonight, swept the
  room and dusted the place up and also did my bedroom. Made
  the bed and finished that job.

9.30 a.m. Had some breakfast. I boiled an egg and some toast, also a slice of marmalade, and ate a lot of marmalade because I think it is good for the bowels. After breakfast had a smoke for a while, then washed up and put the things away, then went out.

11.0 a.m. Got my paper, went to the baker's and got one small loaf. Met a couple of my friends and had a chin-wag and got round to the girl's place at 11.45. Had a look to see if there were any potatoes – none, so I went to the butcher on the corner, bought one small lamb chop and 4 lb. of potatoes and went home loaded. Cooked my dinner and sat down and had a smoke and read the paper till 2. Then washed up and went to my daughter-in-law in Flower Street. My eldest grandchild was there, he is a lovely boy, he likes to hear me sing, he keeps on saying 'more'. Well, I got a nice cup of tea, then went home at 4.0, put the things on the table ready for the girl and her two nippers for their tea, for I tell you they come home hungry, they are good eaters. And after their tea a lot of talking and larking about. I went home at 5.30, buying my paper as I go home. Lit the fire, turned on the wireless, had my tea of bread and jam, sat down and read the paper till my son Arthur came. He comes every Tuesday. We talked till 8.0, then washed up and had a wash and went to the club at 9.0. Met my old chinas, and a game of cards with a couple of glasses of beer and home at 11.0. A couple of biscuits and into bed at 11.40.

Friday

8.0 a.m. Got up as usual. Put the kettle on for a cup of tea, after that cleared the grate out, chopped the wood, and laid the fire ready for the evening. Swept the kitchen out and my bedroom, then put the duster all round. Then got my breakfast.

9.50 a.m. For breakfast I had a fried egg and one tomato. I am not a great lover of tomatoes but still they go down all right. After that washed up, had a wash myself and out we go. Went to the paper shop, got my cigs and paper, went over to the fish shop, bought a plaice for 1s.6d. and also a bloater for my tea. Crossing over the road saw one of my friends. Had a chat for a while and then round to Thirsk St and I bought a small loaf as I came along, the time nearly 12.0. Then washed her things up, made the fire, put some potatoes on, washed my fish, put it in the oven, mashed my potatoes and you have a nice dinner. That over sat down, and a read and a smoke at 2.0. Got up at 3.0 and had a clean up, then went to the door for a while waiting for the girl to come along and when I saw her coming along get inside and put the tools on the table for a cup of tea, that is near enough 4.30. Ten minutes later in come the two hungry merchants and then we got more school for tea and at 5.30 I went home. No papers – oh dear! That's done it. Well, go indoors, light the fire, lay the table, and have my tea which was a bloater and very nice too! Put the wireless on for the news, and you don't get much out of that. Then sat down till 8.0 with a nice Woodbine. Then washed up and cleared the deck. Had a wash and shave and at 9.0 round to the club. Then we had a good chat – what cards! Oh yes, a nice game of cribbage, and our usual couple of drinks and when the bell rings that's your lot. Homeward bound and had a couple of biscuits and so to bed 11.40.

Saturday

8.0 a.m. Got up, made a cup of tea, put a kettle of water on, and scrubbed the stairs down at 9.0. Went out and did some shopping. I bought one long cut loaf 8d., bacon 1s. 8d., 4 eggs 1s. 2d.– 3s.6d. the lot, and ½ marge 9d. Went home and had a rasher and one egg for breakfast. After that washed up, swept the place out, then I went to the paper shop and got Woodbines but no papers. Well, my friend comes every Saturday morning at about 11.30 and we sat down and had a chat about anything, you might say the weather and the strike,[1] which I think was very unjust as there was such a lot of sport. At 12.30 we went out to the P.H. and had a couple of drinks. I left him at 2.0. On the way home I bought one small chop and one kidney for dinner which was O.K. Put the wireless on and heard the boat race – some race! Well, sat down for a while and a smoke, then boiled a kettle of water, washed up everything, made my bed, then waited for football, that lasted till 4.45. Then went and paid Oxford House loan club which is a Xmas club for my son and daughter. Went to the paper shop and had a talk with the guv'nor. Got back in time for the football results and at 6.0 had some tea. I don't go to the daughter's house on Saturday or Sunday but will tell you tomorrow where we go. That will be Sunday. Well, after tea

1. A printing strike, when no newspapers were published.

put the wireless on to the Home Service, washed up, put the things away, and listened to the wireless till 9.0. Then went to the club. No cards Saturday and Sunday. Piano playing and anybody who can sing a song, but it makes a nice evening till 11.0 and then home and finished with the wireless at 12.0, then bed.

Sunday

8.30 a.m. Got up, made a cup of tea, sat down for a few minutes, then started to work on the grate. Cleaned it out, chopped the wood up, and made the fire. Went out and bought one small bottle of O.K. sauce, 1s. Spoke to Mr Gold for a while, then went home and started on the breakfast. I cooked egg and bacon and I think it makes a nice Sunday morning's meal. Well, after filling my tummy I went to work, washed up and swept up and cleared the place in general. All that done have a wash and change and get round to my eldest boy, Flower St. I go there to dinner every Sunday 1.30. I stopped there talking and chinwagging, then the woman next door came in: she and her husband had been down the Row and Petticoat Lane, and showed us what they bought, ash trays and small things like that and my word she can't half jaw. Then Betty the grandchild made a cup of tea, had that with a jam tart. Well, at 4.30 I said, 'Annie, I'm going to slip off the side,' and when I was going she gave me two bananas and two long rolls for my tea, very nice too. I just had a slow walk home, got home at 10 past 5. On goes the wireless and tea at 6.0. Finished tea, sit down till 7.30, then washed up, cleared the deck and out at 8.30 to the club, because being Sunday they close earlier. I get home about 10.40, turned on the wireless with a few biscuits till about 11.45, then to bed.

WEEK'S DIARY NO. 3
21–27 March 1955

Mr Tulier, seventy-one, widower, lives alone in one room, on the first floor of 34 Allenbury Street. Formerly a railway gateman

Monday

7.45 a.m. Got up. Put the kettle on the gas stove. Lovely spring morning, sun shining. Just a little cold.

8.20 a.m. Had breakfast. Nice plate of Quaker Oats first and then a mug of tea and toast. Had a look at the local paper to see if there was a light job, nothing doing, so I sat reading the other part of the paper for a time. Breakfast over, I had a wash and clear up.

9.45 a.m. I got out up Brick Lane to Pearly's the hosier to get a couple of pair of pants the N.A.B. have been good enough to pay for. Had a long chat with the son about different things in life. Brought in a loaf of bread and quarter of corned beef, a packet of tea, and packet of salt – that little bit cost 3s. 4d. Got home about 11.30.

11.45 a.m. The chap across the road came in to shift the mangle belonging to the old girl downstairs, to bring it up from the basement into her room.

12 noon. I went to my daughter's over Hoxton and she had her youngest child taken to hospital on Saturday. Very ill, some kind of gastric. She said she had phoned up and she was comfortable. My daughter and her husband went to see her yesterday but they would not let them in the ward as the child might fret, and they agreed. When I say my daughter, really she is my adopted daughter. Perhaps I can tell you something about her later on, anyway I got home again by 2 o'clock. Had my dinner, some corned beef and veg. I had left from Sunday. After dinner I made the bed and cleared up. Laid the fire, had a wash and went out again.

4.0 p.m. Went back to my adopted daughter's and who should be there but Julie Court, her eldest sister. Very pleased to see one another and talked of years ago. They had a business in Kingsland Rd at one time, but owing to bad health they had to sell out and of course they are not doing much now. Her husband has a light job. One son Joe is married and the youngest is in the Army. Got home again 6.30.

6.45 p.m. Lit the fire, made some tea, had a boiled egg and a couple of slices of bread and butter. Read the *Evening News*, washed up, made the fire up and sat and put a couple of buttons on my shirt and then I read my book about Churchill, or some of it.

10.0 p.m. Made a cup of coffee and into bed about 10.30 p.m.

Tuesday

8.15 a.m. Got up. Don't feel the thing. Change in the weather I
suppose. Anyway, put the kettle on the gas and lit the fire. It
seems a very miserable morning.

8.45 a.m. Breakfast (tea and toast). Don't fancy any Quaker Oats
this morning. Read the *Daily Express* and then swept up and
washed up the breakfast things.

9.45 a.m. The decorator came to have a look at the place. He said
the L.C.C. were going to do it up next week. Then I got my washing together. Then sawed up some wood which I got from a
building site and chopped it up. Saved a few coppers instead of
buying it.

11.45 a.m. Took my washing over to my adopted daughter's. She
puts it in the bag with hers. But the sheets and pillowcases go
best wash only, so she takes them to her laundry for me. On my
way home I take in a bit of boiled bacon and a couple of eggs,
and a jar of marmalade, that cost 2s. 9d. The bacon and eggs I
have for my dinner. Got home 12.30.

2.25 p.m. Went out to the Old People's Club at Penrith House. Met
some old people going in, so I asked them what I had to do and
who to see. So one old chap who said his name was Charlie
Howel took me in hand and put me right, and a very nice old
chap he was. Certainly made me feel at home. Next I saw the
lady, who would be the secretary. All the formalities gone
through I became a member. I saw Mr Howel again and he
introduced me to some more of the old folk. I think this old
chap is in charge of the games, anyway shortly after he came
round with a snack which consisted of a sandwich, a couple of
biscuits and a cup of tea and only charged us threepence. Very
nice. Altogether a very convivial afternoon. Got home just
after 5 p.m.

5.30 p.m. Had to light the fire again because it went out. So while
the fire was burning up I popped across to Dr Hales as I had not
felt any too well all day. Got back quarter past six, made some
tea and had some bread and marmalade for my tea. Read the
Daily Express while having my tea.

7.30 p.m. Washed up dinner and tea things. Made the bed. Had a
wash and sat down for a nice read of the *Evening News* and

T – L

finished my book which has taken me about two weeks to read.
10.15 p.m. Made my usual cup of coffee and into bed about 10.45.

Wednesday

9.0 a.m. Got up, felt a bit better than yesterday. Dull morning.
Looks like rain. Put the kettle on the gas. Waiting for it to boil I
took the ashes up and laid the fire. I didn't light it because I was
going out shortly after breakfast. I knew I should be out some
time.

9.45 a.m. Breakfast rather late this morning, so I had tea, toast, and
marmalade. Read the local paper and saw a light job going, so
when I go out I will phone up. Breakfast over I have a clear up
and have a wash and shave. Now I am waiting for the rent
collector to come. The coal man, he's just come. He left me a
hundredweight, another 7s. 6d. The rent collector is here, now
that's 5s. 7d. He asked me if the decorators have been, so I told
him the foreman was here and he measured up what was to be
done, and he said O.K. they will be in next week.

11.30 a.m. Went out. Phoned up about the light job but it was too
early in the mornings and it was over Poplar. A bit too far and so
I went straight over to my daughter's [adopted] at Hoxton and
stayed some time. In fact I had my dinner there. Stew. And about
half past one she went down to the laundry on the estate to wash
all her woollens, while I washed up the dinner things. Then at
half past two I go to get her bagwash across the road. Help her to
sort it out and she puts them into the drying cupboards. At four
o'clock I go up and put the kettle on. My little grandson has just
come home from school, so I give him and my granddaughter
their tea and take my daughter down a cup of tea. She gets
finished just before five o'clock. I come away and get home 5.45.

6.0 p.m. Light the fire, put the kettle on the gas, while waiting for it
to boil I make the bed. Kettle boils and I make the tea and sit
down to have a boiled egg, some bread and butter, and a couple
of cups of tea.

7.15 p.m. Wash up, have a sweep up. Wash myself and sit down and
try to sort out a perm in the pools for one and sixpence, in
Littlewoods. But I don't seem to get much luck though, but
have a read at some of the news in the evening paper.

10 p.m. Make a cup of coffee and get to bed about 10.30.

Saturday

8.0 a.m. Get up, put the kettle on, take the ashes up, and light the fire. Very dull morning and no newspapers. The strike is still on.

8.45 a.m. Breakfast (tea, couple of slices, and a bit of streaky bacon). I wash up the few things and have a wash and just straighten up a bit.

9.45 a.m. I go out up Bethnal Green Road. I meet a lady friend of mine, Rosie, she tells me she is going over to her son's for the week-end so she wants to get some flowers. So we walk along together, then she goes into the butcher's and gets me a bit of neck and scrag. Then after a little further conversation we say 'Ta-ta'. I make my way towards home. I do a bit more shopping so I have got my meat, Oxo, and flour and veg. Get home eleven o'clock, can't find my key. The old girl downstairs lets me in. I find the key on the table.

11.30 a.m. I go out again over to my adopted daughter's to collect my washing. I ask her if she has phoned up to hear how the baby is going along. All right she says. She makes a cup of tea and we have a chat as to what she can take to the hospital on Sunday. Then while she is doing her work in the house I use the bathroom, which she lets me use every week on Saturday afternoon. We have another cup of tea and I leave at four o'clock.

4.30 p.m. I am home and I put my meat on the boil, of course it has been previously in some salt water to clean it. I like to cook my Sunday dinner on Saturday night because I don't like cooking on Sunday. I get my veg ready and about six o'clock I put them all in together with four Oxos. I have already put a small chop in the oven for tea.

6.15 p.m. I have my tea. I don't get much time to have dinner on Saturdays so for tea I have chop and beans, with bread and a cup of coffee. Finished tea, turn the gas out under the stew.

7.15 p.m. Wash up, make the bed. A sit down to read my book entitled 'Our Old Man' by Toole.

10.45 p.m. My eyes ache and I get to bed.

Sunday

9.0 a.m. I woke up to find my nose is bleeding. I got up and put a

cold water rag on it. After a bit it stopped. I made myself a cup
of tea and as soon as I drank it my nose started bleeding again,
so I went over to my daughter's place and told her I was going
to the hospital.

10.30 a.m. I was in the hospital as casualty. After a while it stopped.
Doctor examined me, gave me some tablets and I have got to see
my doctor Monday, so I had no breakfast. Went back to my
adopted daughter's by eleven thirty and she made me a cup of
tea. Left at twelve thirty, got home and warmed up my stew.

2.0 p.m. I had my dinner. And then I washed the things up, wiped
my face over, afraid to touch it too hard in case my nose bleeds
again, and I have to lie down and go to sleep as I don't feel none
too bright, only I was in hospital sixteen days with the same
thing in Dec. 1952–3.

6.0 p.m. I wake up, make myself a cup of tea, and have a couple of
biscuits out of half a pound I bought this morning, 1s.

7.0 p.m. I go over to my adopted daughter's again and have a look
at the tele., saw Guess My Story and a bit of church stuff. Came
away quarter past nine. Met old Dan Alamino in Hackney Road,
just said good night, that was all. Got home quarter to ten.

10.0 p.m. The fire was out, so I got straight into bed as I was not
feeling quite the thing. The end of a perfect week.

Mr Tulier: Additional Written Note

You may perhaps note in this diary of myself how often I allude
to my adopted daughter. Perhaps it would be as well for me to tell
you how she became my adopted daughter. Well, it is the month of
April 1921. Her family was my next door neighbour. At the time I
with my wife lived in Harold Gardens, a turning in Shoreditch. It
certainly was a bit of a rough quarter but there were still some hard-
working people there. Well, one Saturday night there was a spot of
bother in the street and this child's mother was concerned in it. So
they asked my wife if she would look after the baby till the row
abated. My wife made her a bed on the floor and she never whim-
pered all night. The following morning my wife made her some
bread and milk till such time we got her some proper food. She
was one year and five months old then. Well, we kept the child a
few days because we took to her, and me and my wife had a talk
about adopting her and we agreed to ask her mother about it. We

did so, and the parents were only too pleased. And so we drew up an agreement and that settled that, and although my wife suffered from a form of paralysis in her legs, she was able to take care of this child. Of course, we did not have any children of our own. I might say this child had many illnesses that children suffer from, but with the aid of the doctor and my wife's help she always pulled through. In June 1924 we moved from Harold Gardens, Shoreditch, into Bethnal Green. She always carried our name of Tulier and when she became of school age we sent her to Beesley Road School. She attended school quite regular, passed all her standards, and left at the age of fourteen. She found a job in a cardboard factory and began to bring home a few shillings which helped to buy her clothes. Mind you, she was a very good girl as she grew up, she helped us as we had helped her. Her own mother died about 1934, and unfortunately for both of us my wife died in July 1936. Well, Ivy Alice, that was her christian names, I don't think it matters about telling you her surname, and I her foster father carried on until 1945, and then she got married in the June. She had her first baby in June 1946. Today, 1955, she has three lovely children and a hard-working husband. I don't think that she has ever had any regrets that she was adopted, and I am sure that I have no regrets for having adopted her. And now I am getting along in age my happy times are when I am with her and, as I call them, my grandchildren. I might add that her own father died just previous to her getting married. But for a final word, let me say that my adopted daughter today is devoted to her children and husband, not forgetting she is a good girl to me.

WEEK'S DIARY NO. 4
21–27 March 1955

Mrs Harker, 12 Peacock Street. Widowed, aged sixty-two, living alone

Monday

Got up at 8.30, lit the fire 9.0, then had breakfast, tea, and toast. 9.20 my grandson brought my dinner in to cook. 9.45 cleaned my budgie out and settled her. 10.0 peeled the potatoes. 10.15 started my clearing up, made the bed and washed up. 11.0 put my dinner on to cook and then did a little washing. 12.30 had my dinner, bacon and potatoes, fed the dog. After sitting a while got up and washed up. 2.10 got myself ready to go and see an old neighbour. 2.30 went over to my neighbour. After sitting talking about the family, made a cup of tea and had a cake, after that we finished our conversation. 4.0 washed up. 4.30 left her to come home to catch my daughter's club[1] man but he didn't turn up, so at 5.0 got my tea and sat resting by the fire. Then I got up. 6.30 a friend came in to pay her club. We sat talking about the family, and in the meantime my grandson and his friend came in to take the dog for his night's run. My friend left at 7.15. After that I cleared the fireplace up and tidied up the room. 7.30 sat down and had a read of the paper. 7.45 started to write a letter to my son in Dorset. 9.0 got my supper, a boiled egg and toast, and cleared away. After that I sat and had another read. 10.20 went to bed.

Tuesday

Got up at 8.45 and started the fire. 9.0 got my breakfast which was toast and tea. 9.15 my grandson came in with the dinner and then went to school. 9.30 started to prepare the dinner. 10.0 cleaned my budgie out. 10.15 started my house work. 11.0 put my dinner on to cook which consisted of minced meat and greens and potatoes, cooking for five of us, and then went on with my work. 12.30 took the dinner up. When we had finished my grandson washed up and then went to school and the other on to work. My daughter sat for a while after getting my pension. We talked and she wrote a letter to her son in Africa. At 2.45 she left for work, being on late turn this week, then I made the bed. At 3.0, being a miserable afternoon, I washed up. 6.0 cleared up the fireplace again. Then settled down to have a read of my paper. 7.0 my grandson came to take the dog. After that I sat down and did some writing. 9.0 got my supper which consisted of cold meat and tomatoes. Cleared that away and 9.45 had another read, going to bed at 10.30.

I forgot to put at 11.15 the coalman came, paying him 7s.6d. a cwt.

Wednesday

9.0 got up and started the fire. 9.15 started my breakfast which was a boiled egg and tea. 9.20 my grandson came in with the dinner.

1. Her daughter is an agent of a clothing club – collecting weekly payments for clothing and shoes.

I sent him down to pay my rent which was 12s.3d. and from there he went to school. 10.0 started to do the vegetables for dinner. 10.30 cleaned my budgie out and then carried on with housework. 11.0 I made a sausage batter and started cooking it with greens and potatoes. I also had a letter from my sister telling me all the troubles of the family (she has six children) and then I carried on with my work. 12.30 took the dinner up. At 1.30 my daughter's insurance man called. We had a little talk about the weather and wondered what kind of a summer we would get, then my grandson washed up and the other going back to work. When he had finished he went to school. My daughter didn't come in today. 2.20 I went over to see my old neighbour and spent a couple of hours with her, she is not very well and has a nasty cold. I made a cup of tea for us and had a cake and then we listened to the big race. I like to hear the horses. Then we talked about things in general. 5.15 came over and got my tea and fell asleep to 6.45, then got up and cleared away and washed up and did the fireplace. 7.15 my grandson came to take the dog for a run and I sat down to look at the paper and wrote three letters. 9.0 got my supper. When I finished, sat and had another read, went to bed at 11 o'clock.

Thursday

8.30 got up and got my breakfast. Just as I was finishing my grandson came in with the dinner and then went to school. 9.20 I stood at the window watching the children bring their plants to school. Every year they are given a bulb to grow, and the one that gets the best plant gets so many marks, and it was nice to see all the daffodils going in. 9.40 I started to prepare the dinner. I made a nice stew. 10.0 started the fire going, I had rather a job with it, I don't know if the wood was damp, and then I did my budgie out. 10.30 started my housework. 12.30 took the dinner up. When we finished we sat talking for a time and 2.0 my daughter went back to work. 2.30 made the bed and then had a little rest. 4.0 got myself ready and also my tea. Tea and toast and after clearing away at 5.0 went to meet my daughter and went to the pictures, it was a pretty good picture but an old one. 9.15 got home, got my supper, which consisted of a piece of fried fish, had a read of the paper and went to bed 10.15 feeling a bit tired.

Friday

8.40 started the fire going. 9.0. had my breakfast, tea and toast, and then my grandson came with the dinner. Then went to school. 9.30 started to do the dinner. I made some meat patties with minced meat, they enjoy those with beans and potatoes. 10.15 did the bird and then started my work. 12.30 took the dinner up and fed the dog. Had my dinner, then when we had finished my grandson washed up. 1.45 went to school and his brother back to work. My daughter did not go till 2.45 being on late turn this week so we sat talking. She was telling me her son doing his National Service may be moved farther away, he is already in East Africa, Kenya, where the Mau Mau are. 3.30 my daughter's [club] man called. I gave him a cup of tea and we had a little talk. 4.30 got my tea, toast, cheese, and tomatoes. 5.30 cleared away, washed up, and did the fireplace up, then at 6.0 thought I was going to have a read of the paper, to find there are no papers, they are on strike, so got my book. 7.30 the boy brought the dog back from his run. 9.0 got my supper, a boiled egg and toast. After that I had another read of my book and went to bed 10.0.

Saturday

8.30 got up and had my breakfast, toast and tea. 9.0 cleaned the grate and started the fire and prepared the room to be cleaned. 9.30 cleaned the bird out. 10.0 my grandson brought the vegetables, so I prepared them. 10.30 I made the bed and while I was clearing that up my grandson cleaned the floor for me. 10.0 I put the vegetables on and went on with the clearing. 12.0 my daughter finished cooking the dinner. 12.40 we had dinner. 1.30 they left to go home and 2.0 I went over to my old neighbour and listened to the boat race and then to the big race. Finished up by hearing the football, a good afternoon's sport. 5.0 got my tea, I toasted some crumpets. 5.45 cleared away and washed up. 6 o'clock sat and read, it was easy for the rest of the time. 9.0 got my supper which was ham and tomatoes and tea. After that I sat and read till eleven o'clock then went to bed.

Sunday

9.0 got up and started the fire. 9.15 got my breakfast of bacon and egg and tea. At 10.0 cleared up and washed up, and got myself ready and went round to my daughter's to dinner and tea. At 8.0 my grandson came home with me. 8.30 started a fire. 9.0 got my supper. Cheese and tomatoes and tea. When I finished I had a read till 10.0, then went to bed.

List of References

ABEL-SMITH, B., and TITMUSS, R. M., *The Cost of the National Health Service in England and Wales*, London, C.U.P., 1956.

ABEL-SMITH, B., and TOWNSEND, P., *New Pensions for the Old*, Fabian Research Series No. 171, Fabian Society, 1955.

ADAMS, G. F., and CHEESEMAN, E. A. *Old People in Northern Ireland*, A Report to the Northern Ireland Hospitals Authority on the Medical and Social Problems of Old Age, Northern Ireland Hospitals Authority, Belfast, 1951.

LORD AMULREE, EXTON-SMITH, A. N., and CROCKETT, G. S., 'Proper Use of the Hospital in the Treatment of the Aged Sick', *The Lancet*, 20 January 1951.

ANDERSON, W. F., and COWAN, N. R., 'Work and Retirement: Influences on the Health of Older Men', *The Lancet*, 29 December 1956.

'A Consultative Health Centre for Older People', *The Lancet*, 30 July 1955.

ARENSBERG, C. M., and KIMBALL, S. T., *Family and Community in Ireland*. Cambridge, Mass., Harvard University Press, 1948.

BACKETT, E. M., HEADY, J. A., and EVANS, J. C. G., 'Studies of a General Practice (II): The Doctor's Job in an Urban Area', *The British Medical Journal*, 16 January 1954.

BOOTH, C., *The Aged Poor in England and Wales*, London, Macmillan, 1894.

Life and Labour of the People in London, Vol. 1, 3rd edition, London, Macmillan, 1891.

Old Age Pensions and the Aged Poor, London, Macmillan, 1899.

BOSANQUET, H., *The Family*, London, Macmillan, 1906.

BOTT, E., 'Urban Families, Conjugal Roles and Social Networks', *Human Relations*, Vol. 8, No. 4, 1955.

CHALKE, H. D., and BENJAMIN, B., 'The Aged in Their Own Homes', *The Lancet*, 21 March 1953.

CLARK, F. LE GROS, and DUNNE, A. C., *Ageing in Industry*, An Inquiry based on figures derived from Census Reports into the Problem of Ageing under the conditions of Modern Industry, London, The Nuffield Foundation, 1955.

CLARK, F. LE GROS, Series of Reports on *Later Working Life in the Building Industry, Alternative Work in Later Life*, etc., The Nuffield Foundation, 1954–6.

COLE, D. E., 'The Income, Expenditure and Saving of Old People Households in Cambridgeshire', Paper given to the 4th Congress of the International Association of Gerontology, 1957.

COMFORT, A., *The Biology of Senescence*, London, Routledge & Kegan Paul, 1956.

COSIN, L. Z., 'The Place of the Day Hospital in the Geriatric Unit', *The Practitioner*, May 1954.

DENNIS, N., HENRIQUES, F., and SLAUGHTER, C., *Coal is Our Life*, An anthropological analysis of a Yorkshire mining community, London, Eyre & Spottiswoode, 1956.

DUBLIN, L. J., LOTKA, A. J., and SPIEGELMAN, M., *Length of Life*, New York, Ronald Press Company, 1949.

FIRTH, R. (ed.), *Two Studies of Kinship in London*, Department of Anthropology, London School of Economics, Monographs on Social Anthropology, No. 15, London, The Athlone Press, 1956.

FISHER, R. A., *Statistical Methods for Research Workers*, 12th ed., Edinburgh, Oliver & Boyd, 1954.

FRIEDMANN, E. A., and HAVIGHURST, R. J., *The Meaning of Work and Retirement*, Chicago, University of Chicago Press, 1954.

GLASS, D. V., and GREBENIK, E., *The Trend and Pattern of Fertility in Great Britain. A Report on the Family Census of 1946*, Papers of the Royal Commission on Population, Vol. 6, London, H.M.S.O., 1954.

GORER, G., *Exploring English Character*, London, The Cresset Press, 1955.

GRAHAM, W. L., 'The Aged Sick', *The Lancet*, 6 February 1954.

HOBSON, J., *Problems of Poverty*, London, Methuen, 1899.

HOBSON, W., and PEMBERTON, J., *The Health of the Elderly at Home*, London, Butterworth, 1955.

HOMANS, G. C., *The Human Group*, London, Routledge & Kegan Paul, 1951.

HOWELL, T. H., 'Problems of the Aged and Chronic Sick', *The Medical Press*, 22 December 1954.

HUGHES, W., and PUGMIRE, S. L., 'A Geriatric Hospital Service', *The Lancet*, 21 June 1952.

HUTCHINSON, B., *Old People in a Modern Australian Community*, Victoria, Melbourne University Press, 1954.

JEPHCOTT, P., and CARTER, M. P., *The Social Background of Delinquency*, Unpublished Ph.D. Report, Nottingham University, 1954.

KING, SIR GEOFFREY, formerly Permanent Secretary, Ministry of

Pensions and National Insurance, 'Policy and Practice'. See *Old Age in the Modern World*, 1955.

LEWIS, A. J., and GOLDSCHMIDT, H., 'Social Causes of Admissions to a Mental Hospital for the Aged', *The Sociological Review*, July–October 1943.

LOGAN, W. P. D., *General Practitioners' Records*, An Analysis of the Clinical Records of Eight Practices during the Period April 1951 to March 1952, General Register Office: Studies on Medical and Population Subjects No. 7, London, H.M.S.O., 1953.

MACMILLAN, D., 'An Integrated Mental Health Service', *The Lancet*, 24 November 1956.

MADGE, C., *War-time Pattern of Saving and Spending*, National Institute of Economic and Social Research, C.U.P., 1943.

McEWAN, P., and LAVERTY, S. G., *The Chronic Sick and Elderly in Hospital*, Bradford (B) Hospital Management Committee, 1949.

MOGEY, C. M., *Family and Neighbourhood*, London, O.U.P., 1956.

MYRDAL, A., and KLEIN, V., *Women's Two Roles*, London, Routledge & Kegan Paul, 1956.

PARSONS, T., *Essays in Sociological Theory Pure and Applied*, Glencoe, Illinois, The Free Press, 1949.

RADCLIFFE-BROWN, A. R., and FORDE, D. (ed.), *African Systems of Kinship and Marriage*, London, O.U.P., 1950.

REES, A. D., *Life in a Welsh Countryside*, Cardiff, University of Wales Press, 1951.

RICHARDSON, I. M., 'Retirement: A Socio-medical Study of 244 Men', *Scottish Medical Journal*, 1, 1956.

ROBB, J. H., *The Working Class Anti-Semite*, London, Tavistock Publications, 1954.

ROTH, M., and MORRISSEY, D., 'Problems in the Diagnosis and Classification of Mental Disorder in Old Age', *Journal of Mental Science*, Vol. 98, No. 410, January 1952.

ROWNTREE, B. S., *Poverty: A Study of Town Life*, London, Macmillan, 1901.

Poverty and Progress, London, Longmans Green, 1941.

ROWNTREE, B. S., and LAVERS, G. R., *Poverty and the Welfare State*, London, Longmans Green, 1951.

SAINSBURY, P., *Suicide in London*, Maudsley Monographs No. 1, London, Chapman and Hall, 1955.

SARGAISON, E. M., *Growing Old in Common Lodgings*, The Nuffield Provincial Hospitals Trust, 1954.

SHAW, L. A., 'Impressions of Family Life in a London Suburb', *The Sociological Review*, New Series, Vol. 2, No. 2, December 1954.

SHELDON, J. H., *The Social Medicine of Old Age*, Report of an inquiry in Wolverhampton. London, O.U.P., 1948.

'The Social Philosophy of Old Age', Presidential Address to the Third Congress of the International Association of Gerontology in London, 19 July 1954, *The Lancet*, 24 July 1954.

SHURTLEFF, D., 'Mortality and Marital Status', *Public Health Reports*. Washington, Vol. 70, No. 3, March 1955.

SLATER, E., and WOODSIDE, M., *Patterns of Marriage*, London, Cassell, 1951.

SMITH, SIR H. L., 'Old Age and Poverty', *The New Survey of London Life and Labour*, Vol. 3, London, King, 1932.

THOMSON, A. P., LOWE, C. R., and McKEOWN, T., *The Care of the Ageing and Chronic Sick*, Birmingham Regional Hospital Board, 1951.

TITMUSS, R. M., 'Pension Systems and Population Change', *Political Quarterly*, 81, No. 2, 1955.

'Some Fundamental Assumptions'. See *Old Age in the Modern World*, 1955.

'The Position of Women in Relation to the Changing Family', Millicent Fawcett Lecture, 17 January 1952.

TOWNSEND, P., 'The Anxieties of Retirement', *Transactions of the Association of Industrial Medical Officers*, April 1955.

'Measuring Poverty', *British Journal of Sociology*, Vol. 5, No. 2, June 1954.

VINE, S. M., 'Clinical Pitfalls in the Elderly', *The Lancet*, 16 July 1955.

WELFORD, A. T., *Skill and Age*, An Experimental Approach, The Nuffield Foundation, London, O.U.P., 1950.

WILLIAMS, W. M., *The Sociology of an English Village: Gosforth*, London, Routledge & Kegan Paul: Glencoe, The Free Press, 1956.

WILSON, C. S., *The Family and Neighbourhood in a British Community*, Unpublished M.Sc. dissertation, Cambridge University Library, 1953.

YOUNG, M., 'Distribution of Income Within the Family', *British Journal of Sociology*, Vol. 3, No. 4, December 1952.

YOUNG, M., and WILLMOTT, P., *Family and Kinship in East London*, London, Routledge & Kegan Paul: Glencoe, The Free Press, 1957; Penguin Books, 1962.

Reports

The Ageing Population, Report of the Standing Medical Advisory Committee for Scotland, Edinburgh, H.M.S.O., 1953.

Census 1951: One Per Cent Sample Tables, London, H.M.S.O., 1952.

Census 1951: England and Wales: County Report, London, London, H.M.S.O., 1953.

Census 1951: Report on Greater London and Five Other Conurbations, London, H.M.S.O., 1956.

Economic and Financial Problems of the Provision for Old Age, Cmd 9333, London, H.M.S.O., 1954.

Employment of Older Men and Women, First and Second Reports of the National Advisory Committee, Cmds 8963 and 9627, London, H.M.S.O., 1953 and 1955.

Inquiry into Health Visiting, Report of a working party on the field of work, training, and recruitment of health visitors, London, H.M.S.O., 1956.

Ministry of Pensions and National Insurance, Report for the Year 1955, Cmd 9826, London, H.M.S.O., 1956.

The National Corporation for the Care of Old People, Ninth Annual Report for the year ended 30 September 1956.

The National Insurance Act of 1946, Report by the Government Actuary on the First Quinquennial Review, London, H.M.S.O., 1954.

Old Age in the Modern World, Report of the Third Congress of the International Association of Gerontology, 1954, London, Livingstone, 1955.

Old People, Report of a Survey Committee on the Problems of Ageing and the Care of Old People, The Nuffield Foundation. London, O.U.P., 1947.

Poverty – Ten Years after Beveridge, Planning No. 344, London, P.E.P., 1952.

The Rates and Amounts of National Insurance Benefit, Report by the Minister of Pensions and National Insurance of his Review, Cmd 9338, London, H.M.S.O., 1954.

Reasons given for Retiring or Continuing at Work, Report of an Enquiry by the Ministry of Pensions and National Insurance, H.M.S.O., 1954.

Registrar General's Decennial Supplement for England and Wales, 1931, Part 1, London, H.M.S.O., 1936.

Registrar General's Decennial Supplement for England and Wales, 1951, Life Tables, London, H.M.S.O., 1957.

Registrar General's Decennial Supplement for England and Wales, 1951, Occupational Mortality, Part 1, London, H.M.S.O., 1955.

Registrar General's Statistical Review of England and Wales for the Five Years 1946–1950, Text, Civil, London, H.M.S.O., 1954.

Registrar General's Statistical Review of England and Wales for the Year 1933 (Text).

The Rehabilitation, Training and Resettlement of Disabled Persons, Report by Committee of Inquiry, Cmd 9883, London, H.M.S.O., 1956.

Social Security and Unemployment in Lancashire, Planning, Vol. 19, No. 349, London, P.E.P., 1952.

References to Postscripts, 1963

BELLIN, S. S., 'Relations Among Kindred in Later Years of Life: Parents, Their Siblings and Adult Children', *Proceedings of the American Sociological Association*, St Louis, 1961.

BOTT, E., *Family and Social Network: Roles, Norms and External Relationships in Ordinary Urban Families*, London, Tavistock Press, 1957.

BROWN, R. G., 'Family Structure and Social Isolation to Older Persons', *Journal of Gerontology*, Vol. 15, April 1960.

BURGESS, E. W., 'Family Structure and Relationships', in Burgess E. W. (ed.) *Ageing in Western Societies*, Chicago, Ill., University of Chicago Press, 1961.

COLE WEDDERBURN, D., with UTTING, J., *The Economic Circumstances of Old People*, Occasional Papers on Social Administration, No. 4, Welwyn, Herts., The Codicote Press, 1962.

CUMMING, E., and HENRY, W. E., *Growing Old: The Process of Disengagement*, New York, Basic Books, 1961.

FIRTH, R., *We the Tikopia*, London, Allen & Unwin, 1936.

GLICK, P. C., *American Families*, New York, Wiley, 1957.

GOLDSTEIN, S., and ZIMMER, B. G., *Residential Displacement and Resettlement of the Aged*, Providence, Rhode Island, Division of Aging, 1960.

HARRIS, A. I., *Meals on Wheels for Old People: A Report of an Inquiry by the Government Social Survey*, London, National Corporation for the Care of Old People, 1960.

HOMANS, G., *The Human Group*, London, Routledge & Kegan Paul, 1951.

INGEGNIEROS, S., *Aspetti gerontologici milanesi*, Milan, Commune di Milano, 1958.

KUTNER, B., et al., *Five Hundred Over Sixty*, New York, Russell Sage Foundation, 1956.

LANGFORD, M., *Community Aspects of Housing for the Aged*, New York, Cornell University Center for Housing and Environmental Studies, 1962.

LEMPERT, S., *Report on the Survey of the Aged in Stockport*, Stockport, County Borough of Stockport, 1958.

LITWAK, E., 'Occupational Mobility and Extended Family Cohesion', *American Sociological Review*, Vol. 25, No. 1, pp. 9–21, February 1960.

'Geographic Mobility and Family Cohesion', *American Sociological Review*, Vol. 25, pp. 385–94, 1960.

MATHIASEN, G., 'A New Look at the Three Generation Family', *Proceedings of the National Conference of Social Welfare*, Atlantic City, 1960.

MILLER, M. C., *The Ageing Countryman: A Socio-Medical Report on Old Age in a Country Practice*, London, National Corporation for the Care of Old People, 1963.

PARSONS, T., 'The Social Structure of the Family', in Anshen, R. N. (ed.), *The Family: Its Function and Destiny*, New York, Harper, 1949.

RICHARDSON, I. M., *Age and Need: A Study of Older People in North-East Scotland*, University of Aberdeen (in press).

RICHARDSON, I. M., BRODIE, A. S., and WILSON, S., 'Social and Medical Needs of Old People in Orkney: Report of a Social Survey', *Health Bulletin, Scotland*, Vol. 17, No. 4, October 1959.

ROSENMAYR, L., and KÖCKEIS, E., *Leben und Alter Menschen in Heimstätten*, Vienna, Sozialwissenschaftliche Forschungsstelle, Institut für Soziologie, Universität Wien, 1960.

'Family Relations and Social Contacts of the Aged in Vienna', Tibbitts, C., and Donahue, W. (eds.), *Social and Psychological Aspects of Ageing*, pp. 492–500, New York and London, Columbia University Press, 1962.

ROSSER, C., and HARRIS, C. C., 'Relationships through Marriage in a Welsh Urban Area', *The Sociological Review*, Vol. 9, No. 3, pp. 293–321, November 1961.

SCHORR, A. L., *Filial Responsibility in the Modern American Family*, Washington D.C., U.S. Department of Health, Education and Welfare, 1960.

'Filial Responsibility and the Aging', *The Social Security Bulletin*, U.S. Department of Health, Education and Welfare, May 1962.

SHANAS, E., 'Living arrangements of Older People in the United States', *The Gerontologist*, pp. 27–9, March 1961.

The Health of Older People: A Social Survey, Cambridge, Mass., Harvard University Press, 1962.

SMITH, R. C. F., 'The Effect of Social Problems on the Lives of Old Age Pensioners', *The Medical Officer*, Vol. 97, pp. 303–8, 1957.

SMITH, W. N., BRITTON, J. N., and BRITTON, J. O., *Relationships Within Three-Generation Families*, Pennsylvania State University, College of Home Economics Research Publication 155, April 1958.

STEINER, P. O., and DORFMAN, R., *The Economic Status of the Aged*, University of California Press, 1957.

STREIB, G. F., 'Family Patterns in Retirement', *Journal of Social Issues*, Vol. 14, No. 2, 1958.

SUSSMAN, M. B., 'The Help Pattern in the Middle-Class Family', *American Sociological Review*, February 1953.

'Intergenerational Family Relationships and Social Role Changes in Middle Age', *Journal of Gerontology*, Vol. 15, January 1960.

Swedish Institute of Public Opinion and Research, *På Äldre Dagar*, Stockholm, The Institute, 1956.

TALMON, Y., 'Ageing in Israel: A Planned Society', *The American Journal of Sociology*, Vol. 67, No. 3, pp. 284–95, November 1961.

'Ageing in Collective Settlements', in Tibbitts, C., and Donahue, W. (eds.) *Social and Psychological Aspects of Ageing*, pp. 427–41, New York and London, Columbia University Press, 1962.

TOWNSEND, P., and REES, B., *The Personal, Family and Social Circumstances of Old People, Report of an Investigation carried out in England to Pilot a Future Cross-National Survey of Old Age*, London, London School of Economics, 1959.

TOWNSEND, P., 'Social Surveys of Old Age in Great Britain, 1945–58,' *Bulletin of the World Health Organisation*, Vol. 21, Geneva, W.H.O., 1959.

The Last Refuge: A Survey of Residential Institutions and Homes for the Aged in England and Wales, London, Routledge & Kegan Paul, 1962.

TREANTON, J. R., 'Adjustment of Older People to Urban Life in France', in Tibbitts C., (ed.) *Ageing and Social Health in the United States and Europe*, pp. 167–73, Ann Arbor, Division of Gerontology, University of Michigan, 1959.

VARCHAUER, C., *Older People in the Detroit Areas and the Retirement Age*, Eerdmans, 1956.

WILLMOTT, P., and YOUNG, M., *Family and Class in a London Suburb*, London, Routledge & Kegan Paul, 1960.

WOODROFFE, C., and TOWNSEND, P., *Nursing Homes in England and Wales: A Study of Public Responsibility*, London, National Corporation for the Care of Old People, 1961.

WYNNE GRIFFITH, G., 'The Needs of Old People in Rural Areas', *Journal of the Royal Society for the Promotion of Health*, Vol. 7, No. 4, 1958.

YOUNG, M., and GEERTZ, H., 'Old Age in London and San Francisco: Some Families Compared', *British Journal of Sociology*, Vol. 12, No. 2, pp. 124–41, June 1961.

Index

Abel-Smith, B., 187n., 207n.

Admission to hospital, causes of, 206–10, 229–30

Admission to welfare Homes, causes of, 211–14

Admitting Officers, welfare Homes, 210

Age:
  admission to hospital by, 207–9
  admission to welfare Homes by, 212
  change in household composition with, 34
  frequency of medical consultation by, 64–5

Age differences, 40

Ageing, consequences in the community, 148–50

Amulree, Lord, 206

Arthritis, 64

Assistance, National, 167, 176–87, 219–20

Attendance allowances, 219–20

Aunts, unmarried, 122–4

Authority of men in family, 160–1

Avoidance, and in-laws, 99–102, 130–1

Bachelors. *See* Single people

Bedridden people, 219–20, 230

Bereavement:
  consequences of, 201–2
  and loneliness, 196–9

Bethnal Green, 236, 238, 239, 240, 242, 248, 250
  attachment to, 145–6
  description, 21–4
  electoral wards, 260
  housing, 21

old people at work in, 172

population changes, 22

representativeness, 230–1

special Census survey of household composition, 34, 41, 96

social changes, 231–3

work, 23

Bethnal Green Old People's Welfare Committee, 144

Birthdays, 135–6

Birthplaces, 146

Board money, 76–7

Boarding-out schemes, 221–6

Booth, C., 162

Bosanquet, H., 226

Brighton, 146–7

British Legion, 144

Broken homes, 232–3

Bronchitis, 64

Brothers, seen less often than sisters, 121
  See also Siblings

Burial:
  cards, 98
  customs, 134–5

Census, 1951:
  Bethnal Green sample and, 18
  female domestic servants, 120n.
  hospital population, 207
  household composition, 33–5
  social class, 160

Ceremonial and the family, 133–8, 233

Change, family and society, 231–4

Child:
  birth of second, 245
  compensation for spouse, 250
  death of causing loneliness, 198–9

MORE ABOUT PENGUINS
AND PELICANS

Penguinews, an attractively illustrated magazine which appears every month, contains details of all the new books issued by Penguins as they are published. Every four months it is supplemented by *Penguins in Print*, which is a complete list of all books published by Penguins which are still available. (There are well over three thousand of these.)

A specimen copy of *Penguinews* can be sent to you free on request, and you can become a regular subscriber at 4s. for one year (with the complete lists) if you live in the United Kingdom, or 8s. if you live elsewhere. Just write to Dept EP, Penguin Books Ltd, Harmondsworth, Middlesex, enclosing a cheque or postal order, and your name will be added to the mailing list.

Some other books published by Penguins are described on the following pages.

Note: *Penguinews* and *Penguins in Print* are not available in the U.S.A. or Canada

THE PSYCHOLOGY OF HUMAN AGEING

D. B. Bromley

Infant and adolescent psychology have been very thoroughly explored: but the study of ageing lags behind.

A gerontologist, who is scientific adviser in this field to the Medical Research Council, fills a gap in the literature of psychology with this new introduction to human ageing and its mental effects. Dealing with the course of life from maturity onwards, Dr Bromley examines many biological and social effects of human ageing; personality and adjustment; mental disorders of occupational and skilled performance; adult intelligence; and age changes in intellectual, social, and other achievements. A final section on method in the study of ageing makes this book an important contribution for the student of psychology as well as the layman.

IN THE SERVICE OF OLD AGE

Anthony Whitehead

Mental illness and old age are fundamental social problems, and our attitudes towards the aged and the mentally ill are yardsticks of the humanity of our society. Today the plight of those who are both old and mentally ill is truly terrible. This book is concerned with this growing problem, and with suggestions for alleviating the distress of many elderly patients in their last few precious months or years.

In his foreword Russell Barton writes: 'In this timely book Dr Whitehead has described our attempts at Severalls Hospital to develop an enlightened, hopeful and humane service for the elderly mentally ill. . . . His purpose is to inform public opinion of what can be done and to stimulate self-scrutiny by authorities who should be doing more. The competence, sincerity and humanity are as unmistakable in this excellent exposition as they are in the wards of the psychogeriatric service which he has developed.'

FAMILY AND KINSHIP
IN EAST LONDON

Michael Young and Peter Willmott

The two authors of this most human of surveys are sociologists.

They spent three years on 'field work' in Bethnal Green and on a new housing estate in Essex. The result is a fascinating study, made during a period of extensive rehousing, of family and community ties and the pull of the 'wider family' on working-class people.

'Probably not only the fullest, but virtually the only account of working-class family relationships in any country. The general reader will find it full of meat and free of jargon' – *New Statesman*

'This shrewd – and in places extremely amusing – book combines warmth of feeling with careful sociological method' – *The Financial Times*

'Observant, tactful, sympathetic, humorous . . . I really feel that nobody who wants to know how our society is changing can afford not to read Young and Willmott' – Kingsley Amis in the *Spectator*

'No short account can do justice to this book, charmingly written, engaging, absorbing' – *British Medical Journal*

Obviously there have been changes in the two districts under survey during the last five years. This edition in Pelicans, with its fresh introduction and simplified appendix is justified by the standing the report has achieved as a modern classic of sociology.